CISTERCIAN STUDIES SERIES: NUMBER ONE HUNDRED

PETER OF CELLE

SELECTED WORKS

CISTERCIAN STUDIES SERIES: NUMBER ONE HUNDRED

PETER OF CELLE
SELECTED WORKS

Sermons
The School of the Cloister
On Affliction and Reading
On Conscience

TRANSLATED BY HUGH FEISS, OSB

CISTERCIAN PUBLICATIONS
KALAMAZOO, MICHIGAN
49008

© Translation copyright, Cistercian Publications, Inc., 1987.

The work of Cistercian Publications is made possible in part by support from Western Michigan University to the Institute of Cistercian Studies.

Available in Britain and Europe from

A. R. Mowbray & Co Ltd
St Thomas House   Becket Street
Oxford OX1 1SJ

Available elsewhere (including Canada) from
Cistercian Publications
WMU Station
Kalamazoo, Michigan 49008

Library of Congress Cataloguing-in-Publication Data:

Peter, of Celle, Bishop of Chartres, ca. 1115–1183.
  Peter of Celle, selected works.

  (Cistercian studies series; 100)
  Bibliography: pp. 189–190.
  1. Theology. I. Title. II. Series.
BX1749.P34213   1987   230'.2   87-6579
ISBN 0-87907-600-3

Typeset by Solaris Press II, Rochester, Michigan   *Printed in the United States of America*

To the monastic communities of Engelberg, Switzerland
and St Anselm's, Washington, D.C.

CONTENTS

ACKNOWLEDGMENTS

THESE TRANSLATIONS rest upon the work of distinguished scholars of the Benedictine Congregations of St Maur and Solesmes. The first and only collected edition of Peter's works was produced by Dom Ambroise Janvier in 1671 and accompanied by part of a preface by Dom Jean Mabillon. Reprinted in the *Patrologia latina* of Migne, this edition was the basis for what little study Peter received until this century. In the difficult conditions of the mid-1940's, Dom Jean Leclercq published *La spiritualité de Pierre de Celle* (Paris: J. Vrin, 1946), which included an introduction to Peter's works, a study of Peter's inner life and his language, and a synthesis of his spiritual doctrine, in addition to several editions. Since Dom Leclercq's pioneering work, Peter has been studied by other scholars as an important representative of the theological activity of twelfth-century monasticism. Outstanding among those who have pursued the investigation of Peter's works is Dom Gérard de Martel, whose excellent editions and careful studies are the indispensible basis for inquiry into Peter's life, works, and thought.

Dom de Martel has personally assisted the present translation with advice about which works to translate, help with the Latin text, suggestions regarding translation, and offprints of several articles. Without his generous help this work would be an even less worthy reflection of the work of Peter and the scholars who have studied him. The errors that remain in spite of all this help are entirely my responsibility.

Peter of Celle was a busy abbot and churchman, who found time to write only when he was incapacitated or on a temporary retreat to a haven like the charterhouse of Mont-Dieu. My responsibilities are much less, but this translation would never have been finished had it not been for the hospitality of two monastic communities where most of the work was done, St. Anselm's Abbey, Washington, DC, and Engelberg Abbey, Obwalden, Switzerland. Furthermore, the exemplary Benedictine life of these two communities was an ideal setting in which to appreciate the monastic ideas of Peter of Celle. Nothing is more impressive in Peter's writings than his appreciation of patterns of religious life (Cistercian, Carthusian, canonical) different from his own, and so he would no doubt approve that this

iii

translation by a member of the Swiss-American federation of Benedictines be dedicated to the Benedictines of St. Anselm's (English congregation) and Engelberg (Swiss federation). I would like to thank especially Fr Bruno Becker OSB and Fr Thomas Blättler OSB for their expert help.

H. F.

Engelberg
Corpus Christi, 1984

INTRODUCTION

F OUR TOPICS are discussed in this introduction: Peter's life and character, his writings and his style, his theology, and technicalities regarding the translations included in this volume. The section on Peter's writings includes summaries of and orientation to the works translated here. Dom Jean Leclercq has devoted a study to Peter's spirituality, so that will be treated only obliquely. This introduction contains generous samples of the works not translated, especially Peter's letters and sermons.

LIFE[1]

Early Years

Peter was born early in the twelfth century at Aunoy-les-Minimes near Provins.[2] The family, which included at least two other sons, was related to Agnes of Baudement, the sister-in-law of the king of France.[3] Peter had a niece named Heloise, who married a relative of hers, Pierre de la Tournelle. The marriage was criticized as incestuous, and Peter, then abbot of Celle, was assailed for having approved of it. He vigorously defended himself and the marriage in letters to Hugh, the archbishop of Sens, and Alain, the bishop of Auxerre.[4]

Although his family was of the lesser nobility of Champagne, Peter, as abbot of Celle, met opposition from two monks of great family, who found it humiliating to be under a superior of Peter's lesser social status. The prior of Clairvaux wrote to Bishop Henry of Troyes to ask for his help on Peter's behalf against these two troublemakers:

> The abbot of Celle, a religious man who fears God, a good man with good recommendations from good men, notable for his life and literary ability, is linked to us with such familiarity that he is not one among others, but one singled out from the rest. . . . He finds the abbey which he resides over dishonored and disturbed by the wickedness of some of its inhabitants. He wishes to lead them back to the way of truth, but it is easier to inform the ignorant than to reform the depraved. Among their numbers are two notorious and noisy troublemakers who by their insults

have constantly wasted their own lives and the lives of
others. Trusting in their noble lineage, they nourish
scandals and multiply dissensions because they have been
caught in the works of their hands.[5]

Little is known about Peter's education. In a letter he wrote to the
monks of Cluny when he was abbot of St Remi, Peter lamented the
sad decline of that great monastery and urged its reform, especially
the abolition of the custom of taking food and drink after compline.
In the course of this lament, Peter mentioned that as a young man he
shared in the monastic life at St Martin des Champs at Paris.[6]

Montier-la-Celle

Peter left Paris for the monastery of Montier-la-Celle, where he
may already have received his early education.[7] The abbey of Celle
had given bishops to Troyes and St Robert to Molesmes and Cîteaux,
and it was a place of some religious and intellectual importance.
Before many years Peter became abbot there. It is clear that Peter was
an energetic abbot, whose concerns and contacts extended beyond his
own monastery. A staunch supporter of Alexander III, he wrote to
Henry, bishop of Beauvais, the brother of the king and a former
monk of Clairvaux, to urge him to support Alexander against the an-
tipope and preserve the unity of the church: 'Do what you can and
must in accord with the dignity of your office, the nobility of your
ancestral blood, your religious order, the requirements of your Christian faith'.[8]

Peter wrote to monastic communities to praise their zeal or to urge
them to stricter observance and asceticism. To Peter the Venerable,
for example, he wrote a long letter which included a condemnation
of Cluniacs who were eating meat without permission.[9] To Hugh,
the next abbot of Cluny, to the Cistercians of Clairvaux and to the
Carthusians of Mont-Dieu he sent letters of praise, friendship and exhortation. He was on very close terms with Mont-Dieu, which
several of the monks of Celle had joined.[10] He was active in trying to
establish a foundation of this charterhouse in the archdiocese of
Lund.[11] He must already have achieved some fame as a preacher, since
Theobald, archbishop of Paris, asked him to send some sermons for

Advent, which Peter was slow in supplying because of burdensome occupations and short winter days.[12]

Abbot and Episcopal Vicar at Reims

In 1161 Peter's friend, Henry, bishop of Beauvais, was called to the archbishopric of Reims. Probably at Henry's urging, and with the support of Henry the Liberal, count of Champagne, Peter became abbot of the imposing monastery of St Remi (Remigius) of Reims in 1162.[13] As abbot of St Remi Peter functioned as the vicar general for the archbishop when the latter was away. Peter's duties involved him in settling a civil disturbance[14] and, perhaps, in preaching to the clergy.[15]

All the while, Peter continued his efforts on behalf of the Carthusian foundation in Denmark. One of his monks, Fulk, who had accompanied him from Montier-la-Celle to Reims, was ordained a bishop to help Archbishop Eskil of Lund. Peter wrote on Fulk's behalf to Alexander III:

> The bearer of this document was formed in the womb of our humility and received the religious habit from us in the monastery of Celle. He long suckled wine there from bitter breasts, and now by the grace of God he has advanced to the episcopal position. He is sincerely embracing the task and burden of the office enjoined upon him. . . . When your Lord and Master sent the apostles to preach new things, he also enabled them to work wonders. Fulk does not ask you to grant the power to work miracles, but that your authority may work with him and in him so that he may be more easily granted credence by unbelievers.[16]

When Fulk went back to France from Rome, Peter detained him at Reims, so that the abbot might further instruct the new bishop and in order to have Fulk consecrate churches, ordain clergy, and confirm Christian people, in the absence of the bishop, away in Rome.[17] Then Peter sent him on to Eskil with a letter of recommendation.[18] After Eskil retired and entered the abbey of Clairvaux, Peter continued to write him.[19]

Alexander III

Peter corresponded quite frequently with Pope Alexander III. In one letter which survives he pleaded with the pope not to make Henry of Marcy, the abbot of Clairvaux, the bishop of Toulouse. Henry, Peter wrote,

> like a true religious has taken his own measure and fears he is inadequate. Repudiating this marriage, he prefers to be shoeless and to receive in his face the spit of every sort of reproach just as Jesus did, rather than to abandon the sweetness of the vine, the olive tree, and the fig of the profession he has taken upon himself. . . . So let apostolic permission be granted to this man to work in the paradise of the cloister of Clairvaux for unperishable food. . . . He has taken upon his shoulders the ark of God's covenant, in which is the rod of the cross which flowered in the apostles, grew new leaves in the crowds of reborn believers, and bore fruit in the martyrs, confessors and virgins. . . . What an unhappy change where rottenness is received for sweet odor. . . . Let not the apostolic ear listen to Martha complaining against Mary sitting at Jesus' feet. Martha was concerned about her constant ministry and didn't taste the cup of wine flavored with holy contemplation and continual meditation on God's law.[20]

In another letter written just before a church council, Peter gave Alexander a straightforward admonition about the responsibilities of the bishop of Rome, upon whose shoulders rests the burden of all Christendom. He reminded the pope that the state of the Christian people will reflect the quality of their priests, and he urged him to eliminate the twin evils of indulgence and avarice.[21]

For his part Alexander III often issued mandates to Peter (usually in conjunction with others) to settle disputes, vindicate rights, and work for reform. Although the pope mandated Peter much less often than Archbishop Henry of Reims, the numbers of charges entrusted to Peter indicates that he was of some stature in Alexander's eyes.[22]

England

Peter was involved in the conflict between Thomas Becket and Henry II both directly and through his friends John and Richard of Salisbury. About 1148 John spent some time with Peter at Montier-la-Celle, and John dedicated the *Policraticus* to him. Becket became archbishop of Canterbury at the same time Peter became abbot at Reims, but even before these promotions they had exchanged friendly correspondence.[23] When, in 1163, John went into exile in France, Peter invited him to stay at St Remi and John accepted his hospitality.[24] Peter could have written to John what he wrote to the Bishop of Exeter who was also threatened with exile: 'if that great beast vomits you out of your land, a new home has been prepared for you among us. You can have everything without gold and silver. Your will find in it an abundance of books and the leisure to study as well.'[25]

Among other English exiles who spent time at Reims was John's brother Richard, who later became a canon at Merton. For him in 1179 Peter composed *The School of the Cloister*. When Becket had been murdered, Peter wrote to the two brothers that he was not sure what happened to them. He was, however, confident, he said, that just as the brothers had often drunk from the chalice of the Lord in the eucharist, so they would also not be afraid to drink of it in the suffering of martyrdom. Richard was about to take the religious habit and Peter was glad of that, although he wished Richard had stayed at Reims. However, he mused, 'vexing bodily absence may be a stimulus for greater desire, and where bodily sight has been broken off, prayer may continue'.[26] Later Peter wrote to John that he himself would like to join the throngs of pilgrims to Thomas Becket's tomb. This letter like most of Peter's abundant correspondence with the two brothers, is full of warm assurances of friendship and prayers.[27]

Final Years

As the days of his abbacy at St Remi drew to a close and the infirmities of old age began to be a bother, Peter undertook a fairly

extensive remodeling of the abbey church 'to the honor and beauty
of the house of God and blessed Remi'. Peter's renovations involved
reconstruction of the apse and the facade and were of some importance in the history of architecture.[28]

In June, 1178, Peter of Pavia, cardinal of St Chrysogonus, sent to
Alexander III a letter containing a list of eleven French churchmen
whom he thought were suitable to be cardinals. The list included
Peter's friends Henry of Marcy, abbot of Clairvaux, Simon, the
prior of Mont-Dieu, and Bernerède, abbot of St Crépin, as well as
Peter himself. The Cardinal of St Chrysogonus described the abbots
of St Remi and St Crépin as 'learned and prudent men who are
without a doubt by far outstanding among the other abbots of their
land and order in integrity and religion'.[29]

Peter was not made a cardinal. The ill-health which kept him
from accepting an invitation to attend the III Lateran Council may
have been a factor in his being passed over.[30] His friends the abbots
Bernerède and Henry were, however, appointed the cardinal-
bishops of Albano and Palestrina respectively. Bernerède was a dear
friend and frequent correspondent of Peter, who was saddened to
lose his friend. For his part Bernerède was sorry to be separated
from his friends and monastery. Peter encouraged him:

> Your consolation is greater than your desolation. You
> have left behind a small flock and received the noble car-
> dinals as friends and companions. You have left the
> niche of the cloister and received the city which is
> mistress of the world. Who does not know that the
> status of an abbot is inferior to that of a bishop? Who is
> not aware that although the bodies of the martyrs Cris-
> pin and Crispinian are buried at Soissons, the more
> sacred relics of Peter, the prince of the apostles, and
> Paul, the teacher of the gentiles, are in Rome.

Peter then urged Bernerède to let his feelings be moderated by his
rational estimate of the situation. He ended by asking pardon for
taking up so much of the cardinal's time with the letter and excused
himself by recalling the long hours he had spent in conversation
with his friend Bernerède.[31]

In October 1181, John of Salisbury, the bishop of Chartres, died.

His friend Peter was called from Reims to replace him. Peter was bishop for only a short time, for he died 19 February 1182. His body was buried next to that of his dear friend and predecessor at Chartres, in the abbey of Josaphat. From the time of his episcopacy only two letters survive. One of these, to the General Chapter of Cîteaux, is an eloquent entreaty for prayers:

> Let your holy association remember that I am one of the students of St Bernard. . . . Although absent, I am prostrate at the feet of this holy congregation. I implore your support, which is hoped for, requested and desireable. Yours I was, am, and always will be. . . . You nourished me at Celle and loved me at Reims; will you abandon me at Chartres?[32]

Character

In the preface which he wrote for the first edition of Peter's collected works (1671), Dom Jean Mabillon singled out what he considered the essential elements of Peter's faith and character. Dom Mabillon's outline will serve as a guide for what follows, parts of which will receive fuller treatment later in this introduction.[33]

A first characteristic of Peter's inner life was his piety. Mabillon singles out Peter's devotion to Christ and to Mary. It was particularly Christ's passion which elicited Peter's devotion. He wrote, for instance, to the abbot of Villiers that he understood the abbot was often sharing in 'the chalice of our sister, which is the passion of Christ.'

> This is a bitter draught for those who drink it, but it contains within it the better hope of salvation. Nothing is safer for those going toward heaven than to follow the street stained by the blood of Christ, to gaze at the marks of the nails. . . .[34]

Peter's devotion to Mary was more subdued. It is manifest primarily in his sermons for Mary's feasts and in his polemic with Nicholas of St Alban's. Other elements in Peter's piety were his love of the great liturgical feasts,[35] and his reverence for the eucharist.

With his devotion to Christ Peter combined a remarkable capacity for friendship with his fellow human beings. This is patent in what Dom Jean Leclercq called his 'letters of friendship', penned to such men as John of Salisbury, Bernerède of St-Crépin and Thomas Becket. The esteem which Peter elicited from his friends is clear in a letter from Gérard of Péronne:

> I call you my abbot not out of insolence, but out of friendship. My conscience presumes to call you mine because it feels that I am your servant. Your esteem made me your intimate, intimacy made me a friend, friendship made two to be of one mind. . . . Charity . . . made equal friends out of two unequal persons. . . . As Christ is my witness, I have no one with whom I am more in accord in the heart of Jesus Christ. Although the division of our order separates us, charity binds us, for it is not the color of our habits but the love of hearts which effects this unity or unanimity. . . .[36]

Peter's brotherly love was not reserved to his friends, but extended as well to people in need whom he tried to solace and help.[37]

With tender devotion to Christ and loyalty and affection toward his friends Peter combined a forceful and sincere dedication to the truth and good of the Church as he saw them. He stoutly defended the rights and liberties of the church and urged the clergy to be above reproach by avoiding avarice, favoritism and immorality. Voicing two favorite themes of twelfth-century reformers, he both congratulated Thomas Becket for having stripped himself in order to follow Christ who hung naked on the cross and also recommended to the archbishop the patience of the primitive Church.[38] In his correspondence as well as in his practical activities as abbot and papal mandatory Peter showed himself to be discreet, humble and patient.[39]

Mabillon, like others since his time, singled out Peter's love of solitude and contemplation.[40] Peter frequently expressed a longing for the quiet seclusion of a monastery. He cherished the days he spent with the Carthusians at Mont-Dieu, where he could focus his attention on God in prayer and reading and find rest from his usual cares. The word "contemplation" occurs frequently in his writings, as do other expressions used by medieval writers to describe the life of prayer.[41]

However, three notes of caution should be sounded. First, Peter gives few clues about his own experience of prayer. Secondly, his vocabulary is not precise, so that it is difficult to know what he means by contemplation. Thirdly, Peter 'was a very striking figure in the church and was considered a very capable man. He was often charged by Alexander with ecclesiastical affairs and appointed arbiter between laymen. . . .'[42] For three decades he held high offices, championed reform, and remained in contact with many prominent persons. All this suggests that he had an exceptional aptitude for leadership and practical affairs. It seems highly likely that Peter did not have an unqualified distaste for such activity. People, including monks, usually have a hand in their own fate. A person with a penchant for active ministry may also relish intervals of quiet retreat without feeling called to withdraw permanently into seclusion.

WORKS[43]

Letters

About one hundred seventy-five of Peter's letters survive. His collected letters were first edited in nine books in 1613 by J. Sirmond, whose edition was reprinted by Dom Janvier in his edition of Peter's collected works. Sirmond's edition was included by Migne in the *Patrologia latina,* but the order of the letters was changed, and the number of books was reduced to two. In 1850 C. Messiter edited a large collection of letters from a manuscript of St John's College, Oxford.[44] He attributed this collection to Walter, abbot of Montier-en-Der (Dervy), but they were, in fact, the letters of Peter of Celle. Dom Jean Leclercq has edited five letters of this collection which were not included in the *Patrologia,* along with two others exchanged by Peter and the abbey of Anchin.[45]

The letters edited by Dom Leclercq provide a representative sample of the content and recipients of Peter's correspondence. In 1165 Peter sent a note to the aged Abbot Goswin of Anchin. He asked:

> When you have put off corruption, don't discard compassion. When you have emigrated from the valley of tears to heaven, let not feelings of mercy cease to exist in you. . . . Most holy father, pray for me, your friend,

and for your holy community and ours, so that Jesus
Christ may deign to send into us the Spirit who proceeds from the Father, so that consoled by him we may
cease from our evil works and devote ourselves to good
works. In this may we follow in the footsteps of your
holy way of life and embrace the example of perfect
religion.

One hopes Goswin lived to read it. A reply from Alexander, his
successor, described the old abbot's exemplary death.

Another of these letters was addressed by Peter from the
charterhouse of Mont-Dieu to five monks of Clairvaux. Peter had
gone to Mont-Dieu, in his terms, so that Rachel might bear better
offspring than those heretofore conceived by Leah. Rachel's offspring are Joseph and Benjamin, who stand for good reputation and
good conscience respectively. Peter also wrote from Mont-Dieu to
his own community at Celle, urging them to 'moral integrity,
monastic observance reception of guests, pure love, jubilation in the
divine praises, obedience to one another, and so forth, fulfilling the
precepts of the Gospel and the Rule of blessed Benedict', in oratory,
cloister, chapter, refectory, dormitory, and other places of
customary activity. In another letter to Celle Peter observed that he
had written in a humble manner, so that all the less sophisicated
might understand. Retelling a dream he had had, he wrote of the
theology of the eucharist and the Incarnation and he described the
last hours of Jesus' life, saying that by meditating on them
throughout the Mass one might tie down the wandering human
heart.

In a letter to Hardwin, abbot of Larrivour, Peter described the
liturgy at Mont-Dieu. He began with protestations of friendship
and praised the Carthusians to whose monastery he had come, poor
and ignorant. The contents of another letter, which was accompanied by the gift of a gold ring, are clear from the title: 'Of a friend
to a friend about friendship'. The final letter of this selection was to
Becket, when he was still chancellor of England. Becket seems to
have asked that some sermons be written down and sent to him.

Monastic observance, friendship, mutual support—these, along
with practical business matters, were the concerns of Peter's letters.

Sermons

Peter evaluated his own sermons — ninety-six of which have survived[46] — in a letter to a monk of St Bertin:

> You wish to have our sermons, which the four winds of heaven have tossed around in varying degrees like useless and superflous feathers. If you have read them, have you not found them bloodless in ideas and weak in vocabulary? If you haven't seen them, who persuaded you to seek them so insistently, since once you've found them you'll reject them? Does curiosity or diligent study impel you to beg the greens and tasteless husks of an old man, although you are sitting at the table of rich Augustine, kind Gregory, wealthy Jerome, glorious Ambrose, Bede well stocked with all coins, great Hilary deeper than the sea, Origen of the sweetest-sounding eloquence, and so many others? I am unworthy to gather crumbs under the table of these men. If new things please you there are the writings of Master Hugh, St Bernard, Master Gilbert, and Master Peter, which are wanting neither in roses nor in lilies. Our writings do not draw from the depths nor do they approach the heights, for our words are parched and perhaps sterile. Frequently I have put stylus to tablet with this intention, that on the vigils of solemnities I might occupy myself at least for half an hour in contemplation of the coming joys and withdraw myself from the tumults of the secular cares which oppress me. However, you will find many of our sermons unfinished after an hour, sometimes because of my negligence and sometimes because of unwelcome occupations. I give birth to unfinished and imperfect offspring. . . . However, be merciful, for they did not obtrude themselves, but under compulsion they shamefully became public.[47]

Peter was being overly modest here. Although the small number of surviving manuscripts suggests his sermons were not best sellers, it is also clear that they were well regarded. Archbishop Theobald

of Paris asked him for copies, as did Becket, and Matilda, abbess of
Fontevrault.[48] The sermon was the medium to which Peter's talents
were best suited. In his sermons his imagination, his penchant for
metaphors, and his familiarity with the Church's tradition served
him well, while the limits of the form and the need to communicate
with an audience of varied capacities imposed a beneficial discipline.

The vast majority of his sermons are devoted to the great feasts of
the liturgical year: Advent (1–6), Christmas (7–12), Purification
(13), Lent (14–20), St Benedict (21), Annunciation (22–28)[49], Passion and Palm Sundays (29–33), Holy Thursday (34–41), Easter
(42–49), Ascension (50–52), Pentecost (53–56), the feasts of John
the Baptist, Peter and Paul, Mary Magdalene (57–64), Transfiguration (65–66), Assumption (67–75), St Bernard (76–77), St Nicholas
(78–79), All Saints (80), commons of saints (81–82), synodal sermons to clergy (83–93), and a few miscellaneous (93–95).

The four sermons translated in this volume are a sample of the
thoughts which Peter shared with his community during the two
weeks leading up to the celebration of Easter. The first, for the fifth
Sunday of Lent (S 29, Passion Sunday) speaks of following in the
footsteps of Christ, who followed the path marked out by his
Father's will. In all, Jesus took fourteen steps from his conception
to his burial. In walking this path he bore the judgment which our
sins deserved. His cause freed us from the accusation of sin and
eventually it will liberate us from all sinful deeds.

The sermon for Palm Sunday (S 33) considers the theme "in your
minds you must be the same as Christ Jesus" [Ph 2.5]. Peter pictures
Christ on calvary, abandoned by almost all his disciples. To find out
Jesus' mind, we can ask the bride, or Mary his mother, or Mary
Magdalene, or John the Evangelist, who rested on Jesus' breast at
the last supper. One can recognize Jesus by the signs of his passion.
Contemplating them, one should be filled with compassion, which
is symbolized by the myrrh with which he was anointed and by the
left hand of the spouse which was under the head of the bride. The
right hand of the spouse is the glory of heaven. To reach that glory
one should take advantage of the Lord's mercy while it is available.
There will come a time when the Lord will set aside the
powerlessness of the Incarnation for the severity of judgment.

The sermon for Holy Thursday concerns the eucharist: who and where the bread of angels is; how, when, where, by whom and why it is to be eaten. In the eucharist Christians receive the body, soul and divinity of Christ, who was conceived and born of the Virgin Mary. The greatness of this mystery requires that one participate in it worthily and devoutly.

The brief Easter sermon asks the angels where they were during Christ's passion. They reply that he did not need their help to complete his work of redemption. By assuming our nature and death, Christ has redeemed all that could be redeemed at any price. He values all the little ways in which we share in his passion. Although the festival of Easter pertains especially to our race, the angels also participate in it and we should try to imitate their purity as we celebrate with them.[49]

These four sermons exemplify Peter's homiletic art. He had a vivid imagination and employed some telling symbols (e.g., walking in Jesus' footsteps), although at times his symbols become overly complex or confused (the superimposition of John the Evangelist, Mary, Mary Magdalene and the bride of the Canticle) or even a bit shocking (the imagery from the Canticle applied to touching Christ). The imagined dialogues between his assembly on the one hand, and John the Evangelist or the angels on the other, are effective. These particular sermons show a tender devotion to the mysteries of Christ's life and a sophisticated Christology. Peter effectively relates Scripture and church teaching to Christian living.

Treatises

Peter wrote four scriptural treatises which have been edited recently by Dom de Martel. These include two commentaries on the book of Ruth and two treatises on the tabernacle described in Exodus 25–28. The second of the tabernacle treatises is a resumé of a work of Bede the Venerable.[50] A fifth treatise, *The Book of Breads,* dedicated to John of Salisbury, is a lengthy discussion of the biblical references to bread. Often the content is of theological interest.[51]

The treatises which are translated here are what Dom Leclercq termed 'monastic *opuscula*'. Of the four Peter wrote the only one not translated here, the unfinished *On the Purity of the Soul,* was edited for the first time by Dom Leclercq.[52] In the first part of it, Peter discusses the nature of heavenly purity and how the Christian may approach to it by being melted down by love and conformed to the image of the Son of God. In heaven there will be no growth in purity of charity, but neither will there be any boredom where charity, the vision and God, and joy are perfect. The second part of the work treats those elements of corruption in Christians' lives which impede their progress toward heavenly purity. Growth toward purity begins with a rejection of the devil's enticements toward avarice and indulgence. From this beginning one advances according to the law of justice, becoming progressively servant, disciple, son and friend. At a third stage, one takes the offensive against the forces of evil through confession of one's sins. In the unfinished third part of the work Peter compares martyrdom and virginity. The latter involves virtue in the conscience and a good reputation manifest in public comportment. A pure heart is necessary for contemplation.

The School of the Cloister, one of Peter's last works, was composed for Richard of Salibury in 1179, and Peter referred to the work in two letters to Richard. In the first Peter told his friend that he was suffering from a kidney complaint. Moreover, he was so preoccupied and starved for reading and leisure that he wondered how he could take the measure of claustral discipline. If the religious serving under the rules of Augustine or Benedict keeps their precepts, he will have his reward. The whole of claustral discipline can be summed up in a word: 'that nothing be done, said, possessed, without the abbot's permission, that the eye not go out of the prescribed limits, that the hand not move toward what is illicit, that the foot not run toward what is prohibited.'[53] In a second letter Peter wrote that he had completed part of the work and was hurrying to get it ready for a messenger, when some friends dissuaded him from sending a fragmentary work. If another reliable messenger turned up in a few days, Peter went on to assure him, Richard would have the whole treatise.[54]

The completed version of *The School of the Cloister* is prefaced by a dedicatory letter to Henry of Troyes, the count of Champagne.[55] This letter tells how illness gave Peter a chance again to experience and appreciate the full round of claustral discipline, enabling him to write about claustral discipline as Augustine wrote about Christian discipline. He includes the customary apology for his lack of style and ideas, as well as an apology for his order. A prologue written to Richard of Salisbury acknowledges that Peter had not often been able to live the discipline he describes. Apologizing for his wordiness and other shortcomings, he claims he prefers the gentleness of Gregory the Great to the harshness of Jerome. Finally, he assures Richard of his friendship, of which the treatise is a token.

The Discipline of the Cloister is quite well organized. The first two chapters treat the bibilical origins of the claustral discipline legislated by Augustine and Benedict. Chapters 3–10 compare the disciplines of philosophers, Jews, Christians, claustrals and angels, and expound upon the nature, aim and hardships of claustral life, which is a share in the cross of Christ.[56] Chapters 11–17 develop a series of metaphors for the life of the cloister: stadium, vestibule, treasure room, earthly sanctuary, royal chamber, gibbet, market place. Finally, Peter summarizes some essential elements of claustral discipline: silence (18), reading (19), confession (20–21), prayer (22–23), meditation on death (24–26). He concludes with a treatise on communion (27), an epilogue, and an exhortation to claustrals, which is drawn partially from Gregory the Great. The chapter on the eucharist and the exhortation may have been earlier works of Peter's which he incorporated into *The School of the Cloister*.

The work which Dom Leclercq entitled *On Affliction and Reading* sets out to discuss three tests to which recruits to Christ's army are subjected in their rooms: bodily affliction, reading and prayer.[57] Peter urges the necessity of moderate asceticism and discernment regarding forms of temptation and sin. This leads him to a digression on confession. Most of the work is devoted to reading, without which life in a monastic room would be unbearable. This includes a series of metaphors showing reading as the keeper of Lady Wisdom's keys, a hostess who sets out a variety of breads suitable to every taste, and a maiden seeking a suitable lover. He offers some suggestions about the particular benefits of reading Genesis, Exodus and Joshua. The work concludes abruptly with a description of the benefits of the solitary life, which is driven home with a rather repulsive comparison of self-discipline to a butcher shop where the solitary gathers money to redeem his soul by selling parts of his flesh and blood.

Peter seems to have been writing this treatise especially with eremitical or quasi-eremitical religious in mind. The word *cella,* which is translated here as 'room', occurs quite often in the text. The word might refer to an individual room in a monastery, to a small monastery, to the small, individual dwelling of a Carthusian, or, by a play on words, to the abbey of Celle. Jean Leclercq has suggested that *cella* might be thought of as the basic local unit where one lived the religious life, a unit which took different forms in different orders.[58] Since in *On Reading and Affliction* Peter seems to distinguish the solitaries for whom he writes from claustrals, by the word *cella* he probably refers to a eremitical dwelling.[59]

On Conscience is the least organized and most studied of Peter's monastic treatises.[60] He wrote it at Celle at the request of Alcher, a monk of Clairvaux. In many of his works St Bernard had spoken of conscience, and perhaps this prompted Alcher to ask Peter to write a work dealing specifically with the nature and development of a good conscience.[61] The treatise begins with the customary apologies for incompetence — Alcher's request has called Peter back from a distracted way of life — and poor style. The particular stylistic fault which Peter singles out is prolixity. This he justifies by saying that it will help draw the reader into self-knowledge. Peter admits that he doesn't have a mind for clear distinctions and definitions, so he will proceed by way of descriptions. In any case, his concern is to promote not science, but a good conscience. [C 1–20]

After this long beginning, Peter describes conscience as 'knowledge of self, either anticipating good or wary of evil'. This description implies a starting point, self-knowledge, and a goal, to do good and avoid evil. To clarify this description Peter offers an etymology for 'conscience': knowledge of the heart (*cordis scientia*), in the sense not of interiorized knowledge of extrinsic things, but of the moral knowledge by which one knows oneself in and by oneself. In this description Peter seems to enfold three features: a moral capacity or act, a form of knowledge, and moral earnestness. Self-knowledge in this sense is consciousness of the created image of the creative Image of God (see C 49–53), finite wisdom and holiness brought about through grace, and God-given purity cleansing the soul to make it conceive God's Word. (C 21–23)

Later he offers a series of metaphors for conscience. She is a queen who banquets with her lord and king. Her appearance symbolizes all the moral qualities of a good conscience. Conscience will have no misgivings at the judgment (C 25–28). The indwelling of the Spirit makes the good conscience a microcosm of heaven, indwelt by the Trinity, whose contributions to conscience are fear, instruction in the commandments, and finally reciprocal friendship (C 31–40). Conscience is a mirror in which the soul sees its current state and a tablet on which the deeds of one's past life are engraved (C 47–49).

In the rest of his treatise, Peter differentiates and describes various states of conscience. First, he distinguishes the good, bad and intermediate consciences. The last, the state of a convert who has confessed his evil ways and is struggling toward a holier way of life, is of particular interest to Peter (C 58). This leads him to discuss the pauline theology of law in relation to conscience and culpability (C 59). He then turns to the origins and characteristics of a good conscience, which is developed only by the exercise of discretion, upon the foundation of humility (C 61–66), and to matters of special importance in the treatment of novices (C 67–70). The work concludes with a discussion of four kinds of conscience: claustral (C 75–90) including digressions on confession and eschatology, secular (C 91–94), infernal (C 95–96), and heavenly (C 97–98). *On Conscience*, like several of Peter's treatises, has no proper conclusion.[62]

Peter's interest in conscience is one indication of a pervasive concern for interiority. Conscience is the sanctuary of self-awareness, self-possession and the intentionality which animates one's activities. The meaning and religious value of prayer, tears, confession and good actions are determined by the intention and devotion which give rise to them.[63] Because he was so conscious of the relations between inward and outward action, Peter was equally insistent in condemning hypocrisy and in recommending good example and good reputation.[64]

Style

Peter's writings have not received high marks for style.[65] He himself frequently acknowledged their stylistic limitations: lack of order and clarity, deficiencies 'in worth of ideas and grace of words'.[66] Such disclaimers were conventional, but they were also true in Peter's case. Nevertheless, he obviously expected his works to be read by interested contemporaries.

By the time he became an abbot, Peter's style was set; allowing for differences in genre his ideas and style are homogeneous throughout. A vivid and fertile imagination was one of his greatest assets, but it was also his greatest liability.[67] The same could be said of his mastery of rhetorical conventions: varied vocabulary, alliteration, parallelism, symmetry. By modern standards at any rate, he was not the disciplined master of his thoughts and rhetoric. As a stylist he lacked the discretion and moderation which seem to have characterized him as an abbot and churchman. He was not a logical writer, and does not seem in fact to have esteemed logic very highly.

While acknowledging Peter's limitations as a writer, Dom Leclercq has seen extenuating grounds. Peter's aim was to familiarize his readers with the subject-matter, rather than to instruct them about it, to contemplate rather than to exhort. His forte was biblically-inspired symbolism, not abstract thought. He was dealing with truths which cannot be expressed clearly and logically in words, but which may be given affective expression in order to arouse fervor. Peter practiced a 'higher philology', and his spiritual exercises are 'mixed together in a confusion which corresponds to an order superior to that of logic.'[68]

It is certainly true that there was a theology practiced by claustrals which is recognizably different from that which developed in the schools of Peter's world. However, this theology was in no way incompatable with logic and order. As the writings of St Anselm and Richard of St Victor show, it was quite possible for claustrals to produce theological writings which were logical and lyrical, orderly as well as imaginative, profound as well as contemplative.

Even if Peter's style has its shortcomings and his thought is not strikingly profound or even original, his work is of interest for the history of theology and spirituality. Furthermore, some of his presuppositions and convictions which were taken for granted in the twelfth century will seem striking, challenging or usefully irritating eight centuries later.

Trinity

Peter seldom discusses the Trinity, and he even recommends that one avoid attempts to penetrate the mystery.[69] Yet, he mentions the Trinity often enough to indicate the importance in his faith and devotion of the mystery of the Triune God. In *On Conscience* Peter wrote:

> These three, the Word, the Lord and the Spirit of his mouth create, strengthen and adorn the heaven of conscience. The Lord creates, the Word strengthens, the Spirit adorns. Yet, the Trinity together do these things, which by us and in us according to our different merits are distinguished singly. Whatever the Father does, the Son and Holy Spirit do simultaneously. But, behold, having put a seal on the mystery of the Trinity, let us turn our attention to the trinity or arrangement of conscience.[70]

Later in the same work, Peter is drawn back to the subject of the Trinity:

> A good conscience lays as its foundation the triune God, three in persons, one in essence. Shunning reckless discussion and expanding the veneration of faith, the faithful soul worships, adores and venerates this triune God, preaches him even at the cost of shedding her blood, follows and loves him.[71]

As the Trinity is the foundation of a good conscience, it is also the term of a twofold movement facilitated by the grace of tears. Tears 'incline the Son of God toward us and raise us to the true Trinity by the intervention of the Holy Spirit'.[72]

Christ

If the Trinity is in the background of Peter's thought and devotion, the figure of Christ is everywhere in them. 'One should always and in all things have recourse in the beginning to the beginning. The beginning was in the beginning with God, and the Word was of the beginning and the beginning of every word.'[73] The Word is the Son and Image of the Father. There is nothing 'more beautiful, more desirable, better or purer' than this Image,[74] which served as the pattern for the creation of humanity in the image and likeness of God. This likeness of God has been obscured by sin, through which humanity wandered off into a region of unlikeness.[75] Then 'God showed himself to be our friend when we were poor, since because of the great love he had for us, he brought it to pass that his only Son became incarnate'.[76]

The Word, immutable in his divinity, chose to assume the human condition, subject to temporality and vanity. The Word came into this distant region in order to receive a kingdom and to reign over men and angels in a single kingdom. He was born of the virgin by the overshadowing of the Holy Spirit. 'In the virgin's womb Word and flesh were so joined to each other that henceforward one no longer spoke of man or God, but of the man-God inseparably one person.'[77] Thus did Wisdom depict the form of the new, reformed humanity by means of a new kind of conception and birth. The incarnate Word accepted the full consequences of mutability and advanced in time and with time, 'in age and wisdom before God and men'. [Lk 2:25][78] He was circumcised, offered in the temple, baptized by John. He fasted in the desert, was tempted by the devil, and was transfigured before his disciples. He preached and worked miracles.[79]

Finally, Jesus came to the last days of his earthly life. The Father did not spare his Son but handed him over for us all. The Father let ruthless men beat his well-beloved Jesus, treating 'his Son as though he were an enemy, in order to bring about the reconciliation of those who were at enmity with him'.[80] Jesus accepted this discipline of peace freely and obediently.[81] Choosing to conquer by patience, so that he might conquer by power, he poured out his blood on the cross.[82]

'He descended into hell as a powerful champion, powerfully equipped to free his faithful.' He broke the iron bars of the abyss and cut off the head of the dragon. From the dragon's belly he extracted the patriarchs and prophets, a treasure hidden there since the beginning of the world.[83] Then he rose in triumph from the grave: 'O flesh, O man, congratulate your sister, that is, your nature, which has been glorified in Christ. Put your trust in the spouse of your sister.'[84] His ascension was the consummation of his incarnation and the reward of his passion.[85] Now he is above, below, and beside those who dwell on earth.[86] He brings them healing, enlightenment and peace.[87] In the end he will come as the fearful judge, to pass definitive judgment on every human life.[88]

The successful outcome of Jesus' case assured a favorable settlement of humanity's case, which he made his own.[89] Jesus

> paid off all our debt with interest, not merely a hundred times over, but infinitely more. He did this so that on the scales of the cross the gift would outweigh the sin, and the overflowing grace of pardon would remit not only original fault but also actual sins.[90]

Christ is not only the mediator between God and humanity; he is the source of unity within humanity as well.[91]

Imitation of Christ

All the mysteries of Christ's life are examples for his disciples to follow.

> Your conception is an example for us, so that by your Spirit we may conceive fear of you. Your birth is an example for us, so that we may give birth to your love. Your life is an example, so that we may keep poverty, innocence, humility, gentleness, charity and chastity, mercy and piety. Your death is an example for us, so that we may preserve obedience and patience. Your resurrection is an example for us, so that we may believe in the resurrection of the flesh. Your ascension is an example for us, so that we may hope for the glorification of bodies and souls.[92]

By following Jesus' example, Christians repaint the image and likeness of God in themselves. When their death is assimilated to his death, the wax of their humanity will be sealed with the form of the body of Christ. In heaven this image of God will be indestructible as crystal.[93]

It is above all the passion of Christ which Christians must imitate. They should constantly meditate upon it, so that they will know the path he followed and be stirred to follow in his blood-stained footsteps. Meditating on the external events, they will come to know his inner mystery and have the same mind as he did.[94] Never should Christians recall Christ's passion without deep feelings of compunction, devotion and compassion. This compassion takes practical form in bestowing benefits on Christ's poor and in sharing in the sacraments of Christ's body and blood and confession.[95]

In a special way claustrals carry the sufferings of Christ within themselves. 'Jesus set up the cloister to represent his cross. Just as he bore the discipline of our peace in his body, so we must bear the same reproaches he did when we leave the camp of this world for the cloister.'[96] Every form of claustral discipline flows from the cross: as Christ was stripped and nailed on the cross, so the claustral must strip himself of the lust of the flesh and stretch out toward his beloved. As Christ nailed to the cross could move nothing but his tongue, the claustral is to be attached to the cross by the fear of God and confine his movements to confession and prayer.[97]

Finally, in heaven Jesus himself will be the fulfilment of every claustral discipline. There

> the breast of Jesus is the refectory; the lap of Jesus, the dormitory; the face of Jesus, the oratory; the width and length, the height and depth of Jesus, the cloister; the company of Jesus and all the blessed, the chapter; Jesus' account of the unity of the Father, Son and Holy Spirit and the opening of the mystery of his incarnation, the lecture-hall.[98]

Church and Sacraments

The Church is the body of Christ. Vast and beautiful, she extends to all lands and will last for all ages. Like Noah's ark in the flood, the Church is the vessel of truth in the midst of the world. Her four corners are the gospels and the cardinal virtues. She saves all those who turn from their evil ways and enter her by faith and the works of faith. Through the Spirit she is joined to the Godhead in wedlock and called the spouse of the Lamb.[99]

In the house of the gospel there is a table where each day the faithful are served the bread of angels. There we find a baptistry where bodies and souls are washed of all infection. There those who are contrite and make a sincere confession receive the pardon for which they ask. There a stove gives warmth, burns away superfluity, and illumines the dark. There is a place hidden for contemplation, meditation and intimate conversation. Finally, there is a pool of tears and an ash heap where the last things are remembered.[100]

> Consider the beauty of the church: the washing of baptism, the anointing of chrism, the consecration of the Lord's body and blood; and many other things, which it is more simple to look at each day than to explain now. Adorn your bedchamber, Sion, by worthily and faithfully cherishing the church's sacraments, by wisely providing selected, appointed ministers, by living an ordered and devout life, by keeping the faith, by holding to the truth, by seeking peace.[101]

Three of the church's sacraments were of special interest to Peter and his contemporaries: confession, eucharist, and ordained ministry.

Confession

By Peter's day confession had attained the form which it kept in the Roman Catholic Church until recent times. Confession was a largely private action which could be repeated and which concerned not just flagrant sinners, but all Christians. The theology of the sacrament was less settled.[102]

Peter occasionally showed his acquaintance with the theoretical and analytical aspects of christian penitential doctrine. He spelled out the stages of the moral act: sensory imagination offers an enticement and allures consent, consent leads to action, practice to habit. The essential elements of confession he listed as contrition, confession and satisfaction. There are different degrees of culpability, stemming from different sorts of temptations, circumstances and sins.[103] However,

Peter's usual concern was the practice of confession in the cloister, which he thought should be more conscientious than the 'clumsy and negligent' confession of worldly men.[104] Generally, he seems to have envisaged the claustral confessing to his superior, a practice which combined three elements which later centuries distinguished: (1) sacramental confession, (2) spiritual direction, (3) private *culpa* in which a monk acknowledged his external infractions of the rule to a superior.[105]

Frequent, sincere and candid confession brings many benefits: humility, antidotes to sinful pleasure, wise advice.[106] The decisive argument for the use of the sacrament, however, is that it is the divinely established means by which the baptized receive forgiveness of their sins, recover their baptismal purity and are continually re-formed in the image of Christ.[107] To refuse to confess one's sins is to disobey the command of a merciful God, who has offered an opportunity for forgiveness which is available only as long as life lasts and which serves as a rehearsal for the last judgment.[108]

Peter was aware of resistance to confession: 'aptly is confession compared to a desert, since by regulars as well as by the people of the world it is more deserted than frequented'.[109] Peter analyzed the psychological barriers of twelfth- (and twentieth-) century Christians and claustrals to the sacrament and tried to refute them. Because of shame one may fail to disclose one's sins or their occasions. But one should not be ashamed to disclose one's shamefulness to a discreet confessor who is a compassionate doctor, guardian and consoler. Secondly, even if the superior is strict and inflicts severe penances, fear of the much greater punishment of hell should overcome human fear. The wrath of God is more to be feared than that of a superior. A third obstacle to confession is the presumption of those who trust complacently in God's mercy, while refusing to obey his command to confess their sins. The final impediment is despair, which leads one to think his sins are too great or too long-standing to be forgiven.[110]

The Church weeps for the sins of her children. It is a characteristic of monks that they too weep for their sins.[111] It is especially characteristic of monks that they seek to know themselves[112] through self-scrutiny and self-disclosure, through contrition and confession. By these means they will learn to distinguish and combat the demon-vices which oppose their efforts to follow Christ.[113] As the claustral's conscience is progressively refined in the fire of confession, he advances from fear, to submission to the words of truth, to the perfection of love.[114]

Communion

Some of the finest passages translated in this volume concern the eucharist, which is the heart of Christ's body, the Church.[115] The eucharist was very important in Peter's life and devotion and formed a frequent theme of his preaching and writing. The eucharist provides the unifying thread of the *Book of Breads* and the subject for the final chapter of *The School of the Cloister.* The eucharist was also the topic of one of Peter's most theological expositions, his *Sermon 40* for Holy Thursday, which will serve as the basis for the following summary.[116]

Unlike angels, who are eternally nourished by the sight of God, human beings can ascend to God only by human and visible signs. At the thought of bread, which is preeminent among such signs, Peter broke into a prayer:

> O Lord, always give us this bread, this daily, supersubstantial bread, which descends from heaven and gives life to this world . . . , the bread which the Father stamped with his seal and sent into the world. Behold, Lord Jesus! Your little ones, whom the Father gave you, your children whom you acquired by your blood, seek bread and there is no one to break it for them. . . .

Because Christ the priest offers himself to God the Father, human beings can celebrate their reconciliation. The eucharistic bread is Christ's body, which he broke on the cross by freely laying down his life and breathing out his spirit. In the person of the priest Christ breaks this same bread mystically on the altar, by renewing the faith in Christian hearts and by conferring the effect of his passion on Christian souls. He offers this eucharistic bread with the same words he used at the Last Supper.

Those who partake of this bread ought to be taught the truth of catholic doctrine regarding it. This truth includes ten points.

(1) *Institution.* As apostolic tradition teaches, the sacrament was instituted by the Lord at the Last Supper. Because of his wondrous love he offers to the faithful his glorified body under the veil of mystic appearances.

(2) *Form.* When a catholic priest with the proper intention says the words of institution over wheat bread and wine mixed with water, the bread and wine become Christ's body and blood. All that precedes or follows the words of institution is praise of Christ or prayer.

(3) *Sacramentum and res.* The sacramental sign is the visible appearance of bread and wine. The reality which the sign contains and signifies is the body of Christ. The reality which is signified but not contained by the sign is the unity of the Church among those who have been predestined, called and justified.

(4) *Manner.* The manner of sacramental eating is twofold: for the good, who believe in God and remain in him by holiness of life and unity of faith, it brings salvation. For the evil it brings damnation.

(5) *Conversion of the substance.* After the consecration one sees bread and wine, but one believes most certainly that the only bread and wine there is the bread of angels.[117]

(6) *Fraction.* The mystical breaking of the form of the bread is to be believed rather than discussed.

(7) *Substantial or mystical immolation.* Christ was immolated once by the death of the passion. He is immolated daily by the memory and recollection of that same immolation.

(8) *Cause.* The eucharist was instituted to bestow increase of virtue and medicine for daily weakness.

(9) *Frequency.* The eucharist should be received by one who is not in grave sins or attached to sinning. It should be received at least three times a year, or better, each Sunday, or even daily.

(10) *Minister.* The sacrament is validly confected even by a sinful priest, but not by a heretic who is outside the Church.

Regarding these points two observations may be added. Peter saw the eucharist, like everything else, in eschatological terms. It is the foretaste of the heavenly banquet, where the blessed will join the angels in feasting on the vision of God: 'Would that in receiving [the eucharist] I might have a foretaste of how sweet the Lord will be in heaven.'[118] Secondly, Peter insisted with equal emphasis both on the need to receive the eucharist worthily and on the importance of receiving it regularly. One who is worthy should approach; one who is unworthy should withdraw and purify himself. In no case should one keep away from the sacrament. It is sufficient for a lay person to receive communion once a year, but devout claustrals who never have enough of the sight of God receive communion daily. Those religious between these two extremes of annual and daily communion should take into account opportunity, custom and solemn feasts. They are impelled toward receiving the sacrament in virtue of their baptism, their religious profession, and their ordination, but above all by the love of Christ manifest in his incarnate life and death. In receiving communion religious should strive to purify their hearts through compunction and confession and to receive the Lord with a devout intention.[119]

Priesthood

The nine synodal sermons are a synthesis of Peter's theology regarding the ministry of bishops and priests. The clergy form an ordered hierarchy, which is fashioned according to the pattern of the ranks of angels. The pope is at the summit of this hierarchy, the vicar of Christ, and a bishop with the rest of the episcopal order. After him come patriarchs, metropolitans, archbishops, bishops, priests, deacons and so forth. The image of the glory of the vision of God should shine on the face of the bishop, who ought to be an example of right living, of Jesus' patience, humility, poverty, chastity and charity. He should be distinguished in doctrine and wisdom, as well as in virtue, reading and prayer. 'A person who desires to be a bishop desires a good thing, to pray and to read, so that he may be filled with wisdom and be perfect in propriety.'[120] Bishops should ordain only worthy men and see to it that those ordained serve as faithful and prudent stewards. Priests ought to be responsive to the wishes of their bishops, in whose tasks and powers they collaborate. They come together for consultations, to judge whether anything being done in the ecclesiastical province is contrary to the gospels or the canonical decrees.

Those who have the care of the Christian people whom Christ has redeemed at the cost of his blood have a great responsibility. They have received a task which no man merits: to reform the image of God and carve out his likeness in souls. Theirs is the power to bless, baptize, and forgive; above all, they are ministers of the eucharist. The celebration of the eucharist is a reflection of the Father's eternal generation of the Son. When a priest holds the eucharist in his hands, it is like a mirror whose spotless surface reflects back the priest's own shortcomings and urges him to conform his life to Christ's. This mirror is also like a shield, offering protection from the Father's wrath and from the assaults of the powers of evil.

In order to fulfill their task of watching over Christ's Church, the clergy must devote themselves to pastoral care, to reading and contemplation, to meditation on the Scriptures, to purity and religious living, and to compassion for those who are suffering. Above all, priests should be worthy celebrants of the eucharist. If they fall into sin, it is not enough that they confess their sin; before they approach the altar they should also amend their hearts and their deeds.

Claustral Life

The School of the Cloister was addressed to a canon regular of St Augustine. It speaks of the followers of St Augustine and St Benedict,[121] and Peter would have considered it applicable to Carthusians and other new orders as well. In Peter's world all religious were cloistered, but the term did not mean quite what it did, for example, among the Carmelites of the nineteenth century. The walls of Montier-la-Celle and St Remi were not quite so impermeable. In any case, Peter felt that the followers of Augustine and Benedict agreed on essential points and differed only on accidental ones.

Peter specifies these substantial elements in *The School of the Cloister:* silence, reading, confession of sins, prayer and meditation on death.[122] Clearly, none of these 'substantial elements' was or is the exclusive prerogative of claustrals or religious. This suggests either that these essential elements were not what made religious life distinct from ordinary life, or that the specific form they took among claustrals was what distinguished religious and laity. In the latter case, the specific claustral form of these disciplines would be that given them by the Rule and customs of the community where the monk or canon was professed.[123]

At several other places in the same work Peter gives longer lists of basic components of religious life, most of which are also not specific to claustrals:

3:2: religious statutes: silence, fasting, seclusion, restrained and suitable conduct, compassion, fraternal love, paternal reverence, reading, persistent prayer, meditation, recollection of past evils, fear of death, purgatory and hell.

7:1: claustral discipline: weeping for sins, subjugation to one's superiors (obedience), to plot against no one, to love God and neighbor, to preserve innocence and sanctity, to obey God always, to long for heaven.

10:1: necessary 'expenditures': patience, austerity in food and drink, cheap clothes, continuous silence, obedience, seclusion, continence, and the like.

17:11: marrow and joints of claustral discipline: silence, lowered gaze and becoming gait, continuous sitting in the cloister, intervals in choir, standing before God in fear and trembling, eating and drinking within the limits of sufficiency, sleep sufficient for digestion, chastity, no superfluity, humility, obedience, charity, faith, hope.

From these five enumerations one can formulate a fairly specific summary of Peter's notions about the components of claustral life: austerity in food, drink, clothing, sleep and speech; external conduct which is humble and will appear seemly to outsiders; seclusion; fraternal love and obedience to superiors; fear and awareness of death and hell; fear, obedience and love of God; confession and sorrow for sins; prayer in choir and in private; perseverance.[124]

Action and Contemplation

Peter was not much concerned about the theoretical question of the relationship between contemplation and action. Because of this indifference and his fluid use of both words, he was able to state the relationship differently in different contexts.

Writing to Archbishop Theobald of Paris regarding some sermons which Theobald had requested of him, Peter excused his tardiness by observing that action and contemplation cannot coexist.

> Your Prudence knows that the quiet of contemplation does not coexist with the distraction which secular occupations bring to the mind. The cloth is too narrow to cover both; one is not able to do both. Although everyone has two eyes on his forehead, one cannot separate them in such a way that they no longer do a single task, but one looks to heaven and the other to earth. Much less can one simultaneously direct the one glance of reason and intellect to such disparate objects that with the same mind he deals with heavenly things mystically and treats of earthly things as well.[125]

On other occasions Peter spoke of the union of action and contemplation as an ideal or a possibility. He praised the true quiet of the order of Cîteaux, 'where Martha is joined to Mary, where, in the words of the wise, the one acting must rest and the one resting must act'.[126] Peter consoled Bernerède with the observation that "charity rests in secret and works in public. It imitates the one who works for six days and rests on the sabbath. . . . Charity is a gift which neither dries up in being poured out nor runs out in being distributed.'[127]

Thirdly, Peter could go so far as to envisage the virtual identity of action and contemplation. In the *Book of Breads* he observed that when human beings work they do not rest, and when they rest they do not work, because they live within the flux of time. In God there is no time; his working is more tranquil than any rest; his rest works incomparable effects. A human being's action or the rest of his contemplation should aim at being a distant reflection of this divine unity. One should strive to rest by acting, and to act by resting.[128]

Fourthly, Peter saw action as a necessary presupposition of contemplation:

> The first day pertains to conversion, the second day to confession, the third to profession, the fourth to mortification, the fifth to devotion, the sixth to prayer, the seventh to vocation or contemplation. For we never collect the harvest of contemplation unless we have first

sown the seed of justice; no one rests on the seventh day
who has not worked during the previous six days.[129]

Although it is difficult to synthesize these different statements, it
seems clear that Peter saw Christian life in this world, in or out of the
cloister, as involving both contemplation and action. In this life one
may have just a foretaste of the joy, vision, concord and peace of
heaven,[130] which are the reward of both work and rest, action and
contemplation.[131] 'Meanwhile, here we long for grace. . . .; there,
like on a mountain of contemplation, we receive the glorified face of
Jesus. Here we wait; there we see.'[132]

Schools and Philosophers

For Peter the essential advantage of the claustral life was that it was
more likely to bring one to heaven than was ordinary secular life. As
a result of this conviction he esteemed all forms of claustral life. He
was singularly free of defensiveness and animosity in his relations
with the different religious groups which had sprung up alongside
his own traditional Benedictinism.

Toward non-claustrals Peter did not always display the same im-
partiality and esteem. He does not appear to have had a positive view
of the Christian layperson's chances and salvation. At the end of the
On Conscience he distinguishes the consciences of claustrals, people of
the world, the damned and the blessed. The life of seculars is distant
from the purity and quiet of the cloister. Secular life is unstable and
changeable; seculars are involved in errors of 'the forum, the tavern,
the theatre, and brothel'. Family life and business affairs inevitably
involve one in sin. However, lay people who confess their sins are
'gathered back by penitence into the lap of the Church which weeps
because of the sins of her sons'.[133]

Schools were one segment of life for which Peter showed little en-
thusiasm. His longest comment on the schools is a letter to John of
Salisbury. John had returned to Paris as an exile from England. He
had told Peter that exile in Paris was not without its compensations.
Peter wrote back to John, 'his cleric':

The place where there is greater and more ample pleasure for
the body is truly an exile for the soul. Where indulgence

rules, the soul is morally enslaved and afflicted. O Paris, how suited you are to trap and dupe souls. . . . My John was aware of this, and so he called it exile. Would that you would see this exile for what it is and hurry to your true love, not by word and speech, but by work and truth. There in the book of life you would not see figures and letters, but instead the Godhead as it is and truth itself face to face, without the work of reading, without tiring out your eyes, without fallacy or error in understanding, without concern about retention or fear of forgetting. O blessed school where Christ teaches our hearts by the word of his truth, where we apprehend without study and reading how we ought to live happily for eternity! There no book is bought, no master reimbursed; there are no tortuous disputations, no involved sophistries. There the solution to all questions is clear. There all reasonings and arguments are fully understood. There life confers more than reading; there simplicity is of more use than quibbling. . . . In a word, there every objection is solved, since the one who offers the bad objection of an evil life is answered with 'Go, you accursed, into the eternal fire. . . . '.[134]

Most of Peter's passing references to schools and philosophers are disparaging: 'the studies and doctrines of philosophers, which glory only in the appearance of words';[135] 'the seductions of philosophers';[136] 'secular literature puffs up';[137] 'forests of arguments';[138] 'vain philosophy, stupid stories and genealogies, and interminable questions'.[139]

Peter's attitudes toward the schools (and pagan writers) seem to be compounded of several elements. First, Peter himself had been educated in the schools. All his life long he benefited from what he had learned there, and he explicitly recognized the legitimacy of monks using the knowledge they had gained before they entered the monastery. In the cloister 'grammar, dialetic, rhetoric, music, arithmetic, geometry and astronomy are seasoned with the strong salt of divine Scripture. Customarily they inflict death, . . . but with an admixture . . . of grace they provide healthful nourishment.' These liberal arts can help the claustral to understand the Scriptures and to refute the errors of heretics.[140] Peter himself was not ashamed to cite classical authors like Seneca, Horace and Plato.[141] He could also make use of the techniques of logic and the vocabulary and methods of scientific theology.[142]

Peter's education, however, was primarily biblical and patristic; he had been well 'educated by the skill of the catholic Church'.[143] He had a phenomenal command of the biblical text, as is evident in the way he weaves together dozens of scriptural quotations and allusions on practically every page of his writings. Morever, he could practice the traditional techniques of biblical commentary according to the four senses. Even into his treatises he sometimes incorporates a consecutive exposition of a scriptural passage.[144] Peter also read and cited Church Fathers like Jerome, Augustine, Gregory the Great and Bede, and he spoke positively of theologians who were his contemporaries.[145] Peter's familiarity with the Bible and the Fathers was no doubt primarily the result of public and private reading in the cloister. Reading, Peter insisted, was an essential element of claustral discipline. Without it life in the hermit's room, and no doubt in the cenobite's cloister, was hell on earth.[146]

A second element in Peter's attitude toward the schools and secular learning is his conviction that such knowledge seems to deflect people from self-knowledge. It profits little to know about the whole world and not know oneself. 'Many seek science, few seek conscience. And if it happened that conscience were sought with as great an effort and care as is doubtlessly expended on vain and secular knowledge, it would be grasped more quickly and retained more fruitfully.'[147] To know oneself in God, God in oneself, and oneself in oneself are the great questions. These questions are to be addressed in the school of solitude and self-discipline. Rarely are they broached in other schools, and even more rarely are they answered.[148]

Peter objected to the attention which schools gave to pagan authors. He gave the pagan philosophers credit for their self-control and single-mindedness, but, though they 'abandoned the obstacles of the flesh and the burdens of the world', they 'sowed in a spirit which is not of God'. The philosophers were presumptuous; they rejoiced in novel

words and opinions; they aimed to acquire human glory and
favor.[149]

The School of Christ

Ultimately, Peter's distrust of the schools and the philosophers
resulted from his single-minded devotion to a single master, Christ;
to a single textbook, the Bible; and to a single goal, heaven. Jesus'
school is in heaven, but he offers, as it were, extension courses on
earth, primarily in the school of the cloister.[150]

Scripture contains all the knowledge the claustral needs. 'A lack of
content will never drive us to the alien harvest of secular philosophers, whether we are dealing with the nature of souls or even of
bodies, or of the ethics of good morals, or the logic of speaking cor-
rectly, decorously and truthfully.'[151] The superiority of the Bible extends to its style. Sacred Scripture does not use a great deal of verbal
makeup, 'but nevertheless it is not all inferior to those studies and
doctrines of the philosophers which glory only in the appearance of
words'.[152]

Jesus' teaching in the Scriptures is directly concerned with helping
his disciples reach heaven. The concerns of earthly masters are less
ultimate. This was an important concern for Peter, for whom the
reality of the last things was extraordinarily vivid.[153] One enters the
gates of the world at birth; eventually, one will exit the world
through the gates of death. To prepare for this final exit, one enters
the gates of the cloister. One hopes to enter the gates of heaven. This
hope is centered on Christ who shaped the gates of the cloister by the
way he lived, who passed through the gates of death, broke the gates
of hell, and finally opened the gates of heaven at the ascension.[154]

Doctrinal Authority

The feast and doctrine of the Immaculate Conception of Mary
were just coming into prominence at Peter's time. The feast had been
celebrated in England before the Conquest, but it aroused controversy
afterwards. From England it was introduced into Lyons. St Bernard
opposed this innovation, writing the canons of Lyons that, contrary

to their usual exemplary prudence, they had introduced 'a new feast, of which the ritual of the Church knows nothing, which reason does not approve, and which no tradition recommends'. Bernard was willing to grant that if Jeremiah and John the Baptist were sanctified in the womb, such a privilege was no doubt Mary's as well. But he saw no grounds in authority or reason to assert that Mary was sanctified at the moment of her conception. To have been conceived without original sin, Mary would have had to have been conceived not by human intercourse, but by a divine miracle. In any case, to introduce such a feast would require the prior approval of the authority of the apostolic see.

Among those who championed the feast was the Englishman, Nicholas of St Albans. There survive a letter of Nicholas to Peter and three letters of Peter to Nicholas.[155] In seconding St Bernard's opposition to the feast, Peter makes clear his views about the authorities for church doctrine. The most fundamental authority is Scripture. 'Whatever is not supported by the foundations of Scripture is without any strong or stable support.'[156] Secondly, during her earthly pilgrimage the Church has certainly introduced new decrees and solemnities. However, the see of Peter and the roman curia are the principal holders of the keys of heaven. If you coin some opinion 'which the see of Peter has not approved, to whom it belongs to approve or disapprove the order of the universal Church, I plant my foot and do not go beyond the constitutional boundaries'.[157] Thirdly, Nicholas had denied St Bernard the veneration due him as a wise and holy man who honored Mary highly by his writings and who saw to it that every cistercian basilica was dedicated to her.[158] Fourthly, Peter invoked the authority of the Fathers of the Church, in this case St Jerome.[159] Finally, Peter employed arguments of theological reason. It is more to Mary's honor that she overcame the temptations of concupiscence, than if she had never felt such temptations. Moreover, if Christ was tempted, she surely was.[160]

Peter implies the relationships between the first four of these authorities in *On Affliction and Reading:*

> Since the Holy Scripture is inspired by the Holy Spirit,
> nothing sprouts in it which is not rooted in its holy
> origin. Whatever steely or leaden shavings the enemy

has tried to introduce by vigorously filing heretics or
wrongheaded interpreters have already been pored over
and examined in the expositions of teachers and the
scrutiny of councils and aired by preachers.[161]

The polemic with Nicholas of St Albans shows Peter using
reasonable argument to convince an opponent whom he treated with
respect and even with affection, although he disagreed with him
sharply. Peter's distrust of disputation was not absolute.[162] Despite
its rejection of 'philosophical and secular reason', the following text
implies that reason has a theological role, 'provided it relies on its
beloved who enlightens the darkness of reason itself with . . . the
light of faith'.[163]

O animal man, climb up onto the citadel of reason, since
you are not yet able to scale the heights of contemplation. Compare everything bodily or whatever spiritual
creature is accessible to your mind with the body of the
Lord, and then weigh them honestly on the scales of the
sanctuary, that is, not by philosophical and secular
reason, but by catholic faith and divine precision.[164]

Peter's attitude toward novelty is similarly ambivalent. In the
dedicatory letter to John of Salisbury which accompanied the *Book of
Breads,* Peter declared that novelty which departed from the footsteps
of the Fathers in faith or morals by using new words and formula-
tions should be anathema. But he was also proud of the new things
he discovered and included in his book: 'if by the enlightenment of
the Holy Spirit I was able to grasp anything which was somewhat
new, . . . I did not reject it'. Perhaps a bit shocked at himself, he added: 'I did not write this book on the breads of Holy Scripture in
order to make a big name for myself, like the names of great people
who glory in worldly philosophy'.[165]

TRANSLATIONS

The writings of Peter of Celle are sometimes difficult to translate
because of his luxuriant imagery and peculiar vocabulary. His
sentences are long, but this is usually the result of a concatenation of
coordinated elements, which in the English translation must often be

divided up into separate sentences. These shortened sentences, the divisions into paragraphs, and the omission of a few utterly redundant words are the only alterations introduced for the sake of greater readability. The translation of *The School of the Cloister* has been made much easier by Dom de Martel's edition, notes and faithful French translation. The other texts presented more difficulties.

There is no modern, critical edition of the sermons, and the text reprinted by the Migne leaves much to be desired. The original edition of Dom Ambroise Janvier was probably printed from a transcription made by Dom Alexis Eduart in 1643 of a manuscript belonging to St Remi at Reims. In 1774 a devastating fire destroyed much of the abbey library, including, it would seem, the manuscript of Peter's sermons. More than half of Peter's sermons are preserved in the manuscript Douai B. M. 504, and a few of his sermons are to be found in four other manuscripts. For some, including *Sermon 44* translated here, no manuscript version survives. For the other three sermons translated here Douai B. M. 504 provides a text. The manuscript is a twelfth-century text from the abbey of Anchin. *Sermons 29, 33, 39* are found in it and in no other manuscript.[166] Dom de Martel has kindly checked the text of some suspect readings of the *Patrologia Latina* against this manuscript. In the list which follows, the sermon number and paragraph are indicated first, then the location and the reading in PL 202, then the reading in the MS Douai B. M. 504 adopted for the translation, together with its location in the manuscript.

S 29:2 725D: apprehensione	97va: appensione
S 33:6 737A: talis est, inquit,	106ra: Talis est inquit
Sponsa sive Maria	Sponsa sive Maria
Domini Mater, sive	mater Domini, sive
Maria Magdalene,	Maria Magdalene,
sive ipse Joseph:	sive ipse Iohannes.
S 39:13 764BC: desiderium ad	111va: desiderium ad deum . . .
eum . . . stratum est	deum . . . stratum sunt

The translations of the two opuscules, *On Affliction and Reading* and *On Conscience* are based on the text edited by Dom Leclercq from MS Troyes B. M. 253 in *La spiritualité*, pp. 193–239. In a number of places a comparison with the partial text of *On Conscience* in Migne or other considerations raised questions about the text. Once again Dom de Martel has kindly checked these places in the printed text against the manuscript readings in MS Troyes 253 (= T) and, for *On Conscience,* in the superior MS Lisbon Alcobaça 232 (= L).[167] In the following list the first column gives the paragraph numbers of the translation; the second, the page, line and reading in Dom Leclercq's text; the third, the readings provided by Dom de Martel from the manuscripts or conjectured from the context.

On Affliction and Reading

5.	232:14: jacunda	jocunda (T 75vb)
8.	233:22: scaturientem laqueum	scaturientem, laqueum (T 76rb)
16.	236:22: id praevaricationem	in praevaricationem (77rb)
18.	237:10–11: significatis profectibus virtutum peragra tabernaculum, cum	significatis profectibus virtutum peragra, tabernaculum cum

On Conscience

2.	193:15: defecatus	defecatae (L, T)
2.	193:20:quia	quin (L)
3.	193:21: hic	hinc (L)
3.	194:3: lata quiescat . . . ut sole lata	laeta quiescat . . . ut sole lustrata (PL, L, T)
4.	194:6: carnes	carnis (PL, L, T)
5.	194:14: detrahit	retrahit (L)
5.	194:27: circumliniendae	circumliniendo (L)
6.	195:6: saltat (T)	psaltat (L)
15.	197:34: super	subter (L, T)
16.	198:10: excludit abundantiam	excludit angustiam (PL, L, T)
16.	198:12: penetralibus	penetrabilibus (L, T)
16.	198:14: in generationem et generationem	in generatione et generationem (L, T)

16.	198:16: quae sunt sufficientia	quae sint (L) sit (T) sufficientia
21.	199:32: philosophicae	philosphiae (L, T)
21.	199:33: consecratur (T)	conservatur (L)
22.	200:7–8: Si enim non longe a se peteret et se intra seipso doctore, . . . inveniretur?	Se (*sic*) enim non longe a se peteret et se intra se, seipso doctore, . . . inveniret? (L, T)
28.	202:17: a miseriam. Si unde	miseriam si unde (L)
30.	203:19: eius	cuius (L, T)
31.	203:27: formant	firmant (L, T)
33.	204:15: urgitur	urgetur (L, T)
33.	204:22: dolabrum (T)	dolam (L, PL)
35.	204:37: unanimitatem (T)	unanimitatis (PL, L)
37.	205:27: delinitis	delinitio (T, PL) delinicis (L)
47.	209:36: in eo faciei (T)	in eo forma faciei (L)
48.	210:16: conice	coniice
49.	210:23: quorum	quarum (L, T)
49.	210:31: desiderii, huius	desiderii. Huius (L, T)
51.	211:14: in conscientia ubi pulsanti	in conscientia. Ubi pulsanti (L, T)
54.	211:33: cum uno effecta (T)	cum eo effecta (L)
57.	213:2: renovent urbella	renoventur bella
58.	213:28: mundatione (T)	in undatione (L)
61.	215:16: momenti nec	momentaneae (L, T)
66.	217:25: difficultas (T)	difficultatis (L)
68.	218:7: posset	possent
70.	218:38: anhelita	anhelitu (L, T)
79.	222:20: respectus (T)	respectu (L)
79.	222:22: fertile (T)	sterile (L)
80.	222:26: plenis (T)	penis (L)
82.	223:31: Dux	Duo (L, T)
82.	223:32: ubi	tibi (L, T)
82.	223:34: Domini	Deum (L, T)
83.	224:13: monachus, sanctus, eremita	monacus sanctus, heremita (L, T)
92.	227:20: vitis	vitiis (L, T)
94.	228:8: quem	quam (L, T)

95. 228:21–28: quia mors in olla
    ista *facit cum possit . . .*
    in glorificatione. Quod
    confotum. . . .

quia mors in olla ista.

Quod confotum (The
lines omitted here are
not found in the
manuscripts L, T, and seem
to be omitted in MS Paris B.
N. 2597 as well. They are
omitted from the transla-
tion.)

96. 229:3: desidenorum

desideriorum (L, T)

97. 229:12: linor non obsumat

livor non obscurat (L, T)

All Scripture references are given according to the numbering of the *Jerusalem Bible*. The scriptural texts are translated from the Latin text of Peter's works, both because that text is the best indication of Peter's own understanding of the passages and also because he often quotes rather loosely. Peter's text is saturated with biblical quotations, allusions and vocabulary. To avoid cluttering the text, only direct quotations and a few other important scriptural references have been noted in the translation. Further scriptural references can be found easily in the editions of Dom de Martel and Dom Leclercq.

TRANSLATIONS

A SERMON FOR
PASSION SUNDAY

(fifth sunday of lent)

Judge me, O God, and decide my case against an unholy people' [Ps 43:1].[168]

1. DEARLY BELOVED BROTHERS, following in the footsteps of Jesus, we come to his passion. Would that we were not going to leave him in his passion, until seeing the end with Peter, we have unending fellowship with him. His footsteps are stamped and sealed by the pouring out of his blood which flowed off his feet so that, O good christian, your foot might be dipped in the blood of the lamb. Take note of this and say with Job: 'My foot has followed his footsteps. I have kept to his way. I have not departed from it, nor have I deviated from the commandments of his lips' [Jb 23:11]. One follows different footsteps with Jesus in heaven, on earth, on the sea, in the underworld: the glorious footsteps of Christ in heaven, the pure ones on earth, wondrous ones on the sea, powerful ones in the underworld. Notice his power in the abyss. He broke the iron bars. He cut off the heads of the dragon which was lying there. From its belly he extracted the riches which it had swallowed up. He filled his net with the fish of the patriarchs and prophets. With a strong hand and an outstretched arm he recovered the treasures hidden there from the beginning of the world.

2. These are the footsteps and this the walk of God in the underworld. Like a powerful champion powerfully equipped, he killed the Antichrist with the sword on his thigh. He went through the infernal workshops, leaving nothing behind which was rightfully his and taking nothing which belonged to his adversary. He was as just in leaving none of his own behind as he was devoted in taking them away. That he did not free everyone was not because it was impossible, nor because of cruelty or forgetfulness. Rather, it was the result of justice and truth, in accordance with the indications of an honest scales. So much for the footsteps of Christ in the depths of the netherworld.

3. Now take a similar look at him walking on the waters, and notice the miracle of the Man-God, or rather, of the God-Man. Truly, the corruption of sin was not in that body, which was more celestial through spiritual sanctification than terrestrial through

the earthly indwelling. Hence, no oppressive feeling weighed it down to the neglect of his resolve or with a resultant incapacity to accomplish his good pleasure. He could do something effortlessly, just as easily as his mind could wish it. Therefore, when he wished he walked on the waters. So much for his footsteps on the waters, where he walked without leaving any footprints, where he put his footsteps without any trace. Peter and the others who are like Peter know how to follow his footsteps, so they say in the church: 'My foot had followed his footprints.'

4. We must now examine the footprints of his humility and walk upon these sands, for the psalm says of them: 'Complete my steps on your walkways, so that my footsteps will never deviate.' [Ps 17:5] Walkways are restricted routes, middle routes for the two feet, as it were. Not inappropriately are Jesus' ways called walkways rather than routes, because on this road there is no deviation, no giving rein to what is unlawful. This way said: 'I am the way' [Jn 14:6]. It is difficult and narrow; there are few who find it. Hence the prayer of the one who said: 'My foot has followed his footsteps'. He prayed, 'Complete', that is, direct my steps all the way to the end; that is, direct my actions 'on his walkways'; that is, in his chaste examples and works of piety, 'so that my footsteps will never deviate' from love and imitation of you because of a temptation or suggestion of the enemy.

5. What exactly are his footsteps? Listen to what they are. He was conceived of the Holy Spirit; that was the first step. He was born of the Virgin Mary; the second step. He was placed in the manger; the third step. He was circumcised on the eighth day; the fourth step. He was offered in the temple; the fifth step. He was baptized by John; the sixth step. He fasted in the desert for forty days and forty nights; the seventh step. He was tempted three times by the devil; the eighth step. He preached and worked miracles; the ninth step. He was transfigured before his disciples; the tenth step. He was sold by his disciple; the eleventh step. He was crucified; the twelfth step. He died; the thirteenth step. He was buried; the fourteenth step. These were his steps on earth.

6. O Lord Jesus, 'you have made know your ways to me. You will fill me with happiness by your countenance'. [Ps 16:11] These ways

are beautiful, and all these walkways are peaceful. Therefore, 'Complete my steps in your walkways', where the observance and nobility of the route are such that a just man can hardly hold to the observance and a wise man can scarcely maintain the nobility with a firm step. So let us follow Jesus who was conceived of the Holy Spirit, by accepting the same Spirit's grace of inspiration. Let us follow him who was born of the Virgin Mary, when by the help of that grace we join our free wills to grace. Let us follow him who was placed in the manger, by having a humble opinion of ourselves. Let us follow him who was circumcised, by cutting off the superfluities of our first birth. Let us follow him who was offered in the temple, by making our bodies into temples of the Holy Spirit. Let us follow him who was baptized by John, by cleansing ourselves in confession. By our abstinence let us follow him who fasted in the desert. Let us follow him who was tempted, by resisting temptation. Let us follow him who preached and worked miracles, by taking our stand on the word of God and of doctrine. Let us follow him in his transfiguration, by conforming ourselves to the body of Jesus. Let us follow him in his suffering, by bearing every injury patiently. Let us follow him who was sold, by renouncing our pleasures and binding ourselves to the divine commands. Let us follow him who was crucified, by mortifying our vices. By dying to the world let us follow him who died. Let us follow him who was buried, by waiting for the future judgment in peace. Hence: 'Judge me, O God, and decide my case against an unholy people.' [Ps 43:1]

7. My dear brothers, listen to Our Lord as he says: 'Judge me, O God', etc. Let yourselves be inwardly moved, as you consider how devout is the meaning of these words. The one speaking is Jesus, the son of the virgin, the man without sin, who says in today's gospel: 'Which of you will accuse me of sin?' [Jn 8:46] Imagine yourself in the chapter of the scribes and pharisees, stripped and exposed to the rod of correction or the staff of punishment, saying to the abbot: 'Judge me, O God.' For the Jews stripped him, Pilate whipped him. O piety of heart, O agitation of the lights of heaven and earth! Pilate whipped Jesus. What did Jesus do? What did he say? What did the lamb bleat out? 'Judge me', etc. Brothers, the apostle says: 'Each one will bear his own judgment' [Ga 5:10], yet Jesus bore our judgment,

not his own. He made our judgment his own, not by sharing in our crime, but by reason of the anointing of God and man. He offered his back in place of ours, so that sinners might construct there a structure of sorrows and wounds. He sustained the discipline of our peace, and he took away the accusation of the crime of which we were accused.

8. He says, 'Judge me, O God', etc. How? 'And decide my case against an unholy people.' For my case is the redemption of men, my case is man himself, whom I have come to liberate. Therefore, my God, decide my case, so that in this decision one may grasp what weight my suffering shall have, what is the obligation stemming from Adam's fault, what is the allotment to be weighed out by wrath to patience. Decide my case, so that it may be weighed out in a fair balance, for great deeds are more likely to win favor than are advocates. As a result, the man who was vulnerable to temptation, will find not just pardon, but grace, because of the unfamiliar novelty of sin. For he had not seen any other man sin before he did, nor did he assess how bitter and extreme would be the punishment for one bite of the forbidden fruit. Distinguish my cause from the case of the devil and from the case of the first man. Distinguish the case of man and that of the devil. Distinguish my case, that of the second man, from the case of the first man. Distinguish, so that the benefit will not be like the crime. The crime of Satan remains without remedy. The crime of Adam remains in deed and imputation until my death. But—thereafter, for those of his children whom I redeem, it is eliminated, not in deed but in imputation.

9. What does it mean for a sin to be eliminated as far as imputation goes, if not that it is imputed [to someone else]? What does it mean for sin to be eliminated in deed, if not that one cease sinning and be without sin? But this latter is granted to no one except to the God-Man, who was conceived of the Holy Spirit, and to his blessed mother after the overshadowing of the Holy Spirit, because she was so completely wrapped, clothed, and possessed by grace that thereafter not even the slightest fault found a place in her. In the rest of humanity the death of sin reigned from Adam to Christ's passion with both feet, that is by act and by imputation. But it began to limp, when the nerve in its thigh was pinched, when the charge against us was waived in the death of Christ. After the other foot had

been disabled, when the kindling of sin was sprinkled with the blood of Christ and it was only able to move sluggishly toward evil, it began to weep more intensely. Hence, 'Decide my case against an unholy people', so that by his case man was freed, while the devil is crushed. Man is already freed from the imputation; in the future he will be freed from both imputation and deed. We give thanks to you, O Lord, because your case was so good that
you could make something good of our evil
case, you who live and rule with
the Father for ever. . . .

A SERMON FOR PALM
SUNDAY

Let the same mind be in you as is also in Christ Jesus [Ph 2:5].

1. Dearly beloved brothers, look! Before your eyes is Jesus being led to be sacrificed. What will you say? What will you do? Among all those dear to him there is no one who consoles him. All have left him and fled. O Jesus, alone for our sake, without us you carry the burden and the heat of the day, the crown of thorns, the cross. You carry your blood within the curtain of the sanctuary. On your body you carry our sins up the wood of the cross. You carry fire and wood, so that the fire of your passion may burn up the wood of our mortality. A lion from the woods, a wolf at dusk, a bear, a dog, a unicorn — these enemies rush at you with a spear and gaping mouths, eager to devour you.

2. The daughters of Jerusalem see and weep. The sun hides its face so as not to see such wickedness in Israel. The earth totters, unable to bear it. The dead sense the death of life and rise from the dead, like that dead man who touched the bones of Elisha and came back to life [see 2 K 13:21]. And what about us poor wretches? By the call of his cry and dying gasp the supports of the four corners of the world, that is, the angels or the veil of the temple, are moved. And we stubborn people are not moved to weep, lament, tear our hair, or join those lamenting women who knew how to bewail not Adonijah, but Jesus hanging and dying.

3. Where is Phinehas, where is Peter, where is Mathathias? Do you think the dying Son of Man will find faith on the earth? Lord, your eyes are turned towards faith, but among whom and in whom is faith to be found? The foundations of faith are disturbed and shaken, so that if it were possible even the apostles would be led into error. Where, then, is faith? It almost perished, it almost was removed from the earth. The Lord says to the prince of the apostles: 'Behold, Satan has sought you out to sift you like grain. I have prayed for you that your faith will not fail' [Lk 22:31]. This is a bitter war, in which Jesus struggles all alone against Satan. After his whole body had been wounded and his blood poured out, he was finally overcome and overcame. Thus did Jesus trip up him who on another occasion had caused us to stumble in Adam.

4. Brothers, 'let this mind be in you as is also in Christ Jesus'. Even if we were never worthy to approach Jesus and touch him and sense him, let us at least make our request of the one who sleeps on his breast, who placed him between his breasts, and who says: 'His left hand is under my head, and his right hand will embrace me' [Sg 2:6]. As I said, let us inquire what idea he has of Jesus, and what he sensed in him. Tell us, John the Evangelist, what did he seem like to you? For it has been said of you: 'And he who saw bore witness, and we know that his testimony is true' [Jn 19:35].

5. So tell us about Jesus: how he was seized, when, where, by whom, why. How was he tormented before the crucifixion? Who betrayed him? Who wanted to defend him? What he answered when one of his own followers wished to defend him; with what great fear the same follower later denied him three times; how Pilate had him scourged; how the soldiers wove a crown of thorns and put it on his head and mockingly put a purple garment around him, and hailed him on bended knee, and slapped him in the face? How Jesus himself, wearing the crown of thorns and the purple garment, distinguished not by dominion but by reproach, went out to the Jews; how great was the shout when they repeated: 'Crucify him': How, finally, they crucified him on Golgotha with two robbers; they divided his clothes among themselves; they offered him vinegar; he lowered his head and handed over his spirit?

6. These are Jesus' signs. No one except Jesus showed all these signs. Therefore, it is Jesus you are meeting, if you find someone marked out this way. Such he is, says the spouse, either Mary the mother of the Lord, or Mary Magdalene, or John himself. Such is how my beloved is, and he is my friend, O daughters of Jerusalem. But if you wish to recognize him by fewer signs (since a wise man becomes known through a few) listen: 'My beloved is white and ruddy [Sg 5.10]; white because of his innocence, ruddy because of the punishment he underwent'.

7. Behold, good lady, you have satisfied us by this accurate description of your beloved, your bridegroom. But tell us about his touch, about your sensation of him, how he felt, how his left hand felt, how his right hand felt. For he is far from us, and if for a time we have been unable to see him, much less touch him, we have already

been assured about how he looked. Now add something about touch. For Scripture frightens us a bit and restrains us from touching. It says that he is fire; and he says that those who approach me are approaching the fire. It is a harsh and horrifying thing to put one's hand in the fire. So tell us if we can find him a little meeker on the right side or on the left. You know his right side, because his right arm embraced you. You know his left side just as well, for his left arm was under your head. So, first tell about his left, because from our perspective he slept on the cross with his head to the left.

8. This is a sachet of myrrh [Sg 1:13]. For my beloved will spend some time with me between my breasts, while his left hand is under my head. This is the heap of rocks upon which he pondered that day when his mother, that is, the synagogue, crowned him with a crown of thorns. There Nicodemus came carrying about one hundred pounds of a mixture of myrrh and aloes with which to anoint Jesus' body. One hundred pounds is a gread deal, enough. Jesus' whole body can be embalmed with the amount of myrrh and aloes, to the extent that his lips will be moistened with the first myrrh from this abundance. Truly, your compassion will drench not only the inert members of Jesus; if it is a hundredfold, that is, perfect and complete, it will extend even to his lips, so that he may answer and say: 'I was thirsty, and you gave me drink; I was hungry, and you gave me something to eat' [Mt 25:35]. Similarly, 'You are the one who stayed with me in my trials' [Lk 22:28]. Notice! A contrite and humbled heart had a sachet of myrrh.

9. Notice the great bitterness, grief like the sea, in Jesus' passion. The sachet of myrrh denotes compassion, and this is the left arm. What is the right arm? That of which the psalm speaks: 'The Lord said to my Lord, sit at my right hand' [Ps 110:1]. The right hand of God is blessedness without interruption, glory without end, pleasure without corruption, health without sickness, concord without bitterness, peace without rancor, tranquility without agitation, eternity without fluctuation. This is the right hand of God, because there is full delight at God's right hand, just as here the affliction of miseries abounds. This is the right hand which we do not yet have or know. Nor is the wondrous delight of his right hand as familiar to us as the wretched affliction of his left.

10. Perhaps the fire that we fear will be between his left and right hands. Our God will come as a consuming fire in a fierce storm; then he certainly will not be be as one sleeping, as one dead on the cross or in the tomb, nor even as one glorious after death in heaven. Rather, he will be as the strong man, drunk from wine and roused from sleep, as a roaring lion of whom it is said: 'The lion will roar, and who will not be afraid?" [Am 3:8]. Or again: 'The Lord will roar from Sion and will give his shout from Jerusalem' [Am 1:2]. For he will call out in judgment to the fire to devour the great abyss and to eat up a part all at once, that is, to engulf the evildoers deep down with eternal damnation; to eat up the imperfect, insofar as they are partly imperfect, but not to swallow them by a sentence of eternal damnation. There he will turn aside neither to the right nor to the left by appearing meekly as he did before Pontius Pilate or as he will appear after the judgment has been held. At the judgment there will be severity on his countenance to avenge the injury of the passion, rather than the powerlessness whose form he took up to complete the judgment of the incarnation.

11. So, brothers, 'let this mind be in you which was in Jesus Christ'. You must feel punishment without guilt, innocence without injury. Have in mind the innocent one who forgives: the just one who stands in need; the merciful one who raises you up to the right hand of his seat of majesty. There, brothers, your souls will be carried by the hands of the poor; there you will be taken by confessions, prayers, fasts and other good works.

May you be granted this by Jesus Christ our Lord
who lives and rules with the Father
and the Holy Spirit, God
for ever and ever.
Amen.

A SERMON
FOR HOLY THURSDAY

Man ate the bread of angels [Ps 78:25].

1. Who is the bread of angels, where he is, how he is to be eaten, when, where, by whom and why, it is necessary to see. So it is necessary to say who is the bread of angels which man eats. He flees from the lips of the deceiver and repels erroneous or unclean understanding, but not a humble and quiet spirit which trembles at his word. We may touch and eat this bread with a sincere heart, a chaste body, a holy hand, a purified tongue. The bread is the Man-God, formed from two tithes, that is, from the divine and human natures, conceived in the Virgin of the Holy Spirit and born, made the mediator of God and man.

2. Certainly that woman in the gospel, that is, the wisdom of God or the Virgin Mary, mixed in enough yeast for three; that is, the bond of union inseparably joined the divinity, the soul and the flesh. Wisodm did this through its activity, the Virgin through conception. The baker of this bread is the Holy Spirit, who mixed and united Jesus Christ, the utterly pure bread, from the complete and total substance of the Trinity, as the primary flour, and from the purest and holiest superpurified blood of the Virgin, not in the sieve of human cleverness or merit, but by the overshadowing of the Holy Spirit. He shaped this bread in the condition and form of a man, baked it and took it from the baking oven while keeping the seals of virginity intact, set the most sumptuous delicacies on the angels' table, while also blending a most effective medicine for human weakness. The angelic palate is amazed at tasting it, and asks 'Who is this king of glory?' [Ps 24:8]. The famished human palate is delighted by the taste and satisfied by its nourishment, healed of sickness, incorporated by love. Thus does man eat the bread of angels.

3. Where is this bread: above, below, or beside you? If he is above, go up; if below, go down; if nearby but hidden, look for him; if nearby and in view, take and eat. In fact, he is above, below, hidden and in view nearby. He is above, because he is God on high. He

53

is below, because he is the crucified one. He is nearby, for 'Behold I am with you till the end of the world' [Mt 28:20]. He is hidden, since he is not visible in the form in which he sits at the right hand of the Father, but is in view on the altar in the appearance of bread and wine. In early times he was visible among men, since often he miraculously appeared visibly on the altar to certain people; and he is believed in by all the faithful with greater certainty than that which attends what is seen by bodily eyes. Because he is above and below, he himself is the one who descends and the one who ascends above all the heavens to fill all things. Hence the gospel says: 'You will see the angels of God ascending and descending above the Son of Man' [Jn 1:51]. Because he is near to us the apostle says: 'The Word is near, in your mouth and in your heart' [Rm 10:8]. Because he is hidden, the gospel also says: 'From now on the Son of Man will be sitting at the right hand of God' [Lk 22:69]. Because he appears the apostle says: 'Have I not seen Jesus Christ' [1 Co 9:1] with my own eyes? This was said after the ascension, because earlier he had lived with men, and all flesh saw the salvation of God.

4. He is in heaven, on the altar, in the heart of the Christian. In heaven in his glorified body he sits at the right hand of the Father. He lies on the altar in the hidden mystery, covered with sacred wrappings. When Joseph and Nicodemus removed his same body from the cross and wrapped it in linen with spices, this symbolized the wrapping of the mystery in linen, that is, in the appearances, familar and very pleasing to us, of bread and wine, with the spices of faith, hope and charity and the other virtues or with the scented and sweet-smelling virtues of his most precious body. These scents are very pleasant to the Holy Trinity to whom that sacrifice is offered and to the angelic spirits by whose dedicated service it is taken each day within the veil, that is, to heaven. He is in the heart through faith which works through charity, through a holy life. When such a heart has been accepted, God bestows justice upon it.

5. What of Jesus' body: where does he live, feed, rest? He lives in heaven, as the psalm says: 'You who live in heaven, have mercy on us' [cf Ps 2:4]. He feeds on the altar, he delights in our holy desires, and for our journey he prepares from himself the food which is called viaticum. He will be our satiety in heaven, as it says: 'I will be

satisfied when your glory appears' [Ps 17:15]. He rests in the heart in the noontime of love, if he finds his bed soft, level and clean; that is, if he finds you gentle, just and chaste. So much for the bread: who and where it is.

6. Next something should be said about how it is to be eaten: for it has, as it were, a unique being and a special and retiring way of eating. Thus, the apostle accused the Corinthians, who employed no discernment, of coming to the sacramental reception of the Lord's body casually and indifferently, as if to some food for bodily refreshment. He said: 'He who eats and drinks unworthily, eats and drinks to his own condemnation, without distinguishing the Lord's body' [1 Co 11:28].

7. O animal man, dismount for a while from your assininity and climb up onto the citadel of reason, because, you are not yet able to scale the heights of contemplation. Compare everything bodily and whatever spiritual creature is accessible to your mind with the body of the Lord, and then weigh them honestly on the scales of the sanctuary, that is, not by philosophical and secular reason, but by catholic faith and divine precision. Assess what each is, how great each is, what sort of thing each is, what is the dignity of each, what their utility.

8. What is this but an utterly precious jewel whose price redeems the whole world? When it had been polished by death, it glittered and blinded the eyes of hell. It was a light in the darkness, but the darkness did not grasp it. In fact, the darkness was blinded by its brightness and beclouded by its light. What is this if not an antidote against all poisons and superior to all of them? This antidote even brings the dead back to life. What is this but the body which before the resurrection was made a little less than the angels, because it was subject to suffering and death, but now is raised up above every heavenly height in location, dignity and majesty, and crowned with glory and honor? Of what worth is all that is subject to vanity, that always tends toward non-being, that quickly passes away and is no more?

9. How great he is and of what sort, is known only to that heavenly city which is filled by his greatness and given luster by his beauty. In dignity he is conjoined with God. As for utility, he restores the number of angels, and the salvation of the predestined is completed.

If you consider the quantity of any creature in relation to God, it is reckoned as a grain of dust on a scales [Is 40:15]. If you consider its beauty, it is deformed; its dignity, it is like the soiled rag of a menstrous woman; its utility, it is worthless, for God is not fashioned by his creature, but the creature is blessed by God. Therefore, O man, set this angelic bread apart not only from corporeal foods but from all creatures, by the way in which you honor, cherish, even love, adore, believe in and eat it in preference to all others.

10. This is the manner of eating: receive the chaste bread chastely, the body of Christ as a Christian, the holy bread as a holy person, the pious bread as a good person, the just bread as an upright person, the crucified bread as a devout person, the heavenly bread as a man of the earth. So much for the manner of eating.

11. When is it to be eaten? In tribulation, that tribulation may be lessened; in necessity, that it may be eliminated; in weakness, that it may be relieved; in health, that it may be preserved; in prosperity, that it may be moderate; in adversity, that one may receive strength; in death, that the soul may be directed toward God; in the morning, that it may be with you all day and work with you; at the third hour, that you may keep in your heart the cry of the Jews: 'Take him away, take him away, crucify him', [Jn 19:15] and in compunction the grace of the Holy Spirit may fill your soul. At the sixth hour, that you may fasten yourself to the cross with Christ; at the ninth hour, that you may receive the Spirit sent out from the head and worthily place it in your spirit. Receive the body of Christ fasting, prior to any heaviness stemming from food and drink, so that anticipating your hospitality, he may have the first places for reclining, the first seats, and the first greetings. And as he reclines, let none of the serving girls [thoughts] cause annoyance, let no servile motion intrude the allurements of the flesh by a disorderly movement, but let all things maintain a moderate silence, while his mouth is silent. One's tongue should stick to one's mouth; but all that is inward sits at Jesus' feet, meditating only on what is salutary and concerned with salvation.

12. There are certain established times in which I think one should not abstain, unless there is a reasonable cause, such as a sentence of excommunication or awareness of a mortal sin; if one can make a

confession of sins beforehand and recite the seven penitential psalms, then if it is possible one should receive the body of the Lord. However, the psalmist says: 'Sing to our Lord in confession, sing psalms on the lyre to our God, who gives their food to the animals and to the young crows who call upon him' [Ps 147:7,9]. Eliminate superfluities and the things which are abhorrent to the holiness of his most holy body which never saw corruption, not when it was with the Father before all ages, not when it was born of a mother at the end of the ages, not in the tomb when it arose on the third day, not when by means of this sacred mystery it turns aside to the Christian soul to receive hospitality.

13. When body and soul are purified by holy confession, raised to God by heavenly desire, expanded by charity, touched by neighborly compassion, then is spread that great dining room where the apostles are commanded to prepare the passover. The Apostle teaches the same arrangement when he says: 'Get rid of the old yeast, so that you may be a new batch, just as you are unleavened' etc. [1 Co 5:7].

14. What one should say about the time for receiving is summarized by the psalmist: 'The eyes of all hope in you, O Lord, and you give them food in due season' [Ps 145:15]. Reasons of devotion, faith, established practice and necessity indicate opportunities. So much for when.

15. Where, if not in the holy place, the temple of God, the catholic Church, just as no one took the meat of the lamb outside the house which had both doorposts stained with the blood of the same lamb? The person who believes in his heart in the passion of Christ unto righteousness and confesses it with his lips unto justice puts blood on both doorposts.

16. Now something needs to be said about who is to eat the bread of angels. The apostle indicates who, when he says: 'Let each person examine himself and then eat of that bread and drink of the chalice' [1 Co 11:28]. Those people who have as their own this noteworthly characterisitc of wisdom in what they do, a characteristic which the divine scriptures extol, are always assiduous with every sort of scrutiny in deliberately pondering the outcome of a deed before doing it. Abraham first counted out three hundred battle-ready men from among the members of his household and thus subdued five kings and

rescued his nephew Lot. Gideon, too, at the Lord's command, set aside for the battle against Midian three hundred men who lapped up water with their hands [Jdg 7:5–6]. The legislator Moses also gives orders that when the sons of Israel need to go into battle, before the conflict is joined the priests and chieftans are publicly to test who are suited for battle and who are fearful or less fit for war. In the latter category are those who have built a new house and haven't dedicated it, those who have planted a vineyard and not made it common land, those who are engaged but are not yet married, those who are fearful or fainthearted. After all these have gone back, then each leader will prepare all his own men [cf. Dt 20:2–9].

16. It would be a very long and difficult task to tell about the zeal with which fifty other of God's warriors tested those they chose for any duties. Similarly, the Lord also ordered Moses to choose seventy seniors whom he knew to be elders. Such is the care with which those who exercise designated duties in these worldly matters are tested, though their victory does not produce eternal praise nor the reward of true salvation, unless perhaps some have the intention of offering obedience to God, not because they conquer enemies and kill people, but because they avenge injuries done to God and fight on God's orders. How much more is everything to be tested where negligence runs the risk of lasting danger, and diligence brings an eternal remedy. So let each man examine himself, as though he were about to approach a great battle, not against flesh and blood, that is, against mortal men, but on behalf of the body and blood of the Lord, where war is launched against God if it is received unworthily.

17. Therefore, let him be one of Abraham's household, that is, one educated by the skill of the catholic Church; let him be unencumbered by any baggage of flesh and spirit. Let him be one of the three hundred bearing their crosses after Christ in the faith of the holy Trinity. Let him pursue and capture the five kings, so that he may return and restore the five senses to the service of Christ by the liberty of justice. Let him free Abraham's nephew Lot, that is, let him recover by diligence any virtue lost through negligence. Then let him eat of that bread and drink of the chalice, because when Abraham was coming back from that slaughter, Melchizedek offered him bread and wine.

18. Against Midian, which means 'contradiction' and therefore stands for the devil or the stirrings of the flesh, choose those three hundred who lapped water as dogs customarily do, by putting their hand to their mouth; that is, those who do not live according to the flesh and do not gratify the desires of the flesh. But living on the stingiest and slightest provisions, like dogs pursuing prey, whenever they have been revived they pursue the promised glory as though it were running away. They eat of that bread and drink from the cup, because they do not wish to drink from the cup of Babylon, that is, the pleasure of the flesh.

19. In the new house which has been built but not yet dedicated are those who have decided on a good way of acting but have not yet brought it into effect. In the vineyard which has been planted but not yet been made common is devotion's offspring, partially formed through holy desire but not yet fully formed and brought forth by practice. In the wife engaged but not yet taken is the vow of changing from worldly ways and the promise of accepting a new life, because as long as this is put off, the engaged wife is not accepted. In the timorous and fearful heart we see the person who is afraid where there is nothing to fear and so trembles at a tree leaf as though it were a snake bite and steps back from any vow of holy religion.

20. Once all of these have been rejected, let the rest examine themselves and form up into wedges against the fortified camps of vices. As they fight valiantly against all their assailants who war against the soul, let them eat that bread and drink from the cup. So much for who should eat the bread of angels.

21. There remains the question of why. Why, if not that we may have life and have it more abundantly; if not that we may have the Lord with us; if not that he may be in us for our present justification and future glorification? May he deign to grant us this, who is himself the living and true bread, who descends from heaven and gives life to the pure, Jesus Christ our Lord who lives and rules with the Father and the Holy Spirit.

A SERMON FOR EASTER

1. Although Christ yielded up his soul, exposed his body on the cross and deposited it in the tomb, he did not lay aside his clemency or his power. He rose in power, and in clemency he revisited the apostolic family, with his neck wrung back on his little wings [as a sin offering (Lv 5:8)]. By his glorious consolation he brought relief, either personally or through angels, to minds struck with fear and sorrow. O holy angels, where were you during the passion, what were you doing, why did you not rush to help, why did you let your king be so insultingly discredited?

2. They reply: 'It is obvious he did not need our help. His cause was clear to him, along with the Father and the Holy Spirit. It was hidden from many of us, and it is not for our order to be in attendance unbidden. The good Lord did not wish our joys to interrupt his sufferings.' He did not count as loss what was to be compensated without delay by such great profits. He gave his one body, but he acquired thousands upon thousands. He yielded up his one soul, but how many did he restore and take back to heaven? He was in the heart of the earth for three days, but he acquired eternity and length of days for his family.

3. Who could reckon the price, who could comprehend the human race redeemed at this price? The value of the blood and death and resurrection of Christ flowed back all the way to the angelic peace and even overflowed it. Christ did not leave unpaid for anything which could ever be redeemed at any price. O Christ, you assumed the price from our nature, you paid the price in and for our nature. Your body and blood were ours, only your divinity was exclusively yours. You made up the price from our body, blood and soul. For what, or for whom? For the human race and for all people. How in our nature? On the cross and in the passion. The penalty is ours, the passion is owed for us. It is to be presumed, though without presumption, that this solemn act is ours to spend and to use.

4. Is it not part of our expenditure that in memory of it we have kept vigil, fasted, restrained wanderings and vanities and have been crucified with Christ in many ways? He does not reject our expenditures, small though they be, for he never shuns without renumeration even a glass

of cold water. The use of this solemn act especially pertains to us. The angels, who are gathered for continuous celebration, do not need a devout annual remembrance. The devil, having been conquered, cast out of the world, and despoiled of the booty of so many souls has no festival.

5. Yet we do not exclude the angels by whose ministry we tasted the first fruits of the Lord's resurrection. Rather, we share it with them. They have their stoles, their albs, their radiant faces. O what do they have to do with us, who are in rags, practically naked, whose clothes are worn with age, corrupted with superfluity, ripped with discord? As quickly as we can let us put off the old skin with the old man, wash away the stains with compunction, and stitch together the rips with unanimity.

THE SCHOOL OF THE CLOISTER

THE LETTER ABOUT THIS WORK FROM PETER, THE ABBOT OF
ST REMI, TO COUNT HENRY OF TROYES.

T O HIS LORD AND FRIEND, Henry, the illustrious count
palatine of Troyes, Peter the humble abbot of St Remi,
wishes salvation and every kind of prosperity.

2. If it had not become foolish by its own choice and because of its close connection with a body made from mud, the liberty of the soul would not have needed to be punished with a discipline which bends, levels and binds. This discipline bends what is exalted, levels what is rough, and binds what is wanton. It bends what is untamed, levels what is unequal, and binds what is lax. It bends the mind, levels the body, and binds them both. It bends with humility, levels with equality, binds with religion. It bends with conversion, levels with confession, binds with profession. It bends the shoot on the vine, it levels the surface of the tablets of the heart to receive the commandments of life, it ties the colt at the vineyard, that is, the mind to grace. Finally, it bends the thick-headed bull, it levels the hump-backed camel, it binds the buffalo and the wild ass.

3. After body and soul, each in its own way, were both deprived of the goodness which was theirs by nature, the kindness of God began looking for ways by which to make good the damage caused by such recklessness. Because the cause of such a serious malady is found in the inherent privilege of liberty, he used the healthy method of regular discipline to clip the wings of debased liberty and force down the neck of reckless presumption. What God has arranged in a general way for the whole human race, I have experienced within myself, effected with an altogether gentle kindness. For having set aside the tried and true gravity of our order I was running around in all directions, like a shiftless wanderer. I failed to remove the worldly affairs and earthly occupations which like thieves and robbers steal almost all the resources of religion. But then the hand of the Lord shot the offspring of his quiver into my innards and a dire attack chilled my kidneys and forced me to stay at home. As a result I felt the effects of discipline, and I

began to think about discipline and wrote down my thoughts. The longer I patiently endured discipline, the more spontaneously and diligently, if not eloquently I wrote about it. Augustine wrote about Christian discipline as Augustine and as a bishop. I write as an abbot and monk about claustral discipline. Like a saintly and learned giant he carried the mountains of the deer [cf. Vulgate Ps 103:18] and the minds of the humble upon his shoulders. Like the tiniest ant I carry some cut-up granules to the insignificant little hut which is my treatise, and I prepare a few slight provisions for the coming hunger of winter.

4. So our little work of the discipline of the cloister is not outstanding for style or a striking title, nor does it venture into the argumentative halls of philosophy. Instead, with humble countenance and clothes, in the caves and caverns of the world, it shapes itself to the material of which it treats. So, on what grounds do I send this grimy and ragged treatise to be read by you, a prince most noble, but more to the point, possessed of a very keen intelligence? Trapped by my own words, I prefer to be accused of clumsiness rather than of lying. Let the kind and understanding mind read it, paying attention to the force not of the words, but of their meaning. Just as the power of the mind is greater than bodily beauty, so in a written work one should look for the spirit which gives life rather than for the letter which puffs up. The fruit of the tree is more pleasing than the leaves. Both are good if they are present together, but pretty foliage without fruit is flattery to the eyes rather than nourishment for the stomach. The apostle rebukes the appearance of piety where the virtue of charity is lacking. The Lord, too, when he came to the fig tree which had only leaves and no fruit, cursed it and condemned it eternally. I beg Your Nobility not to pay attention in this reading to what we are, but to what we would like to be.

5. Nor should your prudence be unaware that the lamp of our order is not completely extinct in Israel. It is rather that the eyes of Israel have grown blurred with old age [Gen 48:10]. Elijah complained about Ahab and Jezebel, saying: 'Lord, they have undercut your altar, killed your prophets. I am left alone, and they are seeking my soul.' The Lord gave him this answer: 'I still have seven thousand men who have never bent their knees before Baal' [1 K 19:10, 18].

Thus, lord and dear friend, it is certainly true that although the great virtue of the regular observance of the eminent fathers has slackened off in our times, it has not died out; although there have been departures from it, it has not died; although it has cooled off, it has not perished. Those who seem to men to be nothing or to be insignificant lamps are more in God's eyes than those who seem to be something. I'm not excusing the evil, but I am proclaiming the good. I take away prejudice because I await God's judgment. It is your task to honor God's name not only in holy people, but in the depraved as well.

6. Any person, however contemptible, if he carries your seal, is to be received and honored under the authority of your name, not because he is worthy, but because he is associated with someone who is worthy. So, generally, a worthly person makes someone unworthy worthy; properly unworthy, but improperly worthy; unworthy on his own, worthy because of the performance of an office. I certainly do not want you to spare me where I have committed excesses. But I do ask that you not read my work with weariness; as soon as it begins to be a burden, toss it away from you. Then, if you like, you can take it up another time, or, if it should displease you, condemn it to be shut away in perpetual darkness. People who are poor and proud, but really suffering from poverty, vainly wanting to pretend to glory in order to disguise their poverty and acquire dignity, often trim their cloaks with precious or beautiful furs, not for any utilitarian reason, but to satisfy the curiosity of those who watch them. I have done something similar. Since because of our limitations this work of ours is wanting in the value of its ideas and grace of its words, I have put your name on it as a title, and so decorated its entrance very fittingly. The reader, trusting that only something of excellence would be offered to you, will hurry to read it, not because of the fragrance of the glass offered him, but because of the splendor of so great a prince.

This work of ours on the discipline of the cloister contains the following chapters.

1. It belongs to either the knowledgeable or the experienced to judge of known matters. For the ignorant or inexperienced to deal with unknown matters is presumption rather than exact description. If I claim to be knowledgeable or expert on claustral discipline, I lie. I will not argue the point. I do not deny that I have seen regulars and religious in whose company I was for a while, though I have not kept their virtue. How is it, then, that you ask to hear about claustral discipline from me, when for thirty years I have hardly tasted it with the tip of my tongue. But since charity believes all things, and since I know you ask this from devotion and not as a temptation, I will avoid the problem of refusing and boldly write about what I am not able to observe. I am not particularly ashamed if in this work you recognize me as you have known me to be since your childhood, if only because our age is already declining, and it has less of midday and more of evening about it.

2. I have been wordy in this treatise about claustral discipline, both because of your oft-repeated request and because of the illness which has kept my kidneys under stringent discipline for so long. This work is prepared from common and well-known plants which grow in our gardens, rather than from precious varieties which come from remote places. I have served up more of the honey of Gregory than of the purgative of Jerome. I was afraid that the work would find itself rejected if the purgative was annoying, or its ordinariness demeaning because of the style and the stylist. In repayment for this effort I ask this salary from you: that you read it diligently and remove whatever is offensive and correct what needs correcting.

3. I am paying back with interest a debt which I did not pledge to you, but which you often asked of me. For me the desire of a friend to ask for something is tantamount to a debt. I am adding interest because such a long delay has preceded payment. Thank God who provided the opportunity without which I still wouldn't be rid of that debt. How? A pain in the kidneys which for a long time has kept me under a harsh discipline and denied me the ability to wander here and there. I am glad about my illness and declare: Let us bear

with evils, so that we may do good. Or maybe I should say, let us suffer evils, so we will not commit them. This is part of our claustral discipline, to suffer evils but not to commit them; to return good things for bad. So teaches he who discovered every way of discipline and taught it to Jacob his son, to Israel his beloved. He suffered evils from evil people for their sake, but he returned good for evil and made good people out of evil people.

4. Do not be astonished, my very dear friend, to discover a halting style, because my hand hobbles like my whole body. A shaky hand does not keep to straight lines. What is so surprising if a cripple produces something crippled? It would be more startling if a hunchback gave birth to a person who stood up straight. You, who think and act properly, should excuse Meribbaal's infirm feet just as David did [1 Ch 8:34, 9:40, Ps 81:7]. You should either correct or remove every lame word. It is better to enter into life with one foot than to have two feet and be sent to hell. The jealousy of readers is hell. Envy rightly collapses, when the material evades biting tongues because it is belted with truth, trimly constructed, and armed with reason. The same is true when the material is so deadly dull, ugly in appearance, scraggly in vocabulary, anemic in ideas, that the teeth of envy have nothing to chew on.

5. I do not think my little works worthy of a public viewing, but my secret is mine, my secret is mine [Is 24:16]. Let simple devotion, not misguided eloquence, read my writings, not to applaud but to lament. My dove moans in its hole. The crow caws on its corpses and carrion and croaks: *'cras, cras'* (tomorrow, tomorrow), calling for what is crass. (Thus we read in the account of the Lord's passion that certain people said: 'Behold, he is calling Elijah', although the Lord was saying 'Eli, Eli'.) Or again, maybe the crow is deceiving itself with the promise of long days and years or pledging a delusory penitence. *'Cras, cras,'* that is, never; as the saying goes, 'Today there is a price, tomorrow there will not be.' For myself, I ask for this work the price of prayers and intercessions today and tomorrow.

6. Dear Richard, friend of discipline, as I know by experience, you have more than once disturbed this old man who still studies his alphabet, so that I might collect for you in some literary work what I think. And if I am not forced to rise from my bed by friendship, I am

because of the insistence of the friend described in the gospel [Lk 11:8]. With my mouth shut, I was resting together with my children, my other senses. I must give not what your affection requires, but what I have at hand. I fear that some starvling will come and, finding no fruit but only leaves on the fig tree, will then curse the false hope or promise. Similarly, I suppose, if a queasy person comes along he will pick at each thing out of curiosity and scorn it distastefully. The result will be nausea rather than satisfying taste. But charity believes all, and no one is forced to have my gift. Because of your great love of the inner pith, you even nibble at our tasteless husks. For you alone I collect what God's will has provided, and I hand it over to my mother Rebecca so that from it she can prepare something to eat.

Here Begins the Book of Claustral Discipline.

I. AUTHORS OF THE DISCIPLINES

1. Going back over the rolls of authoritative Scripture, I have found that the prinicpal and greatest authors of this discipline are Moses in the desert, Jesus in the world, and Paul in his assigned office of teaching the gentiles. Augustine and Benedict, two brooks streaming from these sources, have enclosed canons regular and monks in the cloister, like stags and roe deer in an enclosure, or, so to speak, in a park. In Exodus, Leviticus, Numbers and Deuteronomy you should read about the claustral discipline of the Lord's special people and keep with simple understanding the commands which were given to shape their morals. As for the ceremonial directives, which are dressed up with the very fine clothes of Esau, cut them apart and eat the spiritual kernel which is hidden within them.

2. Certainly that discipline was extremely severe, and compared to it our discipline is bearable. In fact, the older discipline was so unbearable that none of the people, neither the weak and common nor the righteous and holy, could keep the commandments of the Law. So Peter declared: 'Why do you try to impose on us a yoke which neither we nor our fathers could carry?' [Ac 15:10]. By contrast our discipline is relatively tolerable, as the epistle of John says: 'Love is

this, that we keep his commandments; his commandments are not heavy' [1 Jn 5:3]. What is our discipline, if not to live according to God's commandments? Jesus is the great and good master, whose chair is in heaven and whose school is in the world. The things he did and taught he inscribed in the gospel as in a book of remedies. He taught claustral discipline to the twelve apostles, his cloistered followers, and to the seventy-two disciples as well. Nor did anyone withdraw from that gospel cloister except the son of perdition and those who said: 'This is a hard message.' 'They went away and did not walk with him any more' [Jn 6:60, 66].

II. APOSTOLIC DISCIPLINE

1. Notice that the apostolic discipline is to be held in esteem everywhere and in all things. This is especially the case when Peter nodded to John, who was reclining at the Lord's breast at the last supper, to ask who was going to betray the Lord. So great was their reverence for the master, so great their obedience, submission and fraternal love for each other, that not a whisper passed among them. The only exceptions were their argument about which of them seemed to be the greatest and the time when they were indignant at the two who sought to sit on the Lord's right and left. Whatever human weakness did in those earthen vessels not yet sufficiently fired by the Holy Spirit, the hand of the potter quickly repaired and strengthened. One time he rebuked them saying: 'O you of little faith, why are you disturbed?' [Mt 8:26]. Another time he consoled them: 'Have confidence; I have conquered the world' [Jn 16:33], and 'Behold I am with you until the consummation of the world' [Mt 28:20]. Sometimes he spoke in parables, sometimes without them. Sometimes he withdrew and spent the night in prayer; one time he hid himself and walked on the sea, so that they thought he was a ghost. Sometimes he returned to his group and lived with them on familiar terms. Once, because of their great hunger, they cracked some grain behind his back and ate it. Another time they collected twelve baskets of fragments from the leftovers of five loaves. They had nothing of their own and declared: 'Behold, we have left all things and followed you' [Mt 19:27]. They wished never to be

separated from him. When he told them, 'I am going to Judea', Thomas told his fellow disciples: 'Let us go and die with him' [Jn 11:16].

2. What shall I say about these canons and monks, the apostles? I would compare them with angelic spirits, except that as long as they had not yet put off mortality, they still ministered to him who was made a little lower than the angels. Once crowned with glory and honor above every principality and power, he was to sit on the throne of his majesty, the throne of greatness. They will sit upon twelve thrones, judging the twelve tribes of Israel. Perhaps they will also judge the angels of whom the apostle spoke: 'Will we not judge the angels also?" [1 Co 6:3]. This hope is stored up in the breast of claustrals, because its realization was promised for such a discipline not by just anyone but by the same Jesus Christ. Peter followed in the apostolate for the circumcised and Paul for that among the gentiles, as Paul himself said: 'The one who was at work in Peter for the apostolate of the circumcision was also at work in me among the gentiles' [Ga 2:8]. The apostle teaches in his rule, that is, in his epistle: 'Those who use this world as though not using it' [1 Co 7:31], and 'Having nothing and possessing all things' [2 Co 6:10], and 'Obey those set over you and be subject to them' [Heb 13:17], and 'Carry one another's burdens' [Ga 6:2], and 'Let no one seek what is useful for himself, but what is useful for another' [cf. 1 Co 10:24], and 'Surpass each other in mutual respect' [Rom 12:10], and 'Let foul speech not proceed from your mouth, and let indecency and foolish talk not be mentioned among you' [cf. Eph 5:3–4].

3. The whole text of the Apostle blossoms with flowers like these. He rules a far-flung and spacious cloister which extends from Jerusalem to Illyria. He has a rod in his hands, as he wrote to certain people: 'Which do you wish: that I come to you with a rod or with a gentle spirit?' [1 Co 4:21]. He hands some over to Satan, so they may learn not to blaspheme. He rejoices with those rejoicing in the guest house, and he weeps with those weeping in the oratory. He is ill with the sick in the infirmary, and he is stung with those who are scandalized in chapter. In the novitiate he addresses his novices: 'My little ones to whom I gave birth through the gospel and with whom I am still in labor until Christ is formed in you.' In the refectory he

chastises his body lest, while preaching to others, he himself become rejected [1 Co 9:27]. Finally, he is always and everywhere found keeping vigils and fasts, in hunger and thirst, in cold and nakedness, in blows beyond number, often in danger of death. He says to those who take care of the guests: 'Be hospitable to one another without murmuring' [1 P 4:9]. To those in the oratory: 'I will pray the psalms in the spirit with the brothers; I will pray the psalms with my mind. I will pray in the spirit and I will pray with my mind' [1 Co 14:15]. To the infirmarians: 'Bear one another's burdens' [Ga 6:2], and 'Receive the sick person in faith'. To those seated in the chapter: 'Reprove, rebuke, entreat' [2 Tm 4:2]. To those in the refectory: 'Do not get drunk on wine, for there lies debauchery' [Eph 5:18]. To the almoners: 'He who sows sparingly will reap sparingly; and he who sows with blessings will reap from blessings eternal life' [2 Co 9:6]. Finally, to all claustrals he shouts: 'Be alert, stand firm in the faith, act mercifully and be strong' [1 Co 16:13]. In this manner nothing which is according to the rule, nothing upright and nothing to which faith can give form, nothing which can imitate Jesus' path, is alien to Paul. One concluding remark of his sums up all claustral discipline: 'Let all your activities be done in charity' [1 Co 16:14].

4. Now let us turn our pen to our special teachers: blessed Augustine and holy Benedict. One was a bishop and canon, the other an abbot and monk. Both were saints; both were teachers and distinguished leaders of the Lord's flock. In some matters our claustral discipline and yours coincide; on other points they differ. Some things pertain to the substance of religious life, others are accidentals. Without the substantial elements there is no religious life. An accidental element can be present or absent because of place, time, cause, person or other circumstances, aside from the decay of religious life. It is left to the judgment of the person in charge to intensify or relax such things, provided peace and unity are preserved. They ought not to be so stressed that weakness is strained to the breaking point, or so relaxed that the rule is violated.

5. These are substantial elements of religous life: silence, about which it is said: 'Let every one be quick to listen, but slow to speak' [Jm 1:19]; reading, about which it is said: 'Until I come, apply yourself to reading' [1 Tm 4:13]; confession of sins, about it is said:

'Confess to the Lord, for he is good' [Ps 106:1]; and 'all things are washed in confession', hence, 'I said: I will confess, and you remitted the impiety of my sin' [Ps 32:5]; likewise prayer, of which it is said: 'If you ask the Father anything in my name, he will give it to you' [Jn 16:23]; then meditation on death, about which it is said: 'Son, remember your final end, and you will never sin' [Si 7:40]. We will treat of all these at greater length below.

III. COMPARISON BETWEEN JEWISH CLAUSTRAL DISCIPLINE AND OURS

1. Just as the commandments of the law written on the two tablets contained the Jewish discipline, so every regular whether canon or monk must live between two inheritances; that is, the framework provided by the Rule and the good customs handed on by his elders. One admits of dispensation, the other does not. A judge judges not the law, but according to the law. However, custom and usage are introduced by the will of those who make use of them and are changed by a contrary decision. If necessity requires that something among the latter be changed, corrected or added, such a change of arrangements is not entirely forbidden. The claustral life is bound by the former as if by the strongest bonds, however, so that neither hands nor feet may move beyond what is allowed.

2. Hence, profession according to a rule and the customs of a place restrains the one bound by its fetters. It places upon the shoulders of the one renouncing the world the gentle yoke and light burden of Jesus Christ. In front of the manger and crib of Emmanuel it ties up the ass and the colt upon which Jesus will be seated as he pursues the hour of his glorification. For both head and members, sufferings come first, then glories. It is recounted that Jesus stood bound before the governor. Since a disciple is not above his master, the true religious voluntarily and freely desires regular discipline in order to be tied back from the appetites of the flesh as if by bands. The bonds of religion are the regular statues; for example, silence, fasting, and seclusion of the cloister, ways of acting which do not attract attention, compassion and fraternal love, paternal reverence, reading and persistent prayer, recollection of past evils, fear of death, the fire of purgatory, eternal fire. Scarcely anyone's thoughts could be so wandering and unruly

that they would not be restrained by such a strong and many-stranded rope. Silence entombs the idle word, the unneccessary word, the word which is out of place. Continual fasting puts to sleep the titillations and provocations which are kindled in the thorns of evil desires. The seclusion of the cloister hinders random and useless wandering in the squares and streets of the city of blood [cf. Ez 22:2]. Restrained and suitable conduct eliminates actions which give rise to evil suspicions in the eyes of those watching. Compassion excludes heartlessness; love, discord; paternal reverence, obstinacy; reading, ignorance; prayer, uncleanness and malice; meditation, sluggishness and drowsiness. The recollection of past evils brings caution about the future, sorrow about the past, and concern about the present. The fear of death is as lethal as is myrrh to dying flies and to worms which do not die but devour the wretched soul. The fire of purgatory calls one back from venial faults, eternal fire from criminal ones. None of these observations is unfruitful in Israel, who, since he fought with the angel, is called not Jacob but Israel.

3. Yet, all the glory of the king's daughter does not lie on the surface; it comes from within, in the golden fringes within the holy of holies, where the cherubim with their heads turned look only upon the propitiatory [Ex 25:20]. The cardinal virtues are the gold fringes, because the hinges of the world are the Lord's. There are also silver columns on golden pedestals, the salutary virtues of a pure heart, a good conscience and unfeigned faith, concerning which it is said: 'I have strengthened his columns' [Ps 75:3]. These support the temple of Solomon, for genuine religion established in the upright mind by regular discipline is not ashamed of the gospel of God, but keeps the gospel's commands like a structure placed upon the shoulders of voluntary observance, as Mary kept all these words.

4. Let us now turn our stylus to the topic of claustral discipline and, as if in one body, describe the form of the beautiful girl, not of Amalek's race, but of the seed of Abraham.

IV. A GENERAL DISCUSSION OF ALL THE OBSERVANCES OF CLAUSTRAL DISCIPLINE

1. Claustral discipline is a spectacle for God, angels and men: for God in the depths of intention, for angels in groans and aspirations,

for men in deeds and words. Man sees the face, God the heart, and angels areas between thinking and doing. Charity from a pure heart and a good conscience and unfeigned faith has regard for God. Holy simplicity looks to the angels while keeping up a good appearance, concerning which it is said: 'With your appearance and beauty, stretch forward, proceed successfully and reign' [Ps 45:5]. As Augustine says: 'sacred and religious expression is pleasing to the holy angels'.[169] Thus, in Exodus, when the Lord was striking down the Egyptians, he did not let the destroyer enter the houses on whose lintel and doorposts he could see the blood of the lamb. Love without pretense and a life which is without quarrelling are for the sake of men.

2. Therefore, claustral discipline which is bedecked with these spiritual endowments never lifts up its head or walks with a haughty air, but like Rebecca before the Lord's gaze it covers its face with a veil of modesty and humility. While it walks along, it says: 'With each of my steps I will proclaim the Lord' [Jb 31:37]. Again, 'I have gone around [the altar] and immolated a sacrifice of jubilation in his tabernacle' [Ps 26:6]. Claustral discipline does not walk, as the impious do, on a detour of vanity and curiosity, but with the angels it ascends the ladder of Jacob with ecstasy of mind and descends by contemplating its weakness. When it sits, it thinks about the throne of majesty, about the throne of eternity, and what it is going to say and do when faced with the dread of God 'on the day of wrath and revelation of the just judgment of God' [Rv 2:5]. If it is standing, let it say: 'The Lord lives; I stand under his gaze' [2 K 3:14]. Or again, 'I will stand before you in the morning' [Ps 5:3], and 'Our feet were standing in your courts, O Jerusalem' [Ps 122:2], and 'The place where you are standing is holy ground' [Ex 3:5]. If it lifts up its head, let it say: 'I have lifted up my eyes before you, who dwell in heaven' [Ps 123:1], and 'I have lifted up my eyes to the mountains; from there help will come to me' [Ps 121:1], and 'As the eyes of servants are on the hands of their masters', and 'as the eyes of a servant are on the hands of her mistress' [Ps 123:2]. If it opens its mouth and lips, let it say: 'My mouth will speak wisdom' [Ps 49:3], and 'Lord, put a guard for my mouth and a door before my lips' [Ps 141:3], and 'Keep your tongue from evil and your lips from speaking deceit' [Ps 34:13], and

'Let no evil speech proceed from your mouth' [Eph 4:29]. If it lends an ear to a speaker, let it not hear of blood or accept reproach against it neighbors.

3. If it eats, before it does so let it sigh with Job, both because of the necessity inflicted through the apple, and because the stomach listens misguidedly to the importuning voice and fashions a confusing and deceptive mixture of necessity and pleasure. Rare indeed is the person who puts a divider and a wall of discernment between necessity and superfluous appetite. If it drinks wine, let it not take poison. As the apostle says: 'Do not get drunk on wine, for there lies debauchery' [Eph 5:18], and 'Take a little wine for your stomach and frequent illnesses' [1 Tm 5:23]. If it sleeps, let it say: 'I sleep, but my heart is alert' [Sg 5:2], and 'I sleep and rest in peace' [Ps 4:8], and 'My flesh rests in hope' of rising for vigils [Ps 16:9].

4. If claustral discipline prays, let it pray in spirit and mind; let it enter its room and close the door and pray to the Father with its heart rather than with its voice, with faith rather than with chanting. If it comes to confession, carrying a flask of water [Mk 14:13], let it bear on the belt of contrition a sharp peg of accusation. With this let it open the land of the heart and lay aside the burdens of the mind. So it will destroy the remnants of Amalek and kill within itself all the agents of wickedness. Let it pour out the sacrificial blood of confession on the base of the altar, so that by the pure blood from the side of Christ it may cleanse its menstrual discharge and hide the idols of its sins under the terebinth of the cross. Let it not pat itself on the back, let it not turn aside to the right by praising its good deeds, or to the left by being silent about the truth or by making up things that are not evil.

5. If [claustral discipline] makes an accusation about a brother's fault, let it be careful that the blade not fall from the handle and wound more than is just, in the manner of Joab, who held the chin of Amasa soothingly, and while he was thus diverting his attention stabbed him in the groin [2 S 20:10]. If the accusation concerns something manifest, let it employ the gentle words of the gentle lamb. The Lord says, 'Judas, are you betraying the son of man with a kiss?' [Lk 22:48]. If the accusation is about a hidden matter, let it take the form of private correction, not public disclosure. If the one

concerned is a powerful person or a prelate, let it keep in mind Nathan's words to David and the two sons of Noah. Nathan, cautiously and indirectly stalked the great lion, and bound up the great king with bonds of artifice rather than of severity. The sons of Noah did not want to see their father's shameful nakedness, and so they covered him up, keeping their backs turned.

6. If claustral discipline reads, it comes to the divine law with friendly simplicity. It eats the grapes on the vine; it does not take them outside by a novel interpretation or by bringing up wrongheaded meanings. It does not labor over questions which, instead of promoting edification, foster strife and the downfall of the hearers. Let it read in order to understand, and let it understand in order to do God's commands. Let it seek there compunction rather than superfluous occupation. Let it chew the essence of the law with the depths of the heart. Once it is fattened in this wax, let it offer fat holocausts with a burnt offering of rams; that is, with the sincere truth and true charity of the apostles and prophets. And since Holy Scripture is a chalice in the hand of the Lord which tips to one side and then the other, sometimes the divine commandments are to be read, sometimes the examples of the saints. For the word of the Lord lives in the sufferings of the martyrs and in the saintly lives of the confessors. But what lies there as though it were dead on the dead parchment, deformed according to the letter, springs to life when what is read is put into practice. If some necessity involves it in external affairs, it comes back quickly, as from a prison, a trap, a furnace, the depths of hell. David sees evil in the city, Dinah sees the women of the region, and Shechem, the son of Hamor, perishes there with his father and his people [Ps 55:11, Gn 34:26]. Thus the belly of claustral discipline, covered with the ivory of chastity, is ornamented with sapphires and gorgeous variety.

7. I think that claustral discipline has been established for the purpose mentioned in the book of Esther. Girls were selected from every kingdom for the king's service. They were placed under careful scrutiny, instructed with great care and anointed with the oil of myrtle and other precious ointments. Finally, when they were thus examined by long very careful attention and embellished with a very becoming appearance, the one who pleased the king spent the night

with him, and came and went at his nod. Thus the great king, the king of kings, the king of all ages, calls his predestined from all nations, tribes, tongues and peoples, from every nation under heaven from the rising of the sun to its setting, from the north and from the sea. He gathers them under claustral discipline and smooths down their disordered habits with the file of the rule. He eliminates the stench of vices with the ointment of a holy way of life. He prepares bodies and minds worthy of the embraces of the king. On the eternally prearranged day, he calls them to the throne and nuptial chamber of glory and the blessed life.

V. THE DISCIPLINE OF THE RULE MAKES REPARATION FOR THE FIRST TRANSGRESSION

1. Human nature, of freedom of choice, was flattened by the original collusion and greatly weakened in its natural goodness, so from the moment a person leaves his mother's womb he needs discipline to restore him step by step, as if by medical remedies. By breaking the very solid gates of the first and the new commandment he has fallen a long way down, he has shackled the nobility of his free will and weakened the strength of his bodily health. The occasion for so great an evil was his failure to observe heavenly discipline. That discipline was not more difficult to keep than to enjoin. Desire did not drag along the appetites, necessity was not exerting pressure, hunger didn't gnaw, the scent of the forbidden tree was not prejudicial to the sweetness of the fruits which had been granted him. Although it is written that the woman saw that the tree was beautiful to behold and sweet to taste, certainly this particular beauty and sweetness did not eliminate the beauty and sweetness of all the other trees of paradise. What the passage does show is that the mind of the woman was penetrated by the serpent's suggestion. For the soul, once assailed or absorbed by temptation, apprehends the thing desired not with judgment but with delight.

2. Constrained not by some heavy burden but by a very easy discipline, and totally and carefully formed by God's hand, human nature could have maintained its health. Once it was badly wounded no remedies short of the blood of the lamb were strong enough to

free it completely. How many medicinal remedies the great physician tried to apply to humanity's wounds Abraham bears witness in the circumcision, Moses in the immolation of sacrifices and in offerings of other kinds, and all the prophets in rebuke and persistent preaching. The disease became chronic, so long did it last and so insufficient were the treatments. His brother's treatment could not cure the sick man; he awaited a lord and saviour, a lord to release the servant, a savior to free the sick man. This saviour sent ahead discipline like Moses' rod, but the rod of his strength he kept for himself on the cross, where his blood poured out quenched the fiery spears of the wicked devil and healed his patient of all fever.

3. He set up the cloister to represent his cross. Just as he bore the discipline of our peace in his body upon the wood of the cross, so we must bear the same reproaches he did when we leave the camps for the cloister. Let us embrace his discipline, like sons following the advice of Solomon, who was very wise. 'My son', said Solomon, 'embrace the discipline of your father; do not reject the law of your mother' [Pr 1:8]. Similarly, the psalmist said: 'Embrace discipline, lest the Lord be angry' [Ps 2:12]. The apostle wrote: 'If you are outside of discipline, you are not sons, but the offspring of adultery' [Heb 12:18]. And he continues: 'At present all discipline seems to be a matter of sadness, rather than joy. Later on those who have undergone its training will be given the ever peaceful fruit of justice' [Heb 12:11].

4. The cloister lies on the border of angelic purity and earthly contamination. If someone passes from the world like a Hebrew from Egypt and brings with him to the cloister some grains of uprightness borrowed from the neighboring arts called liberal, he can use them without being judged a thief. For 'all wisdom is from the Lord God' [Si 1:1], except the wisdom of the flesh, which is at enmity with God. The discipline of the cloister is not fond of the wisdom of the flesh, which instead of helping to build up, promotes the overthrow of simplicity, the cloister's only daughter. After the eyebrows of ostentatious vanity have been shaved off (so the apostle says: 'Let no one deceive you with philosophy and empty deceit' [Col 2:8]), and the claws of greedy rapacity removed, let the inhabitant of the cloister, without misgiving, contract a marriage with all teaching

which is not contrary to faith. But anything that has a savor alien to the cloister, even a wild olive, or just a branch, when it is grafted onto the good olive tree, is sweetened by the oil of the roots and incubated in the womb of wisdom, and so transformed from baseness. Thus grammar, dialectic, rhetoric, music, arithmetic, geometry and astronomy are seasoned by the strong salt of divine Scripture. Customarily they inflict death, as the sons of the prophets call to Elisha the prophet: 'Man of God, there is death in the urn' [2 K 4:40]. But with an admixture of flour, that is, of grace, they provide healthful nourishment. Like Gibeonites they bring wood and water to claustral discipline. By the law of war, the Israelites carry these things back to their cloister from the camp of the Philistines, when instructed in secular letters, they read the divine writings more zealously, understand them more penetratingly, detect the deceptions of heretics more carefully, and defend the simplicity and truth of the faith more forcefully and firmly. When our dweller in the cloister spends his time with these, he is not just passing time; intent on them he puts to flight the idle, empty and superfluous fancies of his heart; buried as far as these go, he sleeps vigilantly. Those are the changes of clothes which Naaman the leper brought with him to the king of Israel [2 K 5].

5. Yet, if we have extracted so many riches from the world, what will we receive from God from whom every excellent gift and every perfect gift comes? He waters the mountains from his heights and paradise with the river which proceeds from the place of delight and then divides into four branches. As a result, each of the four sides of the cloister has its own water source. As it says in the gospel: 'Whoever drinks the water that I will give him, will have within himself a spring of water bubbling up into eternal life' [Jn 4:13–14]. 'He said this about the Spirit which those who believed in him were going to receive' [Jn 7:39]. These four rivers of paradise are known to those who with the apostle Paul are rapt to the third heaven, or to paradise itself, and inebriated by the abundance of God's house and by the torrent of delight. Known, too, are the waters from the fountains of the saviour which delight the city of God with a sevenfold stream. Of these it is said: 'Let your spring be diverted into the streets', and 'From them no stranger drinks' [Pr 5:16–17]. Job calls

these fountains rivers of oil, saying 'When the rock was pouring out rivers of oil for me' [Jb 29:6]. Isaiah, who saw the Lord sitting upon a sublime and lofty throne, lists and names these springs of the saviour or rivers of oil. They are called springs, because He himself promises and sends to his apostles the sevenfold Spirit. They are called rivers of oil, because although the Spirit is in all thing equal to the Father and the Son, he is not from himself, but from the Father and the Son. Hence, the gifts of grace are called rivers of oil. According to his humanity "the Son of Oil" is annointed with that oil of happiness more than are those who participate in him. As Isaiah says: 'The Spirit of the Lord will rest upon him, a spirit of wisdom and understanding, a spirit of counsel and strength, a spirit of knowledge and piety; and the spirit of fear of the Lord will fill him' [Is 11:2]. The gospel light which is so suffused and instilled is not only a lamp, but 'the true light which enlightens everyone who comes into this world' [Jn 1:9]. We have received from his fullness in the outpouring which occurred when the soldier opened his side and blood and water came out. The olive in the press gave out his spirit like oil.

VI. COMPARISON BETWEEN THE CROSS AND THE CLOISTER

But what has this to do with claustral discipline? Clearly every form of claustral discipline flows from the cross. Christ was lifted up from the earth, suspended on the cross, stripped of his clothes, and so stretched out that all his bones could be counted, nailed to the wood so that he could move nothing but his tongue which he kept for prayer and to entrust his mother to the beloved disciple. In a similar way a genuine claustral must crucify his whole self with his vices and lusts. He should raise himself from the ground, as it is written: 'I shall raise you above the heights of the land', and 'I will nourish you with the inheritance of Jacob, your father' [Is 58:14]. He should strip himself, as it says in the Song of Songs: 'I took off my tunic' [Sg 5:3], that is, the lust of the flesh. He must stretch toward what is ahead, not just pretending, but to the separation of joints and marrow, so that the soul melts after the beloved. He should be attached to the wood, so that through the fear of God this mortal body and all its members may be rendered incapable of any evil but capable of every good. Let him retain only the tongue for confession and prayer. What else? Like the prophet let him pass through scoffers and mockers with a deaf ear, just as if he were deaf. Let him not hear the suggestions and temptations which with croaking voice say to leave the cloister, the equivalent of coming down from the cross. In the end let him return his spirit to God who gave it, saying, 'Into your hands I commend my spirit' [Lk 23:46] until the resurrection, so that the torment of wickedness will not touch it. For the 'souls of the just are in the hand of God and the torment of death will not touch them' [Ws 3:1].

VII. IN GENERAL, WHY THE CLOISTER WAS ESTABLISHED

1. After Lucifer fell like lightning from heaven, he never returned there, for he did not have claustral discipline. For claustral discipline is to weep for one's sins and the sins of others, to be subject to one's superior, to obey in all matters, to be on one's guard against ambushes, to plot against no one (for as Jerome says there is not much difference between deceiving in vice and being able to be deceived), to fulfill the first and second commandments of the law regarding love of God and neighbor, to preserve innocence and sanctity, to obey God always, to long for one's heavenly country with all one's desires. When the covenant of proper submission was once broken, the devil fell headlong. From then on, growling and grinding his teeth, he subverted all discipline rather than kept it. So he never obtained mercy, because he never sought pardon or confessed his fault.

2. Man, fashioned from clay and expelled from the cloister of paradise because of his fault, faced the east, bewailed his wounds, and said to God: 'Take from me your blows' [Ps 39:10]. At the appointed and eternally predestined time, at the end of the ages when the way of the saints had been staked out, he returned to the cloister in and with Jesus. Then, subjected to regular discipline, he received not only pardon but his original proper garment as well, and even greater glory. The sons of men who followed him and kept their eyes fixed on their head, learned wisdom from what occurred. By wisdom they could avoid the irreparable fall of the devil, and by living according to the rule as did their predecessors, through the pardon of a merciful God, they had a way to return to their paternal inheritance.

3. I think that this is the main reason why people leave the world to enter the cloister. Those who are deluged with vices and riches will not come to the cloister or to the Lord until the waters have dried up. A person who is in the cloister is in the ark with Noah (his name means 'rest'). One who is without discipline is outside the ark. Only a few, eight to be exact, are saved in the ark. For many are called, but few are chosen to rise on the eighth day in the resurrection of life. In the cloister Jacob lives with Rebecca, that is, with patience. In the cloister Benjamin stays with his father, so that nothing bad can happen to him on the path of sinners where dwells the lion, the wild beast of excessive indulgence, which devours Joseph, sometimes only by a bad reputation, sometimes in fact. In the cloister Jonah is in the belly of the whale. Jonah was in the belly of the whale three days and three nights, and so long was the son of man in the heart of the earth. The claustral is buried with Christ and dies to sin and lives for God in thought, word and deed. In the cloister, Jeremiah, sanctified in his mother's womb, sits alone and remains silent. He raises himself above himself, not in glorification but in contemplation. He takes upon himself the easy yoke and light burden, in order to be meek of heart. In the cloister is John the Baptist who

> Still young fled the crowds of people
> To seek the desert caves
> Lest by even a slight intent
> He blot his life.[170]

Mary was in the cloister when the angel entered and said to her: 'Hail, full of grace, the Lord is with you' [Lk 1:28]. Jesus was in the cloister when he was twelve years old and sitting in the temple. When his mother said, 'Your father and I were seeking you', he answered: 'Didn't you know that I must be about my father's affairs?' [Lk 2:48–49]. The apostles were in the cloister, 'When it was the evening of that day, the first day of the week, and the doors were closed where they were, Jesus came despite the closed doors and stood in their midst and said: 'Peace be with you''' [Jn 20:19]. They were also in the cloister 'when the days of Pentecost were completed, and all the disciples were together in the same place,' etc. [Ac 2:1]. These are the forerunners of the claustral way of life.

4. Therefore, how pious, good, pleasant and safe it is for brothers to live together in the cloister. When brother helps brother, the city is fortified, as it is said: 'Who will lead me into the fortified city?' [Ps 60:9]. The cloister is a city, because there claustrals come together to live good lives; it is fortified, because they live under the protection of the God of heaven. The discipline of the cloister is an iron gate which leads into the city. Those who wander in the wilderness and whose hearts are always roaming will not find the way. Claustral discipline is a rock of scandal and a stumbling stone for those who do not believe the word upon which they have been placed. The discipline of the cloister is a rock twice struck, by renunciation of the world and by religious profession. It provides waters from which people and livestock drink. They are the prudent and simple people of whom it is said: 'Be as prudent as serpents and as simple as doves' [Mt 10:16]. The discipline of the cloister is the cross of Christ. From it no one is taken down before he is dead. The claustral is obedient to the Father unto death, death on a cross. The feet of the person hanging there are attached, so that his steps will not find their way outside the cloister. His hands are shaped for obedience, made of gold for purity, full of jacinth for almsgiving. They distill top grade myrrh for the mortification of the flesh. These hands are not held out to receive money. His eyes are turned toward the Father, towards the disciple, toward his mother; that is, they are always turned toward God, and toward the Virgin Mary, and toward John the Evangelist. God is in possession of heaven; the mother implores her Son; John keeps the gospel. It is a good thing to turn one's gaze from one to the other, now invoking God, now petitioning the Lord Jesus' mother, now reading the gospel of John. The head is inclined, for when He had inclined his head, he handed over his spirit. The claustral always has his gaze fixed on the ground when he is in public. But when his door is closed and he enters his room, there he lifts up his head and turns his eyes to heaven. His back is struck with lashes for sins or evil deeds, in thanksgiving or to offset the passion of Christ. His side is pierced and open, and from it he offers fat holocausts with the smoke of rams. From his side blood flows out on the base of the altar when he confesses his sins to his superior. The water of compunction also flows out to wash away the stains of sin. His stomach is strained, not

by the consumption of unnecessary food and drink, but by the continual purging of fasts. Hence, he says: 'My flesh was consumed, so that my bones stick to my skin' [Jb 19:20], and 'They have numbered all my bones' [Ps 22:17]. Thus, too, his belly is adorned with sapphires. Its skin is not dyed scarlet with blood, but appears to be the color of jacinth because of his mortification. A storehouse for worms is not constructed there but, like a wineskin in smoke, it is shrunk with persistent afflictions. This crucified man is laid to rest by Joseph and Nicodemus, his angel and his superior, and embalmed with a mixture of myrrh and aloes. Thus, just as he did not love corruption in the cloister, so he will not feel the undying worms of hell. Without a doubt he will have angels at his head and feet, who will guard his coming and going and receive his soul as it leaves the body and lead it to rest.

VIII. COMPARISON OF THE DISCIPLINES OF THE PHILOSOPHER, THE JEW, THE CHRISTIAN AND DIFFERENT KINDS OF RELIGIOUS.

1. A spark of the natural good remained in man even after the original planting from God's hand was wiped out. Through the grace of God this spark ran through the reed-bed of all the arts and discovered many disciplines. When people lived in accord with these, the first creation, although not completely restored, was at least not extinguished by being reduced to ashes. Every nation under the sun and every region, according to its capacity, devised for itself a discipline of reason, which was to be the form of life both for the disorderliness of fools and the rightness of the prudent. The philosophers set up their discipline, the Jews received theirs, the Christians theirs, and finally the hermits and claustrals theirs. Different aims separate these disciplines from each other. The philosopher intends to acquire human glory and favor for himself; the Jew, the goods of the earth; the Christian, the hope of pardon and grace; the claustral, the pinnacle of grace and glory. The philosopher scrutinizes the secrets of nature; the Jew, the richness of the earth; the Christian, the promise of life now and to come; the claustral, the fruit partly of the active life and partly of the contemplative life. The philosopher abandons the obstacles of the flesh

and the burdens of the world; the Jew strives to purify the flesh through sacrifices and offerings; the Christian is cleansed from dead works by the sacraments of the church; the claustral abstains not just from illicit things, but even from what is lawful. The philosopher sows in a spirit which is not of God, but his own and vain. The Jew sows in the flesh; the Christian, in faith, hope and charity; the claustral, in the adoption of sons. Presumption aids the philosopher; temporal possessions, the Jew. Faith relieves the Christian; the foretaste of future hope comforts the cloistered religious. The philosopher sharpens his wit; the Jew seeks monetary gain; the Christian invokes the good spirit; religious hope for a golden crown. The philosopher finds joy in novel words and opinions; the Jew, in the letter of the flesh; the Christian, in spiritual understanding; and the religious, in austerity of life. The philosopher eats flour from the mill of cleverness; the Jew, the tasteless husk of the law; the Christian, the flour of the gospel; the religious, the marrow of a good intention. The philosopher scatters, the Jew collects, the Christian distributes, the religious renounces all things. The philosopher teaches in the schools; the Jew, in the synagogue; the Christian, in the church; the religious, in the cloister. The philosopher loves applause; the Jew, money; the Christian, God; the religious, lamentation. The philosopher is like a stag in the forest, the Jew like a bull in the fields, the Christian like a dove in the crevices of the rock, the religious like an eagle in contemplation. The philosopher lives by his art, the Jew by the flesh, the Christian by faith, the religious by the mortification of the flesh. The philosopher disputes, the Jew dreams, the Christian reads and understands, the religious prays. The philosopher captures mosquitoes, the Jew dying flies, the Christian birds, the religious bees. The philosopher spins a spider's web, the Jew incubates the eggs, the Christian repairs Peter's net, the religious weaves liturgical vestments (the pectoral and ephod [Ex 28:15, 4]).

2. If the cementing bond of faith comes into play, the claustral and philosophical disciplines embrace in each other's arms and kiss away from the crowds, for secular occupation and empty conversation impede the intellectual powers and senses of the soul. To have at his disposal all his mental capacities, the philosopher sought quiet, hidden

places. There he should cultivate his mind. With his mind purified, he could present faithful thought, but not such as was leavened with gospel yeast. Instead, like Jacob with his poles with their bark artfully peeled, the philosopher presents a seemingly true design of not one, but many colors. Passing through the senses of the flesh, he reaches the senses of the soul; if he should reach the sense of God and faith, he would be saved. But 'the one who offends in one thing is culpable for everything' [Jm 2:10].

3. Would that through faith and regular observance we afflicted our flesh and loved poverty with severity and diligence as great as many philosophers employed in rooting out from themselves the vices of the flesh. But, because faith cleanses the heart and true penitence roots out all sins through confession, if the exterior finish is somewhat wanting, the interior form of the new creation brings about a complete restoration. For all the glory of the king's daughters comes from within. Religion or discipline merits no reward, unless it is endorsed by grace accompanied by a good conscience. So, let our discipline have in common with the philosopher a fruitful silence, with the Jew a continual sacrifice, with the Christian the shared solace of charity, and with its own profession a special submission to the divine will. Let our discipline, like the philosopher's, exclude concern with worldly preoccupations. Let it, with the Jew's, carry out the worship of one God. Let it commend itself to grace with the Christian's. By interior desire let it rise above itself toward God. Let it fulfill the beginnings of its vows with the philosopher, the middle elements of them with the Jew, their farthest parts with Christians, and their ultimate reaches with a free will joined to grace. Let the claustral harvest what is green with the philosopher, what is fertile with the Jew, what is ripe with the Christian, and what is fruitful with his vow.

IX. THE DISCIPLINE OF ANGELS

1. There remains angelic discipline, which is totally voluntary, which possesses everything with delight and nothing with difficulty or effort. When it ministers to God, it is refreshed; when it attends him, it is satisfied. When it is sent, it hurries along happily; when it

returns, it is received with jubilation. It always proceeds under God, never away from him. Nothing in this discipline is disordered, nothing irksome, nothing irregular. Charity melts and unites all those spirits in the love of God and of each other. When they have been molded together in one spirit, they are as tightly bonded as if there were only a single spirit in the whole multitude.

2. In that order there are nine orders of angels, to whom is joined the tenth order of humankind, so that in the middle of the cloister the psalmist sings a song on a ten-stringed psaltery, on the lyre of the cross and the crucified. The apostle speaks about this harmony: 'If I speak with the tongues of men and angels', that is, with a ten-stringed psaltery, 'but do not have charity', that is, the lyre of the cross and unity, 'I am nothing' [1 Co 13:1–2]. All have their own share in it. 'Until Christ is formed' [Ga 4:19] in us, by that design whereby all the members joined to their head will be made faithful sharers in the divine nature, let us in our claustral room, as though enclosed in a womb, acquire the features by which we will be made like the angels after our mortality has been dissolved. 'Then we will be like God', says the apostle, 'because we will see him as he is' [1 Jn 3:2]. What are these features? Angelic purity, spotlessness, chastity, charity, peace and truth, and all those virtues about which it is said: 'Bless the Lord, all you his virtues' [Ps 103:21]. Prayer should be offered that he who created them in heaven, will give us form in the cloister, so differences in appearances will not separate our dwelling places. For if an angel perceives this visage in you, he will love you as himself.

X. THE FORM OF CLAUSTRAL DISCIPLINE

1. The form of claustral discipline retains the appearance of the angel who announced the resurrection of the Lord. For 'his appearance was like lightning and his clothes like snow' [Mt 28:3]. The timid hearts of carnal folk who do not go to war and disdain to come to the wedding take flight at their initial impression of religious life. They devise fantastic illusions why they cannot do without their customary pleasures. They are preoccupied with the five yokes of oxen to which the gospel refers, or with the house they have bought

and the wife they have married. They excuse themselves from making the necessary expenditures: patience, austerity in food and drink, cheap clothes, continuous silence, the yoke of obedience, unbroken seclusion, perpetual continence, and the like. They call themselves men, but by their manner of life they place themselves among the weaklings. About such people Gregory wrote: 'What will we bearded men have to say, when we see young girls going to the kingdom by the sword?' [*Homilia in Evangelia* 1.11.3; PL 76:1116A].

2. We do not deny the harshness of this discipline of ours, but we say with the psalmist: 'I have kept to the difficult paths because of the words of your lips' [Ps 17:4–5]; namely, 'Anyone who does not hate his father and mother' [Lk 14:26], and 'Anyone who does not renounce all that he possesses cannot be my disciple' [Lk 14:33]. Likewise, the furnace tests the potter's vessel, and no one is crowned who does not compete according to the rules. They flee at the sound of a leaf, even though no one is after them. Touch and taste are more certain judges than sight alone. The discipline of the cloister should be touched and tasted; only then should one judge whether it is good or bad.

3. 'His clothes are like snow.' The clothes of claustral discipline are regular observances. Why are they like snow? Because they extinguish the desires and provocations of the flesh; because they chastise with affliction, but whiten with remuneration. As Isaiah says: 'Though your sins be like scarlet, they shall be white as snow' [Is 1:18]. When? When God distinguishes among kings, good claustrals will be made white as snow, because they will be like the angels of God in heaven, shining like the sun in unending eternity.

XI. COMPARISON BETWEEN THE CLOISTER AND THE STADIUM

1. Not without reason do some think of the cloister as a stadium, and others think of it as a courtyard, or treasure room, or earthly sanctuary, or royal bedchamber, or gibbet, or marketplace.

2. The word 'stadium' is derived from 'standing', because a person in the cloister must be eager to stand fast in virtue and not fall into vices. Thus the Apostle wrote: 'Whoever stands should watch out so he does not fall' [1 Co 10:12]. A stadium is a place where everyone

runs, but only one receives the prize of victory. For, although 'stadium' is derived from 'standing', in fact one runs through the stadium to reach the prize. There the course is completed, as the Apostle said: 'I have fought the good fight, I have finished the course', and so on [2 Tm 4:7]. Therefore, all who have shaved the hair of their heads for Christ and put on the religious habit, run as long as they are still heading toward the goal. But the prize is only for someone who does not change as the moon does, someone who does not depart from the unity of faith and religious profession. 'Such a one will receive a blessing from the Lord and mercy from God his saviour' [Ps 24:5].

3. It is a rule of that stadium that the person who hastens after the prize should abstain from everything. Our law binds us less stringently, since it takes away few things, while allowing many. It forbids fornication, adultery, and all uncleanness, and even marriage itself, since 'he who is without a wife is solicitous for the things of the Lord' [1 Co 7:32]. It takes away intoxication, money, superfluities; it allows what is necessary. Thus Moses commanded Sihon, the king of the Amorites: 'We will go by the royal way. We will not drink your waters, or take anything of yours, but we will pay for all necessities' [Cf. Nb 21:21–23]. A pilgrim and stranger who travels daily from this world to the Father will not accept anything belonging to the prince of this world, even a piece of thread. Hence, as his soul departs, he can say confidently to one who asks back what belongs to him: 'You will find nothing on me, deadly one'. This is the nimble runner, finishing up his race. He runs swiftly toward the odor of the perfumes of the spouse. About this stadium the Lord said to the sons of Israel: 'Every place on which your feet tread will be yours. Your boundaries will extend from the desert and Lebanon and the great river Euphrates to the western sea' [Dt 11:24]. Whoever deserts the world and comes to the cloister has begun to tread upon the world and his own body. This, then, is a desert, 'a deserted land, trackless and parched'. 'Deserted', because of harshness; 'trackless', because of the scarcity of travelers; 'parched', because of the severity of the discipline. But here, 'in the holy place', said the psalmist, 'I will appear before you, O God, in order to see your power' because of the hard labor, 'and your glory' because of eternal consolation

[Ps 63:1–2]. One must begin at the desert of renunciation of the world, run through the Lebanon of chastity and whiteness, or the sprinkling of the blood of Jesus Christ, as it is said: 'Far be it from me to glory except in the cross of our Lord Jesus Christ' [Ga 6:14], where the saints whiten their stoles in the blood of the lamb. Again, one must travel by boat across the great river Euphrates, first through baptism, then through continual compunction. Our course will end at the western sea. So let us not fall along the way before our lives are ended by death. We shall possess every place upon which we have trod, like him who said: 'Having nothing and possessing everything' [2 Co 6:10].

XII. COMPARISON BETWEEN THE CLOISTER AND THE COURTYARD

1. The cloister is called the courtyard. There sacrificial victims are skinned and their parts cut into pieces. There ashes are dumped out, entrails washed, and various burdensome duties performed. So, upon entering the cloister one gives skin for skin, and all that he has for his soul [Cf. Jb 2:4]. This occurs when one takes off the old man and puts on the new, walking in newness of life and laying bare in confession the evils of his former habits. First, he immolates a sacrifice to God by mortifying his earthly members: fornication, uncleanness, lust, and whatever is similar to these. Then, once the skin of all perversity has been removed in confession, he breaks the members into pieces. He conceals none of the circumstances of his sin, but for each submits reasons for accusation and lamentation. The fire of contrition and pentinence devours all these, until they are ashes which he may sprinkle upon his head, saying: 'My sin is always before me' [Ps 51:3], and 'I said to putrefaction, 'You are my father', and to worms, 'you are my mother and sister'' [Jb 17:14]. Compunction is added to these; as though it were water from the side of Christ, it cleans the recesses of the conscience from dead works.

2. The inner courtyard is located near the entrance to the sanctuary, inside the exterior courtyard and outside the first tabernacle, called the holy place. The novice coming to religion is located on the border of reason and sensation; he is no longer in the flesh, but he is not yet in the spirit. While he dwells in between he hears the whispering of the

contending flocks of the flesh and the spirit. He consents to the law of God with his mind, but to the law of sin with his flesh. He hears the whispering of the heavenly flocks, which sing the songs of Sion and prompt him to the sleep of contemplation, while putting to rest the annoyances of the flesh.

XIII. THE TREASURE ROOM

1. The cloister is also the treasure room, where gold, silver and precious stones are stored away. There we have our treasure in earthen vessels; that is, a good conscience in regular observances. In the cloister religious, like businessmen, amass for themselves the treasure of eternal life. To them the noble man entrusts his goods as he is about to go abroad. Every psalm, prayer, confession, tear, fast, all alms, the afflictions of countless labors, do not all these constitute the stock of graces, which is the treasure to be desired in the cloistered community? The eunuch of Kandake the queen is put in charge of these, when someone who has castrated himself for the kingdom of God is given the duties of a prelate. It is not unfitting that such a person, distinguished by modesty and chastity because his loins are girt, is appointed guardian of the spouse of Christ. Such was Joseph in the house of Potiphar, the priest of Heliopolis; such was John the Evangelist, to whom the Lord on the cross entrusted his mother. This was the choice of the apostle, and this is the one blessed Benedict described. Why would the jealous Lord entrust his bride, whom he redeemed with his precious blood and joined to himself in indissoluble wedlock, if not so that his vicar, the friend of the spouse, might faithfully serve and chastely preserve the bride entrusted to his care?

XIV. THE EARTHLY SANCTUARY

1. Let us now enter into the sanctuary which is called the earthly holy place, which the priests entered continuously to fulfill their sacrificial duties. Justice, on pilgrimage in the world, selects for itself pleasant, temporary lodgings in places of claustral discipline. He knocks on the door of the cloister, saying: 'Open to me, my sister.

My head is covered with dew, which I will spray into the air of the cloister, so that dew may linger on my harvest. My locks are moist with the droplets of the night' [Sg 5:2]. These the pious conscience steals away in the hiding place of God's countenance and in the secret haunt of silence. One must run to meet such kind promises with the brisk step of holy desire. One must draw back the bolt of the door, which is the difficulty and lethargy felt by human weakness in the fulfilment of its vows. Such is the earthly sanctuary: to wish to do good, but to be barely able to accomplish it. The heavenly sanctuary is to wish and to accomplish. Hence the apostle writes: 'It is God who gives us the intention and the accomplishment of every good desire' [Ph 2:13]. Likewise, of the earthly sanctuary he writes: 'Willing comes easily; accomplishment escapes me' [Rm 7:18]. Rightly, then, the cloister is called the earthly sanctuary, for there we do not do what we wish, and we do not finish what we do.

XV. THE ROYAL BEDROOM

1. The cloister is also called the royal bedroom. Thus, in the Song of Songs claustral discipline declares: 'While he was reclining, my nard gave off its perfume' [Sg 1:12]. To recline is to lie down to rest. In Isaiah the Lord says: 'I worked with endurance' [Is 1:14]. And in Jeremiah: 'I entreated while I worked' [Jr 15:6]. And in the gospel: 'Jesus was tired from his journey, and so he was sitting by the well' [Jn 4:6]. It was not only that he who stays the same and calmly judges all things was bothered by the crimes of Jacob and by our sins. He was also disturbed by the sacrifices, peace offerings, incense, and songs of those priests whose hands were covered with the blood of avarice and indulgence. Tired out by worldly and evil men he wanted to observe a sabbath, and so sought a place of silence, peace, unity and uprightness. There he established his bedroom. Claustral discipline says: 'This is my rest; here I will dwell because I have chosen it' [Ps 132:14]. Similarly: 'My delight is to be with the sons of men' [Pr 8:31], whose behavior is not animalistic, but rational and spiritual in heaven. This discipline, melted by love of the fawn which leaps across the perfumed mountains, says to him: 'Show me, you whom my soul loves, where you browse, where you lie down at midday' [Sg 1:6–7], when

the spirit is aroused, when the whole mind is red-hot, when unbearable fire blazes in the bones of the lover. Clearly, at midday he feeds and lies down among the clusters of fresh fruit, among lilies, in the forest clearings of minds removed from earthly activities. Young men and young women keep watch at the royal bedroom, holding swords which devour the flesh on the thigh of evil desire, circling King Solomon as a guard against the terrors of the night, lest the howling of wolves and the snarling of foxes break the silence of the middle of the night, when the first born of the Egyptians die.

XVI. THE GIBBET. A COMPARISON WITH THE CLOISTER.

1. The cloister is called the gibbet, where Jesus hung with the robbers. Jesus was there not because he deserved it, but because he chose to be. The thieves did not want to be there, but they were where they deserved to be. Thus, one robber said to the other: 'We are getting what our deeds deserve. He did nothing evil' [Lk 23:41]. Whoever enters the cloister with Jesus voluntarily, chooses to be hung up with the robbers as his evil deeds deserve and their satisfaction requires.

2. The great numbers of claustrals may be divided into three categories. In the cloister are innocent people like Jesus, who are the object of no reproach from God or men. There are also wrong-doers who are repentant; they are with the robber on the right. And there are impenitent wrong-doers, who are with the robber on the left. The innocent suffer to increase their crown, the penitent to merit pardon, the impenitent to the increase of their penalty. Jesus prays on the gibbet; one thief asks pardon; the other thief mocks Jesus. For the good claustral who endures the gibbet, his good conscience makes the penalty, dreadful as it is, easy to bear. The evil man who stands up under the beating without murmuring deserves pardon. The evil man, who is chastised and in despair crackles like a fire in a thorn bush, is damned.

3. Another threefold distinction in claustral discipline should be noted in connection with the gibbet. To be found there is the discipline of the son, whom the Father did not spare, but handed over for us all. Of him Isaiah wrote: 'The discipline of our peace is

upon him', and 'Truly he sustained our weaknesses and bore our sorrows' [Is 53:4]. The merciful Father and God of mercies let fall upon this, his only and well-beloved Son in whom he was well pleased, unremitting beatings, inflicted as if by the fiercest scorpions. The Father treated his Son as though he were an enemy, in order to bring about the reconciliation of those at enmity with him. Hence, the Son declared: 'I have given my body to my persecutors, and my cheeks to those who pluck them. I have not turned my face away from those upbraiding me and spitting at me' [Is 50:6]. O how hard, or rather how gentle, this kindness. Hard, in relation to the merit of the one who suffers; gentle, in relation to the cause and the effect of the suffering.

4. So, the discipline of our peace was upon him who paid off all our debt with interest, not merely a hundred times over, but infinitely more. He did this so that on the scales of the cross the gift would outweigh the sin, the overflowing grace of pardon would remit not just the original fault but also actual sins. Great and heavy was the discipline which caused a very meek lamb to sigh in a soft and gentle voice: 'My father, if it is possible, let this chalice pass from me; but if it is not possible for it to pass unless I drink it, your will be done' [Mt 26:39, 42].

5. If you are a son in the cloister, you should thus have a heart which is ready to suffer and even to congratulate itself on the opportunity, saying: 'For I am ready for the lashes' [Ps 38:17]. If that wolf Judas, perhaps an intimate of yours, should lift his heel against you, do not let him skin away your gentle face, nor peel off the flesh of patience, nor eat away at your inward intent. Satan may openly want to wound your good reputation from top to bottom. If so, then sit on the manure pile of humility and scratch the ulcerous discharge with a shard, attributing it to your fault and not to another's malice. Thus David did not impute the curses to Shimei, but ascribed them to the divine vengeance.

6. The other two kinds of discipline are those of the disciple and the servant. The disciple hears the teaching of the master. The servant, who does not stay in the house forever and awaits the end of his work, is sluggish in listening, indifferent about working. He does everything for appearance's sake; he seeks not grace, but money. The

holy disciple is the thief who hung on the Lord's right; the servant is the thief on the left. The disciple calls: 'Lord, remember me when you come into your kingdom' [Lk 23:42]. In a very brief space of time he had already learned patience and penitence; perfected in a short time, he would be endlessly fulfilled, for his soul was pleasing to the Lord. Hence: 'Today you will be with me in paradise' [Lk 23:43]. So also you claustrals, who perhaps came from the east, caught up in sins at a young age, or from the west and lived in sins until old age, now that you are converted to religious life, hope in the Lord and do good. Say 'Lord remember me when you come into your kingdom'. Likewise, 'My soul clings to you,' following you and obeying you; "Your right hand receives me" [Ps 63:8], because, although I have sinned and merited death, I hope in your mercy which is your right hand'. The one who sits at the right, or even the one hanging at the right, is not outside discipline. He is sitting who keeps the discipline of the cloister with pleasure. He hangs, who has mooing calves, which are not fenced in. Aware of these worldly appetites and of the impulses of the flesh, he does not pursue his lusts. Carnal suggestion is at work, but it is not accompanied by consent or enjoyment. His flesh conceives distress, but does not give birth. Why? Because he is not outside discipline nor outside the right hand. He always says: 'The Lord is at my right, nothing can shake me' [Ps 16:8]. The disciple does not die. What becomes of the slave who is the servant of sin and the penalty of sin? 'Expel the servant and her son. The son of a servant will not be heir with the son of a free woman', Mary [cf. Gn 21:10; Gal 4:30].

7. This [slave] is the claustral who seeks what is his, rather than what belongs to Jesus Christ. He seeks obedience not to Jesus Christ, but to his own judgment. He seeks money. He seeks his own will. He seeks to serve two masters, God and mammon. He honors God with his lips, but his heart is far from him. He comes in sheep's clothing, but inside he is a ravening wolf. His God is his stomach. He has the appearance of piety, but he repudiates its virtue. He is not one of us, although he may be with us within our large number. He chooses to feed the swine of unclean desire, rather than to stay sensibly among his father's possessions.

Let us now go down to the marketplace and buy necessities.

XVII. THE MARKETPLACE AND THE MORAL MEANING OF TYRE. COM-
PARISON WITH THE CLOISTER.

1. The cloister is a marketplace, where are displayed all the goods
useful to the soul, whether for its adornment or its needs. Read in
Ezekiel [chapter 27] about Tyre, which was well constructed and
decorated with all different kinds of things from various peoples and
regions, in accordance with the possibilities of each and the wares of
foreigners. It is beyond our capacity and the scope of this work to
draw out from the pouches and bags of the historical sense the
mystical meanings of these things and explain them. We leave that
on the shoulders of Jerome and Gregory and to other expositors who
have sharp scythes to reap where others have labored. However, I did
purchase for our discipline and cloister the following item which I
am bringing back: those who have pleased God from the beginning
of the world until our time have filled the cloister of religious life,
just as neighboring and remote provinces filled that extremely weal-
thy city. They prepared for our use everything they said and did. If
you seek forceful examples of chastity, you will find countless incor-
ruptible cedars. If you seek those who possess patience, steadfastness,
faith, truth, mildness, piety, obedience, justice, fortitude, prudence,
temperance, and all the other virtues, more numerous than the sands
of the sea and the stars of the sky, they will come to meet you. So we
read: 'O God, your friends have become honourable to me; I will
count them and they will be multiplied more than grains of sand' [Ps
139:17–18]. So, let each one buy from God's good and lawful mer-
chants what pleases him and what is necessary for the feast day.
There will be nothing more to be found in the market, when the
door has been closed and the foolish virgins are told: 'Go to the sellers
and buy some for yourselves' [Mt 25:9]. This will be said not to ad-
vise them, but to confound and mock them. Wisdom says: 'I will
jeer at you when what you feared has happened to you' [Pr 1:26]. Fittingly, then, Tyre (which means 'straits') signifies claustral
discipline, because 'every buyer says, "it's no good, it's no good"'
but is pleased when he comes home [Pr 20:14]. 'Our present tribulation is brief and light, but it produces for us a measureless weight of
eternal glory' [2 Co 4:17]. The provisions of the soul in the cloister

are not less than those of the earthly goods in Tyre. It is scarcely possible either to collect the resources of Tyre or to enumerate the labors of the cloister. What Tyre gathers for the passing glory of this world the religious community suffers with estimable patience in order to acquire blessed life.[171]

2. First one must consider that it is 'situated at the heart of the sea,' [Ez 27:4] where the labor is as much harder as the fear is greater. At its 'frontiers' are Elijah, John the Baptizer, St Augustine and blessed Benedict. They 'built' the religious cloister by word and example and 'perfected' it with holiness and incomparable beauty.

3. 'Firs and cedars' [Ez 27:5], souls which because of their purity and incorruptibility will never rot; and which are sublime because of their contemplation. 'From Senir', (that is, 'by way of the lamp' or 'by the teeth of the watch') or also 'from Lebanon', they construct a cloister, when some have been perfected and their life is a way for others, and a light or a concerned and biting reproof for those who err, as well as a dazzling whitening for those who follow their example.

4. The cloister also receives 'the oaks of Bashan' [Ez 23:6], that is, disgraced sinners, and makes them into 'oars', just as Joshua made the Gibeonites carriers of water in the temple and hewers of wood. Hence, the apostle wrote: 'Set up as judges those who are contemptible in the church' [1 Co 6:4]. "From Indian ivory," because of mortification, and 'from the islands of Italy' or Cypress, that is, struck by the fear of God, they fashion 'thwarts', whose feet carry peace; and 'decks' whose souls stick to the ground.

5. 'Varied linens from Egypt', that is, from the world, 'woven into a sail' [Ez 27:7], when, after they have been converted from worldly things, for the sake of the house of Israel they place themselves like a wall against the difficulties and obstacles of adversaries. Similarly, 'hyacinth', those from the nobility, and 'purple', those from unknown and common, though very hardworking, stock, both 'become a deck tent' for the security and concealment of the sick against storm and rain.

6. 'The inhabitants of Sidon and Arvad' [Ez 27:8], former hunters, rhetors and people who demolished with power (as Nebuchadnezzar exalted those he wished and humbled those he wished) are now our 'oarsmen', steering the ship and drawing it to harbor. 'The wise men

of Tyre are your helmsmen', for when the state is ruled by them things go well.

7. 'The elders and wise men of Byblos', nourished in the order from childhood, 'had sailors to take care of your fittings' [Ez 27:9], since the customs and usage of the cloister are to be sought from them. 'All the ships of the sea and their sailors were involved in your commerce', because claustrals live from the work of seculars. As the apostle wrote: Those who sow spiritual things reap carnal ones.

8. 'Persians', that is, those tempted, drawn and allured by their desires; 'Lydians', those endangered by the devil (thus, 'You are from your father, the devil' [Jn 8:44]) and 'Libyans', those whose mouth is full of cursing, are converted to the claustral 'army', either to test Abel by perserving in evil or transformed to serve the living God. 'Your fighting men have hung up their shields and helmets as decoration for you' [Ez 27:10]. They put on the armor of God in time of war and resist the devil and the vices of the flesh. When they have completed their military service, which is the life of man upon earth, they leave forceful examples of virtues to their successors as did Eleazar, who did not want to pretend to eat swine's flesh in violation of the holy laws.

9. 'The sons of Arvad with your army upon your walls' and 'all around' [Ez 27:11]. The men of Arvad who put off the old man with his actions are guards upon the walls all day and all night. They are never silent, but revolt against the powers of the air. 'But the pygmies who were on the towers hung their quivers on the walls all around. They perfected your beauty.' Note that the Pygmies, who are people a cubit tall, are said to perfect 'your beauty'. Clearly someone who humbles himself like the little child of the gospel is in the towers of peace and security and completes the measure of religious life.

10. 'Greece, Tubal and Meshech are your retailers' [Ez 27:13]. In summary something should be said about the ones already converted to the religious life from all the nations and the many more still to be converted, who from their morals, regions and customs, make many dwelling places in the house of God, so that from many persons of different appearance the body of Christ which is the Church is established and the great Church built up.

11. Perhaps when it is beneath these coverings the very modest figure of claustral discipline does not much please you. You would prefer it more bare, and stripped of the foliage of words, succinct, in the fashion of the world, so the reader will not be impeded by the obstacles of obscure language and lose the sense because of tedium. Would that in this also I could both satisfy your wish and be of use to others. Here, therefore, are the nerves and joints of claustral discipline: strictly enforced silence, rare and reasonable permission to speak, gaze fixed on the ground, a walk which is neither too slow nor too fast, continual sitting in the cloister, intervals of choir, standing with trembling and fear as if before God, eating and drinking held within the limits of sufficiency, sleep sufficient for digestion, chastity governing each person's whole being, the fear of God grounding all actions, the love of God stretching over the heavens, constancy and perseverance in good supporting the walls, purity and cleanness sweeping the cloister clean of all superfluity, humility laying down straw for the feet, obedience guarding the entrance and exit, charity arranging the whole community in order, faith animating, hope refreshing. Believe me, where this discipline is kept and the order does not break down, Jesus stands in the midst of his disciples. Giving them peace he goes in and out with them. He is peace for the one entering into the discipline and for the one going out into eternal life. Let these things be written with the blood of the lamb on the lintels of the houses of claustrals for future generations.

XVIII. THE SILENCE OF THE CLOISTER

1. I am going to repeat myself in order to recommend more fully those things which I think are highly desirable and even necessary for the religious life, such as silence, reading, confession and prayer. The silence of the cloister is neither mute nor garrulous. It should not be mute in the ears of the Lord of might, but should always say 'Turn your ear to the words of my mouth' [Ps 17:1] and 'I called to the Lord with my voice' [Ps 142:1], since it was said to the silent Moses, 'Why do you call to me?' [Ex 14:15]. Our voice will reach the depths of God's mercy if it is the expression of our spirit, alive and entire, groaning in its deepest recesses and calling with a mighty utterance

to the third heaven. Thus, the apostle writes of the Lord: 'In the days
of his flesh, he offered prayers and entreaties with a great cry and
tears to him who could save him from death, and he was heard
because of his reverence' [Heb 5:7]. Such silence has bells, along with
pomegranates, on the hem of the priestly vestment [Ez 28:22],
because, anxious about departure from this life, it prays for refreshment and perfection of eternal life.[172] Similarly, it is not talkative,
because 'in much speaking sin will not be lacking' [Pr 10:19]. If a
tongue which tries to negotiate a slippery spot moves without the
support of the fear of God, it finds it difficult to avoid sliding and it
will most likely fall. Let it not open the doors of the lips, except
perhaps on the sabbath day and the first day of the month in order to
recall future rest and the joys of the saints. In such a silence holy
desires, peace of heart, and tranquility with true purity increase and
multiply, because windy and vain talkativeness, mixed with the ice
and frost of words which sow discords, quickly and frequently
freezes fig trees, vineyards and immature trees, with scandal. By contrast, the seal of silence nourishes the good seed under the shade of its
seal and causes it to reach maturity.

2. This is why, in the Apocalypse, the book which is at the right
hand of the one sitting on the throne, and which is written on inside
and out, is fastened with seven seals. We ourselves and our words are
in the hand of God, closed with seven seals, until our mouth is opened
by the Lamb who was slain and who has the key which opens and no
one closes [Rv 3:7]. Thus, Paul is in chains, 'but the word of God is
not chained up' [2 Tm 2:9]. The Lamb closes and no one opens.
Thus, in the same book of Revelation it says: 'Seal up what the seven
thunders have said; do not write it down' [Rv 10:4]. And in Daniel:
'The words are sealed' [Dn 12:9]. This book is written inside and
out, so that once your lips are closed you will not ponder wickedness
in your room; that is, in the secret places of your heart. It is sealed
with seals, so that no idle word will get out, because we are going to
have to render an account of every idle word. Nor a vain word, as in
the case of those who spoke vain words to their neighbors. Nor a
deceptive word, because deceivers are containers of the worst evils.
Nor a dishonest word, because You will destroy all those who tell
lies. Nor a bad word, since it is written: 'Let no bad word proceed

from your mouth' [Eph 4:29]. Nor schismatic, heretical or murmuring words, because Dathan and Abiram were swallowed up alive [Nb 16, Ps 106:17], and the murmurers perished at the hands of the Destroyer [1 Co 10:18]. And finally, no blasphemous word, for which there will be no forgiveness in this world or the next.

3. There are also seven seals or reasons by which the book of claustral silence is sealed: for tranquility, because of profession, to keep peace, to subdue the feelings and movements of the heart, to detach oneself from secular affairs, to study the law of God, for the sake of contemplation. Where the restraints of silence are weakened, tranquility is disturbed, profession is broken, peace is upset, the feelings and movements of the heart crash upon each other like waves in a wild sea. Anyone who is enmeshed in secular affairs is withdrawn from eternal and heavenly matters. Anyone who is concerned with the deceptions of sophistry and rhetoric does not meditate on the law of God. Anyone who is occupied with multiplying words and vain wordiness does not raise his mind to God. So, retain these seals until the Lamb loosens them and opens our lips. The book of silence which is sealed with these seals is not to be unsealed until it is opened by the Lamb who was slain; that is, silence will be enforced until death. It is unsealed by the Lamb, who is 'worthy to receive virtue', since he is king of virtues; and 'divinity', since according to eternal generation he is consubstantial with the Father; and 'wisdom', which says 'I came forth from the mouth of the most high' [Si 24:3]; 'and fortitude', since he is strong and powerful in battle; 'and glory and honor,' because the Father has crowned with glory the one who became a little less than the angels; 'and blessing', since he receives a blessing from God and he is above all things the blessed God [Rv 5:12]. The Lamb opens the mouths of mute and loosens the seals, so that we may speak of the wisdom hidden in the mystery, and we may say of Christ: 'He did all things well. He made the deaf hear and the mute speak' [Mk 7:37].

4. Therefore, let us read in this sealed book, that is, in silence, and let us investigate what is closed under the seals, as Jacob took away the stone from the mouth of the well, and the angel removed the rock from the Lord's tomb. Let us drink from these waters. So, claustral silence is a good thing.

XIX. READING

1. Reading is chained to this silence, analogously to the way the rings must be fastened to the hooks of the curtains in the Lord's temple [Ez 26:4].

2. For reading is a very rich pasturage, in which small and large animals prepare fat holocausts for the Lord by continual browsing, when they ruminate within themselves the sweetest flowers of divine scripture and have nothing else in their hearts or in their mouths. Thus, constant and attentive reading done devoutly purifies our innards of the bones of dead men and the corpses of thoughts which should be cut out. Even if the fruit of understanding and knowledge does not result from reading, reading is nevertheless always useful in that our minds are occupied and exempted from the vain and useless thoughts which weigh them down and stubbornly intrude themselves. The apostle said to Timothy: 'Be occupied with reading until I come' [1 Tm 4:13]. Further, 'happy is the man who meditaties day and night on the law of the Lord' [Ps 1:2]; just as the bars of the ark were always in the rings [cf. Ex 37:14], so always let the devil find you occupied. For, the unclean spirit only enters a house when he finds it unoccupied.

3. It says in Revelation that reading should not be vain and garrulous, but quiet and marked with the seal of meditation: 'And when the lamb had opened one of the seven seals, I heard one of the four living creatures say as though with a voice of thunder: Come and see' [Rv 6:1], that is, read. The gospel of Matthew, which is the first of the four living creatures, begins this way: 'the book of the generation of Jesus Christ' [Mt 1:1]. What else is beginning a gospel this way than saying: come and see in this book the mystery hidden from the ages and revealed and manifested by the generation of Christ? Come and see the incarnate Word, which hitherto was hidden with the Father and sealed with the seal of divinity. 'And behold a white horse', Christ conceived by the Holy Spirit and born without sin from the virgin.[173] 'And the rider on it was holding a bow', stretched between the divine and human natures against the devil. 'And a crown was given him', so that he who was king of the Jews might be king of the angels. 'And he went away' to the place of Calvary, 'conquering' by patience, so

that he 'might conquer' by power.

4. The one occupying himself with reading becomes a 'white horse', when like a dove he flies about over the streams of water, and like a shorn flock he rises from the wash and puts on the new man who was created according to God in justice and holiness of truth. Further, understanding, which rides the white horse and presides over all the senses has a bow, holy scripture, which is sometimes stretched, sometimes slack. It is stretched when it threatens with punishment; it is slack when it promises pardon. 'And a crown was given him': we already have a crown shaved on our heads, but let us seek glory and a good conscience in our minds. The crown upon the head is constant reading with intent devotion. Hence, Solomon wrote: 'Bind it permanently on your heart, and tie it around your throat' [Pr 6:21], so that it may be 'a circlet around your neck' [Pr 1:9]. The person who meditates on the law has a crown on his head. The person who speaks of the law has cries of joy from God in his heart. The one who is subject to the law has a circlet on his neck.

XX. CONFESSION

1. You ought to rise from reading to confession, and there accuse yourself of violating God's commandments, or of negligence, or of ignorance, or of weakness. However, the confession of claustrals must not be clumsy and negligent like that of worldly men. Confession is water which is not muddy, polluted or brackish, but clear, pure and clean. Like a second baptismal regeneration it purifies those who have not kept their clothes white like snow after the bath of sanctification.

2. Confession is different before a judge, a master, a father. A guilty person looks for an advocate; a servant, the scourge; a son, a friend. The guilty person offers gifts; a servant, compliance; a son offers himself. The guilty person offers penance; the servant, amendment; the son, an offering which brings salvation. The guilty person prostrates before the entryway; the servant, before the door; the son enters the room. The guilty person confesses great and enormous crimes; the servant confesses sins; the son confesses transgressions. Let the guilty person say: 'Don't condemn me' [Jb 10:2]; let the servant

say, 'Have mercy on me, O God' [Ps 51:1]; let the son say, 'Father, I
have sinned' [Lk 15:18], but spare me. The person who withdrew
fell from the status of son to that of servant, and then from the rank
of servant he passed to that of a guilty person. By returning he
changed from a guilty person to a servant, and from a servant to a
son. Thus, by the same steps through which he departed into a
region of unlikeness he returns to likeness to the Father. Because the
image and likeness of God in the soul had been deformed by sin, he
was to seek through confession the seal of his reformation.

3. So let the Lamb now open the second seal in confession: 'I heard
the second living creature say, "Come and see" '.[174] The second living creature is Mark, who roars in the desert like a lion; he is especially concerned with preaching the Lord and the resurrection. Aptly is
confession compared to the desert, since by regulars as well as by the
people of the world it is more deserted than frequented. In this desert
roared that sinner who said: 'I roared loudly because of my heart's lament' [Ps 38:8]. 'And another horse, a red one, went out.'
Allegorically, this is Christ, who is white in his nativity, red in his
passion. Morally, however, it refers to a person who blushes in confusion when he confesses his enormous crimes. Further, someone
who blushes over his corruption is made red by the sprinkling of
blood. Hence, the apostle says: 'What fruit did you have then in the
things about which you now blush?' [Rm 6:21]. The red horse is the
person who bears his confession, saying: I, a sinner, am not worthy
to raise my eyes to heaven; and 'I am not worthy that you should
enter under my roof' [Mt 8:8]; and 'I will bear the anger of the Lord'
[Mi 7:9], because I deserve it; and 'It is given to its rider', namely, the
fear of the Lord, 'to take peace from the earth'. So to him 'was given
a great sword'. This great sword devours the flesh and gets drunk in
heaven. Accursed is he who keeps his sword from blood; that is, he
who does not cut off through confession the sins which come from
flesh and blood. Of these it is said: 'Flesh and blood will not possess
the kingdom of God' [1 Co 15:50].

4. The sword of confession is 'living and effective, more
penetrating than any two-edged sword, reaching to the division of
soul and spirit, and of joints and marrow, discerning the thoughts
and intentions of the heart' [Heb 4:12]. Who could thus express the

power of confession? Who has thus depicted its nature and form? The text said: 'the word is living'. Where is the corpse of confession? Where is the dead likeness that has a mouth but does not speak, that has hands not of Jacob, but of Esau, hands which are hairy and not smooth? Who has feet, but does not walk? As a dead man is not a man, and a dead faith is not faith, so also a feigned confession is not confession but confusion. Let the word of confession be alive, so it may proceed from a living heart and sincere lips, not from the tomb of a dead cadaver which lies buried and rotting.

5. He adds: 'And more penetrating than any two-edged sword'. Grammar, dialectic and rhetoric are the swords with which clerics fight each other. They are certainly penetrating in their teaching and rules. But the word of God and the word of confession are more penetrating than any two-edged sword. Such a word seeks to avoid loss and to acquire gain, since it not only penetrates the depths of a man, but even pierces through the innards of the devil's suggestions and breaks the portals of hell. How? By 'penetrating to the division of soul and spirit', that is, of sensation and reason.

XXI. GENUINE CONFESSION

1. Genuine confession omits nothing, but reproaches all excesses of both the senses and the superior reason. For it is one thing to sin through sensation which we have in common with the beasts, another to sin through reason which is proper to our humanity, and which, by God's arrangement, we have in common with the angels. The sins of sense are those which occur through weakness and catch us off guard. The penalty and penitence for these should be less. Sins of reason, which arise from deliberation and ambition are threatened with a harsher punishment. He [the Apostle in Heb 4:12, quoted in the previous chapter] adds: 'of the joints and marrow'. The joint of soul and spirit is the borderland of reason and sense where it is difficult to discern whether something pertains to reason or to sense. As the apostle declared: 'I do not understand what I do' [Rm 7:15], because in that borderland 'the flesh desires in opposition to the spirit, and the spirit desires against the flesh' [Gal 5:17], that is, against sensation. The living word must mark off this frontier and

pursue and examine sins to the very marrow. At the end he adds: 'It discerns the thoughts and intentions of the heart'. In confession thoughts should be revealed and intentions examined, so not the slightest hoof [cf. Lv 11:3, Dt 14:3] of sin may escape to come into God's sacrifice. Confession concerns both the criminal and the venial. But it is within the capacity of few people to differentiate night from night, that is, between the venial and the criminal, since many things are considered venial which are criminal because of the intent of the sinner. So one should express in confession not just the action, not just the thought, but also the very intention which makes the whole body, that is, the work, luminous or dark. This is the great sword which has been given to the rider of the red horse [Rv 6:4]. Its blade cuts deeply and cuts apart the old Leviathan's scales, which are joined together in such a way that not even a breath of air can pass through them.

XXII. PRAYER

1.After shedding snake skins in confession, after having been washed in the waters of the Jordan with Naaman the leper, after having been anointed a second time with the boy David, one may raise his hands and eyes to God in prayer, in order to obliterate past deeds and take precautions against future ones. The house of prayer is supported, as it were, by two columns if the wrath of God is withdrawn and his grace is granted. Prayer does both: it extinguishes wrath and implores grace. One sort of prayer is laborious, the other is devout. Laborious prayer extinguishes wrath; devout prayer calls forth grace. Yet, neither comes without the other to the throne of grace. Rather, Jacob marries and cohabits with both Leah and Rachel, that is, both laborious and devout prayer. One night he sleeps with Leah, another night, perhaps, with Rachel. From both are born offspring, more numerous from Leah, more cherished from Rachel. Both the former and the latter are reckoned in the seed and the number of the patriarchs, because the one who, like Leah, works more will receive more reward. To the one who, like Rachel, does not labor, reward is imputed, not according to what is merited or due, but in accord with grace. When grace comes first to touch the mind, prayer is said to be pleasing and devout. It is like a morning rain shower. Prayer is laborious, when a person's heart is far from him, and God is far from his heart. A man's heart is far from him, when it is preoccupied with unnecessary cares, lukewarm in religious fervor, or immersed in carnal desires. Similarly, God is far from the heart, when he withdraws his grace, when he defers his presence, when he tests the patience of the petitioner. Laborious prayer is that of which Peter spoke: 'Master, though we have worked the whole night, we have caught nothing' [Lk 5:5]. Job said of it: They dig up death for themselves, as though it were treasure, and when they find it, they rejoice [cf. Jb 3:21–22]. And again Job said: 'I call and you do not hear me' [Jb 30:20]. And the bride in the Song of Songs: 'On my bed during the night I sought him whom my soul loves' and so on [Sg 3:1]. And in the psalm: 'You have confounded your anointed' [Ps 89:38]. Prayer is devout when grace arrives quickly, when it captures the mind, when it is present before it is asked for, when it gives more than we ask or understand. However, when a man has knocked at the door of grace, saying, 'My prayer will come before you' [Ps 88:13] and 'My eyes went before you at dawn' [Ps 119:148], then it is called laborious and an evening rain. The Lord says: 'I will cause morning and evening rains to fall upon you' [Jl 2:23], so I may guard your coming and going. At the time when Jesus prayed during the passion, his sweat became like drops of blood. He also often prayed very peacefully, as he did here: 'Father, glorify your son. And a voice came from heaven, saying: I have glorified him and will glorify him again.' And the Lord said to the crowd: 'This voice has come not for my sake, but for yours' [Jn 12: 28, 30]. And to the Father: 'I knew from the beginning that you always hear me' [Jn 11:42].

2. Whoever imprints himself with the Lord's seal of prayer will be trained in the example of the good teacher in this, as in so many other ways. Revelation continues on this same subject:

XXIII. MORE ABOUT PRAYER

1. 'And when he had opened the third seal, I heard the third living creature say: Come and see. And I saw. Behold, a black horse, and its rider had a balance scales in his hand' [Rv 6:5]. The third living creature

is Luke, the physician and evangelist, who prepares medications for the soul to cure all its ills. He begins his writing in this way: 'In the days of Herod, king of Judea, there was a certain priest Zechariah by name', and so forth [Lk 1:5]. And because in the vision of Ezekiel he is represented by the figure of a bull calf, and the calf is sacrificed to God, he is rightly called a 'black horse', because of the mortification of the cross, which he preached in word and accomplished in deed. For Christ, who was white in his birth and red in the passion, is black in death.

2. He has the balance beam of the cross in his hand, because he has the power to lay down his life and the power to take it up. When the guilt of the whole human race is weighed on this balance against the penalty which the Lord bore in his body, his penalty is found to be more than our guilt. Hence, this penalty of Christ's passion blotted out the guilt of sin of our first parent and of the whole world. And what was his passion, but his prayer and our reconciliation? So Christ rides on the black horse, when raised up from the earth he is suspended on the gibbet of the cross. Let us claustrals or priests imitate him who prays on the cross, by raising pure hands and dove-like eyes to God, confessing the blackness of our sins and getting the jump on death by doing penance. Thus the psalmist wrote: 'Ethiopia stretched forth its hands to God' [Ps 68:32]. The Ethiopian woman, who was discolored by the sun and blacker than charcoal through the afflictions of her flesh and mortification of her members, prays: 'Turn away your face from my sins' [Ps 51:9], and 'my bones dried out like firewood', and 'I have been cut like hay and my heart has dried out' [Ps 102:3–4]. To the soul who prays in this way the Spouse speaks in the Song: 'I have likened you to my cavalry among pharaoh's chariots, my friend' [Sg 1:8]. It is as though the Lord rode ahead of the sons of Israel on a black horse, the pillar of cloud by day, and on a red horse, the column of fire by night. The chariots of pharaoh are the horses [cf. Ps 33:17] which roam the whole world misleading people about salvation: pride, deceit, gluttony and lust, which carry their riders to hell. But the horsemanship of Jesus is salvation. About this it is said: 'The chariots of the Lord are many times ten thousand' [Ps 68:17]. To them the psalmist speaks: 'Bring to the Lord, sons of God', that is, angels, 'bring to the Lord the young of rams' [Ps 29:1], that is,

Christians who imitate the apostles and prophets.

3. The rider of the black horse has in his hand a balance scale on which he weighs what he should ask about things temporal and what about things eternal, how persistently for things eternal and how moderately for things transitory. Hence, there follows: 'And I seemed to hear a voice in the midst of the four living creatures which said: A two-pound measure of wheat for a penny; and three two-pound measures of barley for a penny.' Wheat symbolizes things eternal, barley things temporal. A single, simple prayer, that is, one two-pound measure of wheat, for eternal life. Hence 'one thing I asked of the Lord' [Ps 27:4]. A multiple and diverse prayer, that is, three two-pound measures of barley, for the necessities of temporal sustenance. Hence, 'rescue me from my necessities' [Ps 25:17], O Lord.

4. 'Do not harm the wine and the oil' [Rv 6:6]; do not harm to damnation those baptized in Christ and anointed thoroughly with holy chrism, which is oil, and redeemed by the blood of the lamb, which is wine. And I command you not to harm the soul; as it is said of Job, 'you shall spare his soul' [Jb 2:6]. Nevertheless, I do not wish the one who treads the grapes to be sparing in the pressure of the wine press. In this pressure the unsparing God spares his faithful.

5. So much for prayer. Next something should be said about meditating on death.

XXIV. MEDITATION ON DEATH

1. Nothing is more certain than death, nothing more uncertain. Nothing is more desirable to the good, nothing more hateful to the evil. The event is certain, but the outcome is not. For those who are not of the world, whose way of life is heavenly, departure from prison for the kingdom and passage from disorder to glory are welcome. Then death has intervened, naked truth will manifest the glory of the supreme and indivisible Trinity, the glory of the blessed Virgin, the glory of the heavenly virtues, and finally the glory of all the saints. In this glory everything will be new, sure, abiding, wondrous and lovable. The veil of the present sacraments—which is of hyacinth to indicate the hope of the kingdom, of purple because of the blood of the lamb, of scarlet cloth twice-dyed because of the love

of the mediator of God and men, of finely woven linen because of the purity and indissoluble truth of the catholic faith — will then be removed or rent asunder. It will be removed according to the passage: 'When what is perfect has come, what is partial will be eliminated' [1 Co 13:10]. It will be torn apart, just as in the Lord's passion 'the veil of the temple was torn in two from top to bottom' [Mt 27:51], so that the judgment of the great day may be like midday when the designs of hearts will be discolored and there will be nothing hidden which will not be revealed. No one should be afraid of paying death's debt, when he expects to be endowed with so great a recompense for paying this debt. The debt is what is owed and paid for all and by all. The time and hour of the payment is not in the power and knowledge of the debtor but in the will of the Creator. He has set limits which cannot be exceeded. The creditor and collector cannot anticipate the day and collect the payment of death in advance, nor can the debtor defer or postpone it. This debt or tax is canceled for nobody. It was not even remitted for the Son of God himself, since he was son of man, even though from the beginning he was exempt because of his immunity to sin. For 'the outcome of death belongs to the Lord of the Lord' [Ps 68:20].

2. Therefore, one should always consider and ponder that we pass through death rather than remain in it. Death is a traveler's lodging rather than the permanent residence of the dying. It is the lifting of a burden, not a weight of calamity. It is the breaking off of a punishment, not its continuation. It is the way to the Father, not a byway to the enemy. It is a progress to the homeland, not a submersion in gehenna. It is a healthful draught, not an infernal consumption. Finally, it is an ending, not in destruction but in consummation. Before one's death mortal fault is to be avoided or at least wiped out by confession and penitence. On this side one should prepare what is needed to live happily after death. Death does not swallow up good merits; on the contrary, it brings back even forgotten evils. Death gathers up all past deeds, it uncovers all hidden ones, it designates the eternal tents which are dwelling places, and it gathers souls not where they wish to be, but where they deserve to be.

3. In order to be certain of the uncertain, hold onto the certain and do not follow after the uncertain. For the apostle does not run in

uncertainty, but is certain that neither death nor life can separate him from the love of God which is in Christ Jesus. You will be made certain by certain faith, certain hope, certain love, certain obedience, certain humility, certain chastity, certain observance of Christian religion and your profession. Depict death before your eyes: how horrible its face, how dark and grim its countenance, what tasks each of its members will fulfill in each of a person's members. Whatever strength and vigor there is in the souls and bodies of the damned, they will devour and feed on, as though they were tender sprouts. Thus the psalm declares: 'Death will feed on them' [Ps 49:14]. That the Lord may take us out of the belly of this whale, let us present ourselves before his face in confession, so that he who pierced its jaw with a ring may free us from eternal death. The divinity which lay hidden in Jesus' flesh shattered the molars in death's mouth, when it rashly bit at the flesh of the Word.[175] Even if it bites us like a snake or a horned serpent, if we have the horns of the cross in our hands, if we carry the blood of the lamb over both posts and the lintels, then all that horrible armor described in Job will be destroyed, and its innards, bored through with this spear, will lie open.

4. O sulphuruous pit, O unbearable stench, O distress, O darkness, O heat, O grinding of teeth, O confusion, O sorrow, O despair, O desolation without consolation, evil without end, destruction without rebuilding! If only I might keep before my eyes the compensation which death has in store for evil delights. One should obtain beforehand by prolonged meditation and preparation what reduces the bitterness of death and makes tolerable what is inevitable.

5. For there are remedies which alleviate death: confession of sins and penitence; the rampart of the holy cross against the powers of the air; the viaticum of the Lord's body and blood as comfort for so great and so unknown a journey; the oil of anointing to fuel the lamp of conscience and take away the dense darkness of death; the protection of God, the help of all the saints, and the prayer of the brethren. In the face of these remedies, the second death will either succumb or yield. The first death still rages as usual against mortal man, but it is weakened and does not keep in its nets a soul which it sees surrounded by such troops. Death is afraid of the power of the cross, and it is not aware that the traveler who crosses over with viaticum cannot

run short. It remembers that true confession and penitence have forcefully extricated countless souls from its womb and hellish belly. It remembers that it can never resist God's will. It knows by experience that it can harm neither human bodies nor souls if the help of the saints comes to their aid. It flees fraternal prayers as though they were flaming arrows. Let us ball all these up into lumps to burst the innards of the devil, of death, and of hell, and with Daniel let us throw them into the mouth of the dragon [cf. Dn 14:26]. These lumps are prepared in the cloister by those who always bear in mind that they are going to die, and who like a palm tree multiply their days by looking upward and putting to death the roots of sin within themselves. Over such as these death has no power. For, they have the power to walk on the serpents which killed the sons of Israel in the desert and upon the scorpions which lie in wait for our heel.

6. O soul loosed from the body, where do you dwell? In heaven, in paradise, in the cleansing fire, or in hell? If in heaven, you are blessed with the angels. If in paradise, you are safe from these miseries. If in the cleansing fire, you are troubled by punishments, but you look forward to liberation. If in hell, you await in despair for truth and severity, not mercy. O soul without a body, where is your body now? Where is Abel your brother? Look at the worm, the moth, the rot in the bones which were once yours. What of yourself? Are you asking Abraham to send Lazarus to dip the end of his finger in water and cool your tongue? Are you undergoing the punishments of flame either partially or completely? Is there hope of getting out? O soul, if you are in hell, your eye will not return to see good things. If you are in the cleansing fire, the furnace of Babylon was less hot, even though its flame shot up forty-nine cubits. Some very cruel Ethiopians zealously collect and maliciously pile up from the forest of our evil deeds, wood, hay, straw, pitch and darts. They devote themselves to taking care of the cleansing fire. Until a voice comes from the throne of grace, they cease not torturing the wretched soul.

7. O soul, whether happy or miserable, how useful it would be for the pilgrim soul still in its body to see and hear you, for you have not forgotten our lot and have already experienced yours! Behold, you have the balance in your hand, weighing out what you deserved in

the body and what you have received outside the body. Here below people use dishonest scales, but there justice, without regard for persons, weighs out punishment even-handedly, tilting neither to the right nor to the left. In the present mercy is mixed with justice, and justice with mercy, as God tips the chalice in his hand from the side of mercy to that of justice, and from the side of justice to that of mercy. But in the future judgment justice will be without mercy for those who did not act mercifully. Then there will be no oil for sale. Now it is said: 'Do not damage the wine and oil' [Rv 6:6], because correction and compassion are necessary to cure the man left half-dead by the robbers. In the judgment it will be too late for rebuke, because it will be the time not of sowing, but of reaping. Compassion will be in vain for those who have shown no pity. Like ships carrying apples, the soul in the body smells these things but does not taste them. But one who has reached port already tastes the savor of the future ages.

8. It is also said of meditation on death: 'In my meditation a fire breaks out' [Ps 39:3]. Of this fire it is written: 'Their worms will not die, their fire will not be put out' [Is 66:24]. It is marvelous how when one meditates on death it gives off warmth, although death is in fact frigid and takes away and extinguishes all vital heat. When is a fire lit, if not in winter? Contraries are driven away by contraries, and fire is sought when the numbness of cold is oppressive. What does the warming fire in meditation on death accomplish? Wood, hay, straw and chaff it burns, reducing to ashes vanities and deceiving foolishness, carnal and worldly pleasures. When death occupies the whole mind, it makes the mind count all temporal things for little. Who when he is submerged in water loves the water which submerged him? And do not the concupiscence of the eyes, the concupiscence of the flesh and the pride of life submerge in deepest hell those who have them? In these waters Leviathan swims and lies in ambush, in order either to drown those who incautiously come near it or to burn them up by shooting forth from its nostrils smoke like that from a burning and boiling pot. Hence, it is written in Job: 'From its nostril proceeds smoke like that from a burning and boiling pot. Its breath fans the coals, and the flame goes out of its mouth' [Jb 41:11–12]. Smoke, of which it is written, 'smoke rises in his anger',

causes darkness of vision, but 'darkness is under God's feet' [Ps 18:8–9]. The flame from the dragon's mouth is referred to in the passage: 'Fire came down and they did not see the sun' [Ps 58:9]. This fire is evil concupiscence which fans the coals, when it seduces a soul here below or drags it to punishment in death. In opposition to these 'the nose of the spouse', like the tower which looks toward Damascus, meditates on death against death. For, darts that one anticipates wound less, and there is no beast so savage that is may not be corrected and tamed by persevering training. So when death comes, it is not unknown, thanks to meditation; nor is it unforseen, thanks to watchfulness. Hence, it does not surprise; it does not intrude, but enters our open doors; it comes rather than crashes in; it pokes rather than pierces the side of the sleeper. We receive it politely, not with consternation. It comes as a good messenger, not as a dangerous adversary. It brings a mandate, rather than inflicts a punishment. It does not go beyond the limits of the mandate; of itself it can do nothing. God, the just judge, restrains its jaws with bridle and bit, so that once the outer covering and shell have been broken, the kernel of glory which God has hidden for those who fear him may fill the bellies of the blessed.

XXV. MEDITATION ON DEATH

1. 'And when he had opened the fourth seal, I heard the voice of the fourth living creature, saying: Come and see. And I saw. Behold a pale-colored horse. The name of its rider was death, and the nether world followed him' [Rv 6:7–8]. Notice that in the three preceding instances he had said: 'the first living creature', 'the second', 'the third'. But for the fourth he does not write 'the fourth living creature', but that he heard the voice of the fourth living creature. Now, John the evangelist is the voice of the Word. He begins his gospel thus: 'In the beginning was the Word', and so on [Jn 1:1]. The 'pale horse' refers to him who before the passion began to be fearful and weary, saying: 'My soul is sad unto death' [Mk 14:33–34]. And 'death was the name for him' who now has died for our sins. And in Hosea he says: 'I will be your death, O death' [Ho 13:14]. This accords with those who say: 'His name will no longer be remembered' [Jr 11:19].

2. 'And the nether world was following him', according to the passage: In their judgment 'they placed me in a deep lake, in darkness and in the shadow of death' [Ps 88:6]. Pertinent, therefore, to meditation on death are the death of Christ, the death of the devil, and the death of man.

3. Meditation on the death of Christ kills death: in the devil so he no longer lives; in man so that he will not stay put; in the devil so he will perish; in man so he will not perish; in the devil, so he will not reign; in man so he will not be enslaved; in the devil so he will not rage; in man so he will not be afraid; in the devil so he will not deceive; in man so he will not believe him; in the devil so he may despair of life; in man so that through death he may aspire to life.

4. Meditation on Christ's death is a visit to the sick; meditation on the devil's death strengthens the weak; meditation on one's own death humbles the proud. Meditation on Christ's death is a healthy drink; meditation on the devil's death drains the swelling; and meditation on one's own death restores or preserves health. Meditation on Christ's death is an antidote to poisons; meditation on the devil's death dissolves an abscess; meditation on one's own death applies a dressing to the diseased areas. 'The pale horse' is the one who mortifies himself in these meditations, so that he may punish death with death, and may temporarily submit his neck to death, but then escape in death from beneath the yoke of the one who comes.

XXVI. MORE ON DEATH

1. Regarding meditation on death, the Lord said to Job: 'Have the gates of hell opened for you, and have you seen the dark doorways?' [Jb 38:17]. For God nothing is closed; for him all things are bare and open. He measures the earth with the palm of his hand and holds in his fist all things from the limits of heaven to the bottom of hell. His eternal power enters and leaves all the provinces of his realm without encountering resistance, because he does whatever he wants in heaven, on the earth, and in all deeps. Certainly the gates of death were open for him, so that he entered when he willed and left when he willed. Whomever he wanted he sent in there, and whomever he wanted he called out. Only through Jesus were the gates of death

opened for the saints so that they might get out. It is true that they have been opened through sin so that each person leaving the world inevitably enters through them into the world to come, to punishment or to glory.

2. There are the gates of death, the gates of hell, the gates of the world, the gates of the cloister, and finally, the gates of heaven. The psalm says of the gates of death: 'You who raise me up from the gates of death so I may announce all your praises at the doors of the daughter of Sion' [Ps 9:13–14]. Of the gates of hell the gospel says: 'You are Peter, and upon this rock I will build my church, and the gates of hell will not prevail against it' [Mt 16:18], and 'I will go to the gates of hell' [Is 38:10]. The gates of the world are life's entrance and exit. The gates of the cloister are profession according to a rule with observance and hope of reward. The gates of heaven are the holy angels and ministering spirits, who are sent on behalf of those who receive the inheritance of salvation. The gates of death are penal; the gates of hell, detestable; the gates of the world, dangerous; the gates of the cloister, religious; the gates of heaven, glorious. The Lord passed through the gates of death; he broke the gates of hell; he entered and left the gates of the world without drawing back the bolt; he shaped the gates of the cloister by the way he lived and died on earth; he opened the gates of heaven at his ascension.

3. The gate of death swings on a distressing hinge; the gates of hell on a punitive thing; the gates of the world on a changeable one; the gates of the cloister on a meritorious one; the gates of heaven on a rewarding one. A holy angel guards the gate of heaven; a good superior, the gate of the cloister; daily decline, the gate of the world; the damned devil, the gate of hell; the prince of this world, the gate of death. The key of heaven is glory; the key to the cloister is the rule; the key of the world is vanity; the key of hell is eternal punishment; the key of death is the divine sentence. At the gate of heaven there is rejoicing over the end of labors; at the gate of the cloister, cleansing of sin; at the gate of the world, perilous concern; at the gate of hell, despair; at the gate of death, fear. It is midday at the gate of heaven, dawn at the gate of the cloister, twilight at the gate of the world, evening at the gate of death, midnight at the gate of hell. At the resurrection of the dead the gates of death will be opened, because

we will all arise; but the gates of hell will not be opened, because we will not all be changed. At the end the gates of the cloister and the gates of the world will be opened, and after the judgment, the gates of heaven. For he said: 'Have the gates of death been opened for you, and have you seen the dark doorways?' This was to say: Do you have a clear conscience and is your life so sure of my grace that you await death unafraid, so that when it comes you will swallow it down like wormwood, entering its gates without effort and leaving them without difficulty? 'And have you also seen the dark doorways?' If you have oil in your lamp you will not bang your foot on the dark doorways, because you will direct your steps according to God's word in which there is light and no darkness.

XXVII. COMMUNION IN THE BODY AND BLOOD OF THE LORD

1. In the discipline of the cloister one must not omit a prime necessity, which is to be most deeply etched into the memory. The eucharist has the same place in the body of the Church that the heart has in a human body. A man with an unimpaired and healthy heart lives; a man with a diseased and injured heart dies. So Solomon said: 'Guard your heart with all care, for life proceeds from it' [Pr 4:23]. In the gospel the Lord said of his body: 'Whoever has me for food will live because of me' [Jn 6:57]. This is the life of an angel upon which the angels wish to look; it is the life of a Christian through which he can progress. This life is received in one way by the person who lives in the flesh and according to the flesh; in another way by those who sow in the spirit so that from the spirit they may reap eternal life. It is received in one way by those whose mouths are full of cursing and bitterness; in another way by those who hunger and thirst for justice. To the latter it is said: 'You are not in the flesh, but in the spirit, provided the spirit of God dwells in you' [Rm 8:9]. They say: 'I live now, not I, but in me lives Christ' [Gal 2:20], whom I love with all my heart, all my soul, and all my strength. Such a heart thinks only of God and loves and desires him alone. This soul announces God with each breath and always expresses and desires God. Virtue can do everything through him who strengthens it, but it can do nothing without him who says: 'Without me you can do nothing' [Jn 15:5].

2. A person so occupied with God and for God is nourished daily in the morning hours, at the urging of a holy hunger, by communion in the Lord's body and blood. However, according to the apostle one must distinguish between this spiritual food and everyday bodily food. One needs great discernment to decide when to approach the body of Christ, when to withdraw, when to keep away. To approach Christ is to approach the Lord, the king, the light, the fire, the bread, the vine, life itself. Are you looking for freedom? Approach the Lord. Are you looking for security? Approach the king. Are you looking for clarity? Approach the light. Are you looking for heat? Approach the fire. Are you seeking refreshment? Approach the bread. Are you seeking drink? Approach the vine. Are you seeking the resurrection? Approach life. Have you offended the Lord? Withdraw. Have you acted against the king? Withdraw. Are you blind or dim-sighted? Withdraw from the light. Do you carry in your hands or loins an alien fire? Withdraw, lest fire from the altar burn you. Are you full of murmuring and sated with detractions? Withdraw, and do not approach the bread of angels. Are you drunk with the vine of Sodom and Gomorrah? Withdraw, and don't approach to the wine of the vine of Sorech [cf. Is 5:2b]. Are you dead with crimes and buried in hell? Withdraw.

3. There is a big difference between withdrawing and staying away. To withdraw is an act of reverence; to stay away is irreverence. A man who withdraws says: 'Lord, I am not worthy that you should enter under my roof' [Mt 8:8]. The one who stays away says: 'Behold, you are throwing me out of your sight' [Gn 4:14], and 'My iniquity is too great for me to desire forgiveness' [Gn 4:13]. Jonas, also, fled and stayed away from the face of the Lord. He was swallowed up into the belly of the whale for three days and three nights. And the psalmist wrote: 'Depart from me, all you who do evil' [Ps 6:9]. Then, what end is in store for those who stay away from God? 'All who distance themselves from you will perish' [Ps 73:27]. I will withdraw when I have sinned, but I shall not stay away, provided I have confessed my error and made amends.

4. But one should pay careful attention to when, how, and why one ought to approach communion. The use of this refreshment involves discerning the time for it, determining the manner, and knowing its purpose. Regarding the time three things should be

considered: opportunity, custom and solemnity. Regarding the manner: purification, intent and devotion. Regarding the cause: institution, utility and necessity. The topics just enumerated need to be briefly gone over and explained.

5. Opportunity itself flees and routs preoccupation. It is with inner freedom that one should fulfill this duty and submit to God. Custom remedies lay people's negligence and their excessive lethargy about their salvation. It is sufficient for a lay person to take communion once a year. But devout and attentive Mary sits at the feet of the Lord with our claustrals. Her eyes never have enough of the sight of God, nor her ears enough of listening to him. She receives the bread of angels, the Lord's sacrament, daily, and still she is hungry every day, as it is written: 'They who eat me, will still be hungry, and those who drink me will still be thirsty' [Si 24:29]. An imminent solemnity prompts us to approach communion, for what sort of solemnity is it where there is hunger and want? Where there is no imperishable food which lasts into eternal life, there is need and fatal want. The solemnity of the saints has and supplies a solemn food. So much for the time. Now we will look at the manner, under the headings of purification, intent and devotion.

6. Of a certain holy man it is said that Christ cleansed away his sins [cf. Si 47:11]. The apostle wrote to the Hebrews about Christ: "Supporting all things by the word of his strength, bringing about the purification of sins, he sits at the right hand of the majesty on high' [Heb 1:3]. O my heart, my soul, my mouth, my lips, my jaws, my tongue, my stomach, what is on the altar? Is it not the body which was assumed from the Virgin Mary and conceived by the Holy Spirit; the body which suffered on the cross and was buried in a new tomb; the body which rose from the dead on the third day; the body which ascended above all the heavens and sits at the right hand of the Father on high; the body in which Jesus, the judge of the living and the dead, is going to judge the living and the dead and the world by fire? What, then, of you, my interior and exterior senses? How will you receive something so chaste, so holy, so clean, you who are soiled by such impure menstrual defilements, such condemnable, continual and numberless faults? Your sordidness must first be cleansed with the water of compunction, the fire of brotherly compassion, the hyssop

of faith and the humblest confession, the ashes of very salutary submission and mortification. Regarding this purgation the apostle wrote to the Hebrews: 'We have the confidence to enter the sanctuary through the blood of Jesus Christ, the spotless lamb, on a new and living way which he opened up for us through the veil, that is, his flesh. We have a high priest over the house of God. So let us approach with a sincere heart, in the fullness of faith. Having purified our hearts from a bad conscience and washed our bodies with water, let us maintain the unwavering confession of our hope' [Heb 10:19–23]. If someone has a purified heart, that is a heart cleansed of a bad conscience, and a body washed both by the sanctification of baptism and the compunction of devotion, and an unwavering confession of faith, then he may go in to God's altar confidently, and he may approach the communion of the Lord's body without misgiving. Notice the 'unwavering confession', so that his feet walk a straight line, accusing himself and not blaming his creator or the devil. 'For God is no tempter to evil' [Jm 1:13]. The devil does tempt, but only with permission and not beyond what is granted him. However, 'each one is tempted by being distracted and enticed by his desire' [Jm 1:14].

7. Let us now speak of intention. It is threefold: good, bad, worst. It is good if Christ's body is received with true faith and a conscience pure of all evil, so that the blood of Christ justifies the just man further. He receives to become good. It is evil when it is put into a vessel bitter through hate, unclean through indulgence, corrupted through wickedness. In this case, he who is evil does not receive to become good, but to seem good. He is a hypocrite. It is worst of all when someone approaches the Lord's sacrament irreverently, with a wicked heart, like a rabid dog, not in order to be good, but that the antichrist may lie hidden under Christ. Such a one is a rapacious wolf which under the guise of a sheep's skin devours the lamb. He covers his foulness with fig leaves, not with a view toward pardon, such as the person whose sins are covered and whose evil deeds are forgiven, but as Adam and Eve in paradise sewed together fig leaves, not in accusing, but in excusing, themselves. Thus the intent in receiving the eucharist should be to sanctify the good, to correct the evil, and to move the wicked to compunction. The Lord sends the crystal of his

utterly pure body like small morsels of food to heal the sick, satisfy the famished, nourish and strengthen the healthy. This intention is expressed in the [Mass] prayer which says: 'Let it not be for us a source of guilt leading to punishment, but a saving intercession leading to pardon, a washing away of faults, a strengthening of the weak, a support against the dangers of the world, and the remission of all the sins of the faithful, living and dead.'

8. Let us speak of devotion. Devotion is threefold, involving, respectively, compunction, sighing and tears. Devotion of compunction is a gushing fountain, devotion of sighing a leaping fountain, and devotion of tears is a fountain bubbling over. The first pricks, the second induces a flow, the third pours or drips. Fear pricks, hope draws out, love sprinkles. Fear binds the vein, hope opens it, love causes the humor to flow by means of the throbbing of the spirit. When one has thus been relieved of the blood of sin by tourniquet, knife and the voluntary movement of the heart, let him say to the Lord: 'Willingly shall I sacrifice to you' [Ps 54:8], who stood bound before the governor; who hung on the cross pierced by nails; who, struck by a lance, gave forth blood and water; who offered yourself not under constraint, as though this were something you did not want, but with devotion and freely, because you wanted it so.

9. It is now time to speak of the cause, in which we noted three aspects: institution, utility and necessity. To be considered regarding the institution are the following: by whom, for whom, when and how this sacrament was instituted. By whom? Christ. For whom? The apostles. When? At the last supper. How? Taking bread, he blessed it, broke it, and gave it to his disciples, saying: 'Take and eat from this, all of you, this is my body'. He did the same with the chalice after he had eaten, saying: 'Take and drink of this, all of you. For this is the chalice of my blood, which will be poured out for you and for many. Do this in memory of me' [Mt 26:26–28, 1 Co 11:25]. In the originator I recognize goodness, knowledge and power: goodness, because he wished to do it; knowledge, since as consolation for his absence he prepared for future illnesses an adequate remedy which could be obtained easily after his departure; power, because he could and does do what man can scarcely believe, much less define. In the apostles I contemplate friendship, obedience and

reverence. This friendship was then as tender as a blade of grass, but once they had received the Spirit, it was like a mighty tree. Their obedience was to be given even to the division of soul and spirit, even to death, the cross, beheading. Their reverence was for one who was like a master, a lord, a father, even God. Thus: 'You are Christ, the Son of the living God' [Mt 16:16].

10. As regards the time, I think about the closest bond, the strongest argument, the most excellent gift, which therefore he had kept in reserve and which he had eternally predestined to be given to his friends after his bodily separation from them. The bond is the body of Christ, compounding into one the God received and the receiving Christian. As the apostle said: 'The bread which we bless, is it not a communion of the body of the Lord? And the chalice which we bless, is it not a communion of the blood of the Lord?' [1 Co 10:16]. This is a plausible and necessary argument regarding the divine love, because he would never have given himself to us if he had not loved us specially. What in heaven or on earth is better than Jesus, what dearer, what more precious? He is the best gift and the perfect present descending from the Father of lights. The Father gave Jesus, his Son incarnate, for the human race, but on the condition that they receive him in his assumed humanity, after he had completed his task as legate. Then he added grace to grace, so that in another form but with the same reality he gave this same Son of his, Jesus, not just as a companion for the journey, but as viaticum for their whole pilgrimage. As a result, he who once had redeemed us by his visible passion, would always strengthen us with invisible refreshment.

11. The manner in which the Lord handed over his body to the apostles is taught by the apostle to the Corinthians, and the evangelists show it more fully. He who had created bread itself took bread, and, with the same power with which he had first created it for the bodily refreshment of men, with a thanksgiving to the Father and a blessing with the Father, he changed it into the substance of his body for the redemption of souls and bodies. And the same with the chalice.

12. Now let us look at its utility. 'The preceding commandment was abrogated because of its lack of usefulness and power. The law brought nothing to perfection' [Heb 7:18–19]. Further, 'if formerly

it had been without fault, there would be no reason to look for a second one' [Heb 8:7]. However, 'Christ was offered up once to take
away the sins of many' [Heb 9:28], and 'Offering a single sacrifice for
sins he sits at the right hand of God' [Heb 10:12]. Power is to be
sought against weakness, utility against uselessness. The gospel suc-
ceeds the law, just as strength or health succeed weakness. Is it
strength? Listen to the apostle: 'I am not ashamed of the gospel. It is
the strength of God for the salvation of every believer' [Rm 1:16].
What of the body of Christ? 'You did not wish offerings or sacrifice.
Rather, you fashioned a body for me' [Heb 10:5]. Is the body of
Christ strength? Again the apostle: 'The weakness of God', such as
an assumed body, 'is stronger than men' [1 Co 1:25]. At his head Elijah found bread baked in ashes, and he walked for forty days on the
strength of that food. Do you doubt then, that, with the strength of
the bread which comes down from heaven, you can walk not simply to
Horeb, God's mountain, but to the mountain where God is pleased to
dwell? Therefore, there is strength and health in the body of Christ.
The strength of the eucharist, like health, is incompatible with
weakness. Hence, this phrase: 'Health beneath his wings' [Ml 4:2],
under the wings of the visible appearances of bread and wine, as
under the swaddling clothes of faith in the crib of the altar. Thus, the
angel said to the shepherds: 'You will find the child', who in himself
is eternal, among you, 'wrapped in swaddling clothes' [Lk 2:12], just
as the first Adam was clothed in tunics of skin. What is lying hidden
under these tunics, skins, wings, swaddling clothes? Without doubt
it is strength. For the strength of God was in him. Just as weakness is
excluded by strength, uselessness is excluded by usefulness. Grasp
the apostle's meaning. The ashes of a calf were sprinkled for the
cleansing of the flesh, but this did not lead anything to perfection,
nor did it place anyone at the right hand of God. However, all these
things are accomplished by the living sacrifice, the holy sacrifice, the
spotless sacrifice, which by its threefold effect offers purification,
sanctification, and fellowship which is not merely angelic but divine.
Communion of the Lord's body and the sprinkled blood of Jesus
Christ, the spotless lamb, cleanses us from the great fault and from
every sin. Hence, John the Baptist declared: 'Behold, the lamb of
God, behold, him who takes away the sins of the world' [Jn 1:29].

And in the Apocalypse, John the Evangelist wrote: 'Who washes us in his blood' [Rv 1:5]. Similarly in his gospel he says of this sanctification: 'For them, too, I sanctify myself, so that they also may be holy,' [Jn 17:19]. And the apostle wrote to the Hebrews: 'He who sanctifies and all those who are sanctified are one' [Heb 2:11]. And of his passion he said [in a liturgical responsory]: 'I go to be immolated for you'.

13. Therefore, the eucharist purifies our conscience from dead works, and by the justice of the Lord it sanctifies no less. So, let him who sits at the table of the rich man note carefully the things which are set before him, knowing that one should prepare such things in order to show a chaste hospitality to a chaste guest, a pious hospitality to a pious guest, a just hospitality to a just guest, a pure hospitality to a pure guest, a holy hospitality to a holy guest. So, Peter the apostle wrote: 'Christ suffered for us, leaving you an example so you would follow his footsteps' [1 P 2:21]. We are purified and sanctified, so we are companions of his sanctification, and so, too, will we be companions of his glorification and consolation. Thus, John wrote in his epistle: 'What we have seen and heard, we announce to you, so that you may have fellowship with us, and your fellowship may be with the Father and his Son Jesus Christ' [1 Jn 1:3]. And what a fellowship! Not the fellowship of lions which devour their companions. Nor the fellowship of dogs which growl and grumble in their throats, and bark out loud, and seek to capture the soul of the just man. Nor the fellowship of crows which bite and croak at corpses. But rather a fellowship of sheep which cover what is unclean with fleece, which warms what is cold. And a fellowship of lambs, which to pasture their friends hand themselves over to death. And a fellowship of doves which look upon everything with a straightforward gaze and take away all bitterness and anger and indignation. O fellowship which bears with and takes away our evils and confers upon us its goods; which asks nothing from us besides what it has given; which takes nothing which it has saved for our use; which never defrauds in business, but always offers eternal support; which offers everything that is its own and arranges everything that is ours.

14. So, then, we have said a few things about the usefulness of the eucharist, which purifies, which sanctifies, which bestows fellowship

with God. To conclude, let us look at its necessity. This, also, is threefold: one necessity results from the authority of a decree, another from the obligation of a promised vow, another from the impossibility or difficulty of a thing, of reason, or of a deed. From the authority of a decree: 'On the day you eat, you will die' [Gn 2:17]. By this decree every human being is mortal. From the obligation of a vow: every Christian is bound by the promise of baptism, a canon and a monk by religious profession, the priest and every ordained person by the consecration of holy orders. Because he tasted what was forbidden, the necessity which requires that every man die condemns the one who broke his covenant. As the prophet said: 'The one who breaks a covenant, will he escape?' [Ezk 17:15]. He will not escape. Further, it is better not to make vows than to make them and not keep them. The other necessity arises from the difficulty or impossibility of the thing: what is white necessarily is not black, because nothing white is black at the same time. From the impossibility of reason: a stone is not a man, because a rock is without sensation, while a man is sensate. From the impossibility of a deed: a man cannot touch the sky with his finger. But let us get back to our subject.

15. It is necessary for every Christian to receive the eucharist by reason of the divine decree which says: 'Unless you eat the flesh of the son of man and drink his blood, you will not have life in you' [Jn 6:53]. By the obligation of a vow, we are bound to renounce the devil and his pomps, and to receive communion in such a state of renunciation. The apostle says: 'Someone who receives unworthily, eats and drinks judgment for himself' [1 Co 11:29]. By necessity, then, we must go to communion worthily. The reality which is rendered visible by the sacrament is invisible in its power. The reality manifests one thing and conceals another. Exteriorly, it presents the visible sacrament, interiorly it contains invisible power, which it discloses to the clean of heart. If you approach the reality with your whole self, you will have it all. If you approach by half, you will have half; that is, the sacrament, but not the reality of the sacrament. You will then be the branch on the vine which does not bear fruit, but which is cut off and thrown into the fire. When you are worthy

yourself, approach worthily so worthy a reality. Then he will not be absent who was never absent to anyone who was worthy, but was absent only to him who was not worthy. He approaches worthily who succumbs to no mortal sin and who daily makes humble satisfaction for venial sins.

16. In such bright sunlight our reason sees less or is blinded. It sees less because of the bleariness of natural ignorance, and it is blinded because of the unbearable splendor of the divine work. If reason keeps to its familiar paths, it will not grasp the wisdom of this mystery which is hidden from the eyes of all the living. But if reason relies on its beloved who enlightens the darkness of reason itself with true light — at present the light of faith, later the reality itself — then, filled with his riches which surpass all spices, it will say: By faith and love 'I hold him, and I will not let him go until he leads me into the house of his mother', Mary, 'and into the room of his mother by grace' [Sg 3:4], by whom Jesus the creator and enlightener of reason was conceived and born.

17. So, come, reason, to the altar, not with proud gaze and stiff neck, but with bended knee and face turned toward the ground, adoring the footstool of the eucharist, without disputing or judging why and how it comes about. For the Lord said to Peter: 'You do not know now, you will know later' [Jn 13:17]. Are you better than Peter? Are you on closer terms with God? Peter did not know, though he was a very dear disciple to whom the Father had revealed that Christ was the Son of the living God. He had not yet learned, and you, by arguing, discussing and defining wish to take out the bones of the king and reduce them to ashes, when they are hidden until the time and times [Dn 7:25]. O reason, wait until maturity has come to Shelah, whose name means 'his shade', until in our hearts there arises the daystar who will tell us all that he has heard from his Father and who will cause all of us to be taught by God.

18. It remains to speak of the deed, this wonderful deed, this loveable deed, of which the psalmist wrote: 'O Lord, you have delighted me by your work' [Ps 92:4]. The deed is 'impossible for men': that God would die, that the Lord of glory would be crucified, that bread would become the flesh of Christ and wine his blood. 'But with God all things are possible' [Mt 19:26]. It involves no labor for

God to do great, weighty and impossible things. He can do all things easily, as readily as he wishes them. There is no delay or difference between God's wanting and his doing. But for the God-Man willing, suffering and doing are all different. But this is because of what is ours, not because of what is his; or, you might say, because of what of ours is his, since what had been ours alone by quality of our nature, once it is assumed by him, is made his in worth and adoption. Therefore, in that which was both ours and his, he wished one thing in our way, another in his. But he subjected what he wanted in our way to what he wanted in his own manner, saying to the Father: 'Not my will but yours be done' [Lk 22:42]. Likewise, some things he did in our nature, other things in his own. In our nature he was conceived, born and tired, and in it he suffered and died. But in his own nature he was adored, he enlightened the blind, he cleansed lepers, he raised the dead, and so forth. But, one and the same, he acted in our nature and his, the God-Man, and the Man-God. Finally, he suffered not in his nature, but only in ours; that is, in what of ours was his, not in what of his was his. What he suffered on the cross and what he does in the chalice, if we view it from the standpoint of our nature, seems impossible, but viewed in relation to his it seems easy and possible. This fact, beyond our telling but necessary for our redemption, is loving and holy beyond the reach of any merit.

These comments should be sufficient regarding necessity.

EPILOGUE

It is great labor to put one's hand to heroic tasks, and to continue with Joshua the war against the enemies. But one does not gain great rewards except by many labors. In justice merit and reward walk in step, but in grace reward exceeds merit. Is it not astonishing to be confined within the vault of the cloister for a short while and afterwards to possess eternally the infinite reaches of heaven; to dry out the flesh of clay with abstinence and at the resurrection receive with the angels a spiritual body without any burden; to exchange worldly uproars for angelic melodies; to receive consolation in place of desolation, riches for poverty, glory for subjection, God the Father for one's father, God the Son in place of sons, God the Spirit in place of every relationship and carnal affection? No seller had made such a sale, no buyer such a buy, no merchant such a trade. But it was necessary that Christ suffer and thus enter into his glory. Such was the trade effected and taught by him, who restored both what is in heaven and what is on earth, who learned obedience from the things he suffered, that is, the power and glory of obedience.

This hope is deposited in the breast of claustrals, and it is not cooled by winter cold nor withered by summer heat. It contemplates not the things which occur in time, but those which last eternally. It understands that laborious discipline has an end and that everlasting glory will ensue. After a foretaste of the earnest money, patience will grow sweet; otherwise without hope patience would have been bitter. Boredom will turn into desire, annoyance into delight, delay into longing forebearance. [His seven years of labor] seemed like just a few days to Jacob because of his love for Rachel [cf. Gn 29:20]. On the other hand, there is the person in the cloister who sighs and squeaks like the wheel of a wagon laden with hay, who says: 'This is a hard saying' [Jn 6:60], who turns back like the Jordan, who sighs for the fleshpots, who joins in the revolt of Korah against Moses, that is, against the abbot, who in the army of Gideon drinks water on bended knee rather than lapping it like a dog, seeking not the necessities of nature but his desires. Let someone like this listen: it would have been better not to have known the way of truth than to have turned back after knowing it. They are to be reprehended, corrected and wept over, who break Peter's net and obscure the moon, and subtitute the sweet for the bitter and the bitter for the sweet. They have multiplied beyond counting.

Thus ends the book about claustral discipline.

EXHORTATION TO CLAUSTRALS

'Put on the armour of God, so you can resist on the evil day and stand perfect in all things' [Eph 6:11, 13]. Thus, 'You are beautiful and seemly, awesome as an army in battle order' [Sg 6:4]. Be a battle line, be awesome. Every army which is not in battle order is not awesome. And if it is not awesome, it cannot be the Lord's battle line.

For the things which are from God are ordered. You know that those concerned with military operations arrange the slingers and bowmen in the proper places, the standard-bearers in suitable spots; the strongest troops in support; and the weaker ones in safer places, because they are not strong enough to bear the adversaries' charge. As a result the ordered battle array will be awesome to the enemies, because it leaves open no way of penetrating it. Thus the battle line of God's army must make an orderly advance through the level and rough places of this world, so it leaves no point of entry to the enemy who wants to make an assault. If it leaves an opening, it will, as a captive, hand over its troops to the victor.

The task of arranging the battle line belongs to prelates. They must know the capabilities of all with an instinct born of loving, paternal affection, and not as a pretense for haughty domination. They must place each in his proper place. They must send to the outside those whom they see are strong and proven by their good conduct; not the rough, greedy, inconstant or short-tempered, but the meek and humble. The weak and those fired by the flames of the world they must protect in the bosom of the cloister. If anyone has been hurt by the spear of temptations, they should look after him with healing admonitions. So ordered it will be awesome to him who goes about looking for someone to devour [Ps 5:8].

Furthermore, each of us must order himself, so that he will be beautiful interiorly, so his glory will be from within, and he will be proper and ordered in his morals, and devout, modest, patient, humble, good-natured, compassionate and charitable. The devil intensely detests those whom he sees joined and united by charity. Those lacking charity he attacks with confidence. So Gregory wrote: "No matter what good things are in us, if charity is lacking, the evil of discord opens a breach in our battle formation through which the enemy can enter. The enemy does not fear chastity without charity, because he himself does not burn in the flesh. He is not afraid of abstinence, because he uses no food. He does not fear distribution of belongings, because he needs no riches. But if he finds the true unity of charity in us, he fears it. He is intensely jealous of concord, because he sees it possesses on earth what he lost in heaven. Hence, it is rightly said: 'Awesome as an ordered battle line', because the evil spirits fear the number of the elect which they see fortified with concord.' "[176]

ON AFFLICTION AND READING

I N THEIR ROOMS newly enlisted soldiers of Christ, who fight under the banner of the cross, are subjected to a strenuous, three-fold test: bodily afflicition, by which the body's wantonness is curbed; reading of the New and Old Testaments, by which the soul is fed; prayer of compunction for sins, which, together with a desire for the heavenly kingdom, raises the spirit to God. The gospel mentions two of these when it says, 'This kind is not cast out except by prayer and fasting' [Mt 17:20], and the third when it says, 'You search the Scriptures', by which you think you have life [Jn 5:39].

2. Generally, two things in regard to afflicition require attention: the manner and the fruit: the manner, so that nothing is excessive; the fruit, that no effort is wasted. To afflict oneself without measure is tyranny; to afflict oneself without fruit is folly. Affliction without measure causes a breakdown instead of better conditioning; a fall, instead of upbuilding; wearing away, instead of completion. It merits loss, not grace.

3. The proper measure for affliction is to mount a campaign against one's wantonness, rather than against one's nature; against the cause of sin, not against the creature of God; against the reign of death, not against the instrument of good works. The proper measure is to show kindness to the body, but not to be its servant; to scourge it for its errors, but not to fight an all-out war against it; to rule it, rather than to ruin it; to correct it as a friend, rather than recoil from it with relentless hate as though it were an enemy. The body is only to be afflicted when it actually does, or possibly might, draw away from God. When the sting of temptation becomes stronger, then it should be silenced and its pricks restrained by unyielding abstinence and tireless vigilance, until these fevered passions from Babylon's furnace are banished and every workshop of base desires is undermined.

4. Anyone who has kindled the oven of the spirit of fornication is himself burned the next morning in confession, so that he is paid back seven times over for the evil persuasion, for the law of sin, and for the shameless inflammation of his members. Nor is it enough that

all unlawful desires are driven out of the body. One must carefully investigate whether one fell solely by one's own propensity or also by the concomitant cunning of the Adversary. For, what perusasive argument does the Evildoer offer, to be let off unpunished, even though the doer would not have done his deed, had the Persuader not pestered him? It is right that sin be presented for condemnation; nonetheless, it is also proper that a distinction be made in confession, indicating whether you sinned without anyone else's persuasion or whether you were allured by someone inwardly or from without.

5. Distinctions are to be made about three facts: the manner of the sin, the manner of the confession, the manner of satisfaction. Who, though, is presumptuous enough to undertake to define the manner of sinning, since it is even less conceivable that one know the kinds of sins than that one calculate the number of sinners. There are, however, some general distinctions in the manner and kinds of sins; for example, was there pleasure, consent, deliberation, did temptation come slowly or suddenly, and was it violent or gentle. Briefly, it may by said that pleasure means a gentle, persuasive attraction; consent, turning the mind toward the allurement; deliberation, the agreeable acceptance of the alluring sin. Temptation is an unwary preoccupation, which may be termed slow, if foreseeable by anyone who was not negligent; sudden, if like a robber it undermines the house of a sleeping man; violent, if it crashes down like lightning from heaven: gentle, if like a moth it quietly gnaws away. All these things, which are concealed in confession at the price of accruing evil, must be so strictly collected that one even shakes the dust from one's feet and stores away even the slightest passing thought in order to winnow it in confession. Thus, one should fulfill all justice; that is, beware of all injustice and exercise the fullness of penitence. Finally, when Moses—that is, the superior—orders it, the molten calf must be smashed to bits and drunk down with water, that its memory may perish from the earth through contrition in the heart and confession on the lips, flooding tears, mortification of the flesh, granting alms, singing psalms, punishment with lashes, bending the knees, continuous silence, separation from worldly things.

6. So much for what needs to be noted regarding the manner of bodily affliction. Now for its fruits. Regarding them the Apostle

wrote: "You have sanctification as your fruit, eternal life as your goal" [Rm 6:22]. And elsewhere: 'the fruit of the Spirit is charity, joy, peace, patience, goodness, kindness, fidelity, mildness, self-control, chastity' [Gal 5:22]. These first and purest fruits are gathered from the heavenly paradise, from the fruit trees of sun and moon, from all the trees of Lebanon, from the enclosed garden, from the orchard of nut-bearing trees. They do not lie heavy in the stomachs of those who eat them, but rather cheer the mind. They cause not rumbling in the innards, but rejoicing in the depths of the heart. They do not break a fast, but sanctify it. When consumed they are not used up; but, like the bread which God blessed in the gospel, they grow ever greater although shared by a thousand generations.

7. These fruits are better when tasted than when held in the hand. They heal and they satisfy. These fruits are to be used and enjoyed by those still on the way. But they will only be enjoyed in the greater satiety of our homeland. Certainly they are never eaten in the present life without rinds and shells, because they are acquired with great labor and possessed with great fear. The gladder we are to have acquired them, the more disturbing is our fear of losing them. For nothing is more laborious to acquire than virtues, nothing easier to lose. Nor should you so much as allege the difficulty of the way to make a case against the rind, for the fruit cannot be preserved for a journey if the outer shell is broken. What does the Apostle mean when he says, 'Strength is made perfect in weakness' [2 Co 12;9], if not that the fruit should be kept in its rind? 'When what is perfect has come, what is partial will be shelled off' [1 Co 13:10], because when we take off what is mortal we shall receive immortality. When we see God as he is, we shall receive the fruit of eternity without the husk of trouble and diffculty. This is eternal life, of which it is said, 'You have santification as your fruit, eternal life as your goal' [Rm 6:22]. This is the blessed fruit of Mary, the fruit of her womb, the reward and inheritance of the servants of God, the fruit of the nativity, the fruit of which it is said: 'I have appointed you to go and bear fruit, and your fruit will remain' [Jn 15:16]. For, whatever labor we do must be done for eternity.

8. Now let us look at the second exercise, reading in one's room. What should I say about reading? I consider a room without reading

to be a hell without consolation, a gibbet without relief, a prison without light, a tomb without a vent, a ditch swarming with worms, a suffocating trap. A room without reading is the empty house of which the gospel speaks, where the nocturnal and noonday devils assault the idle hermit with as many thrusts of useless and harmful thoughts as there are hours and moments in the day and night.

9. One who does not devote his time to holy reading disarms his ramparts of a thousand shields which might hang down from them. How quickly and easily is the city of one's room captured if it does not defend itself with God's help and the shield of the sacred page. Jesus, the great hermit, taught you, O good hermit, what weapons are best for opposing your assailant, the devil. Each time Satan tempted him in the desert, he replied with the words of Scripture. As a result, the devil limped away and never recovered, as though a flaming arrow from the hand of a powerful man had been stuck in the thigh of a barking dog. Search in reading's garden for strong herbs to use as medicine against the incursions of bad angels, lest you perish from his poisonous exhalations and inspirations.

10. Take projectiles from your bookcase so that when you are struck you may strike back at the one who struck you and force him to speak. For in the book of Judges, when Judah and his brother Simeon cut off the ends of his hands and feet, Adoni-Bezek declared: 'After the extremities of their hands and feet had been cut off, seventy kings gathered scraps of food under my table. As I did to them, so has the Lord done to me' [Jg 1:7]. Adoni-Bezek, whose name means 'lord of the river', is the one of whom it is said: 'I saw Satan falling like lightning from heaven' [Lk 10:18]. He is called the 'lord of the rivers', that is, of evil temptations. He cuts off the ends of the hands and feet of the kings he has captured. He tries to take away the fingers of those he deceives; that is, their power to discern deeds and feelings, for discernment is like the culmination, that is, the mother of all the virtues. As a result, they are to collect scraps of food under his table; that is, once they have lost discernment they second and obey his suggestions and commit not only the spiritual evils which are the food of his table, but also the works of the flesh. The latter an ethereal being cannot do himself, but those who bear an earthly body

may commit them at his suggestion. Yet he is captured by Judah and Simeon, that is, by confession and penitence. They cut off the ends of his hands and feet, because in confession they hide no evil feeling or action.

11. Reading teaches these things because it constantly tells of the clash of virtues and vices, so that this clash is never passed over in silence. Reading is the soul's food, light, lamp, refuge, consolation, and the spice of every spiritual savor. It feeds the hungry, it illuminates the person sitting in darkness; to refugees from shipwreck or war it comes with bread. It comforts the contrite heart, it contains the passions of the body with the hope of reward. When temptations attack, it counters them with the teaching and example of the saints. By it those who have recovered from infirmity are made strong in battle. Prosperity is kept within bounds by its power, lest we glory in our good fortune. Adversity too is limited, lest we waver in it, for God indeed raises up a strong wind.

12. Reading holds the key of lady wisdom and opens her mistress's writing case to a sober and humble mind. Reading makes accessible the heavenly storerooms of philosophy. From them David returned with his pockets full. So that he would not be accused of the theft, he said: 'In the pocket of my heart I have hidden your words' [Ps 119:11], dividing up the storerooms of the Old and New Testaments, which yield up one thing after another. In front of persistent readers, reading places an inebriating glass, a drink seasoned with costly spices. Reading displays a steaming oven full of different kinds of bread, so that from them each person who hungers and thirsts for justice may be refreshed with the kind he chooses. In the breadbox of sacred reading are breads baked in an oven, breads roasted on a grill, or cooked in a frying pan, breads made with the first fruits and sprinkled with oil, and barley cakes. So, when this table is approached by people from any walk of life, age, sex, status or ability, they will all be filled with the refreshment that suits them.

13. Next, reading takes a golden crown from her head and puts it on the head of her lover. For reading seeks a lover to whom she may offer not merely food, but offspring. She seeks not just any kind of lover, but one who is noble, handsome, and also thoughtful, healthy and holy. For whatever is in her is holy. Since Holy Scripture is inspired by

the Holy Spirit, nothing sprouts in it which is not rooted in its holy origin. Whatever steely or leaden shavings the enemy has tried to introduce by vigorously filing heretics or wrong-headed interpreters have already been pored over and examined in the expositions of teachers and the scrutiny of councils and aired by preachers. Hence, as you amble through the field of Scripture, you will not stub your toe against a rock. Rather, like a bee harvesting flowers, you may concoct from it a honeycomb which will bring sweetness to the taste, light to the eyes, and wonderful scents with which you can sprinkle the walls of your room. For how could the timbers, seats, doors and walls of the room not be suffused with the scent of wisdom, when within them wisdom is constantly studied and read, and comes in and out? If you were concocting the best herbal remedy there, wouldn't even inanimate things absorb some slight scents through the evaporation of the spices? Therefore, you should be afraid to live in wisdom's room smacking of foolishness.

14. It is necessary to lessen or eliminate all the annoyances of reading, just as an attentive nurse quiets a screaming, crying, nursing baby by offering it her breast. So, one should see what is to be read and how. The nourishment of holy books is so fruitful and abundant that in them our every weariness will be countered by as many varieties of readings as there are moments in our lives, however long we live. A lack of content will never drive us to the alien harvest of secular philosophers, whether we are dealing with the nature of souls or even of bodies, decorously and truthfully. The Spirit, who is the artisan of all things, who possesses all the knowledge of speaking, and who is the kind spirit of wisdom, has so arranged his words in the writings of his people that nothing is wanting there of refinement, truth, honor or utility. All that he says speaks of creation or reformation, correction of the guilty, instruction of the foolish, encouragement to those making good progress, damnation for the wicked, and reward for the good. There is no corruption in human beings for which authoritative reading does not offer a remedy. According to the inclinations of various feelings one should read now things new or then old, now obscure, then plain, now subtle, then simple, now examples, then commands, now something serious, then something lighthearted. If the soul is thus compassed about

with such a harmonious variety, it will avoid boredom and receive a cure.

15. The reading of Genesis is for those who wish to retrace their origins and know from what sort of ancestors they came into the world, by what unhappy misfortune they fell from liberty into abject slavery, for what crime they were condemned to the squalor of prison, and other things of this kind. Here, too, with appropriate gratitude you will find out about the first channels of God's goodness, which because of his bountiful fullness, flowed out into the creation of the world and overflowed in the array of the works of the [first] six days.

16. In its original planting God so graced our race with honor, that it was as if he pondered with careful deliberation how he might endow it with better artistry and more desirable form than other creatures received. Because nothing is dearer, better or worthier than a mirror reflecting his image, he created our first parent in his image and likeness. God extended this kindness to give our parent a unique authority for ruling all the things He had created in the world, not in such a way that our parent would be troubled with anxiety, but so that he might use and experience all these things with a delightful endowment of reason and authority. Glory to you, O Lord, because you thus preceded us with your blessings which would never have dried up for all our race, had not there appeared that worm of pride which struck Jonah's gourd and dried up the tender new shoot with the snake's venom and caused our race to fall into sin.

17. In this book also, travel by your reading all the way to paradise and sigh over what was lost. Drink from the four rivers by imbibing justice, prudence, fortitude and temperance. Beware the snaky suggestion, eating the forbidden fruit, the excuse Adam and Eve offered for their sin, Cain's cruelty and despair. Walk with God as Enoch did. Flee the fornication of the sons of God which deserved the flood. Enter the ark at the time of the flood when God is angry with you; that is, stay hopeful in the shadow of God's wings until the evil passes by [Ps 57:1]. Fear drunkenness, which puts one in danger after he has been freed from the flood. Like Shem and Japheth hide a parent's error, instead of laughing at it like Ham. In this manner run through the contents of this book with a deliberate but light step,

imitating the good deeds, avoiding the evil ones, interpreting what is obscure, retaining and committing to memory what is straightforward. Whenever you enter a pleasant meadow of prophetic blessings, loosen the folds of your garment, stretch your belly, open your mouth and extend your hand, then depart with mouth, belly, garment and hands loaded. From such passages you will draw not annual, but continual assurance for years to come. Thus with Jacob, embalmed in spices and dead to the world, you may live for God, to whom all things are alive, saying: 'I live now, yet no longer I, but Christ lives in me' [Gal 2:20].

18. Then come to Exodus and be saddened by the entry into Egypt. Notice with what insistence the prince of this world fosters evils and how the right hand of God encourages virtues. See, too, how — to assist the liberation of his people — God's right hand stirs up from the hidden repositories of his power great signs and wonders against the heads of his enemies, and how he prevails and destroys their names in the turbulent waters. Then admire the foreshadowing of our redemption in the blood of the sacrificial lamb. Observe how the law was given on Mt. Sinai and how it is open to spiritual understanding. By progressions of virtues run through the forty-two stopping places with what they signify. With an angelic mind build within yourself the tabernacle and its ceremonies, then inhabit the heavenly realms by imitating their holiness. Then beware of ungrateful murmuring, and do not seek after the meats and dishes of Egypt. Let the grace of manna be enough for you. Seeing offenses and their punishment, proceed cautiously with Moses after the Lord your God, always and in all things protected by the divine cloud. Leviticus belongs especially to you who live in your room, for in it all things are cleansed by the atonement of sacrifices.

19. By a just and unalterable judgment, Joshua did not let the treachery of the Gibeonites go unpunished, but he remained completely faithful to the treaty. He declared: 'Set them aside and let them live. They may chop wood and carry water for the common use' [Jos 9:20]. Similarly, the soul makes the bodily senses into providers of wood and water when, after having been tricked by their deceit, it accuses itself in confession, with the result that the senses are made subject to the sufferings of Christ through affliction and

draw waters from the well of the heart through earnest compunction. To continue the same image: Benjamin, Manasseh and those sons of Israel who received their share of the promised land across the Jordan and were to divide it by lot, were not able to destroy the Jebusites and Canaanites completely from their midst. Still, they made them tributaries. O you who see God, as long as the senses of your body pay tribute by giving obedience to the spirit which serves God and to true confession, the son of his right hand, do not destroy them by immoderate mortification. They pay their tribute when all their members, intent on divine service and worship, through the mediation of the soul offer their activity and labor to God.

20. After work a rest is welcome. After being burdened all year by what is surely cruel and unrelenting distress, and thirsting in some measure for the silence of my room, which seems like a very desirable haven, I draw deeply from the quiet which has now been granted me. The mind has a more extensive and expansive leisure within the six surfaces of a room than it could gain outside by traversing the four parts of the world. In fact, the smaller the place the more extended the mind, for when the body is constrained the mind takes flight. A brake upon the body expands the mind. If no one prevents it, my mind leaps as high and as far and as deep as it wants; (where disputes and the causes of disputes have been put to sleep,) it does not fear obstructing complaints. However, if any dispute is brought into the room, not on behalf of the body, but with the body—that is, when the flesh has desires which conflict with those of the spirit, and the spirit has desires which conflict with those of the flesh—then, with God as judge, that dispute is to be cut down not with outcry and tension, but in silence and compunction. Of course, where has every matter for earthly delight and vanity, such as can cause conflicts, been removed? Is there only misery? This misery is not reason for despair, since eternal happiness destroys it, now in hope and later on in reality.

21. Here the human heart can be in possesion of itself, once it has narrowed all questions to one. Having excluded other people's business, the heart can tend to its own affairs. To inquire after oneself in God and God in oneself is indeed the one great question, but it is not unsolvable if the search is unending and zealous. Actually, there

is another preliminary question: to seek oneself in oneself. As long as this preliminary inquiry is not yet fully resolved, it makes use of the long argument of solitude and the obvious mastery of the flesh, as though these were a stool for its feet. This inquiry is rarely undertaken by academics in the schools of cities and towns. Since it is hardly ever urged there, it is even more rarely completed. I would not say that this question is never considered by those dwelling in cloisters, but they have less time for this one question, when they are involved in many necessary as well as unnecessary questions, and a crowd of people forcefully impels superficial and jabbering disputants to solve questions which have been raised. By contrast, our solitary inquiry goes better in silence and is more perfectly studied in solitude. It is a matter of the heart, not the lips. That is where the Spirit speaks to Paul and the Lord to David the prophet. When the Lord draws our hearts to himself or binds himself to us, he solves our problem more sweetly and clearly than can be told. He is our sole master and does not enter the city, but dwells with the beasts in solitude. He says, 'Now the door is closed and my children are with me in bed' [Lk 11:7]. For he condemns cleverness, but he loves simplicity. He says 'I will lead my soul into solitude and there speak to her heart' [Ho 2:14].

22. Because I am a new and infrequent dweller in my room, I can't speak of the pleasant attractions of solitude, but it seems to me that if the dough is offered as first fruits it is holy [cf. Rm 11:16]. I do not reckon it among those pleasures which are boring when one has them, and desired when one does not have them. A room has one of two qualities, depending on the way of life of those who dwell in it. It is a hard place for carnal people, but a pleasant one for spiritual people. It is a prison for the flesh, a paradise for the mind. It is a market where the butcher sells small and large amounts of his flesh to God who comes as a customer. The more of his flesh he sells, the greater grows the sum of money he sets aside. Let them therefore increase their wealth and fill their purse by selling their own blood and flesh, for flesh and blood will not possess the kingdom of God. Voluntary mortification of the flesh is the redemption of man's soul, which is the riches of the saints. The Lord says, 'He who loses his soul will find it' [Mt 10:39]. Although what the apostle says is true, 'I do not find

good in my flesh' [cf. Rom 7:18] nevertheless I can make a good profit from the flesh and acquire glory for it, if I remove wantonness. Yet, the flesh is childish and extravagant, unless it is restrained by the yoke of discipline and granted no independent management of itself and its belongings.

ON CONSCIENCE

To his very dear brother, Alcher, monk of Clair-vaux, brother Peter of Celle wishes salvation and good conscience.

THE RELIGIOUS MIND inquires with religious curiosity about the religious conscience, so that it may know, and indeed have, a good conscience. I take up the question more in order to learn than to teach. Called back by your inquiry from the deviation of the revolving world, I make the question my own. A blind man and a beggar, I set about like a mole to dig deeply, striving to reach the light of conscience, although I lack the light of knowledge. It is striking how the little creature uses its hands and even its feet to cast off the oppressiveness of the weight and darkness and seek the freedom of the air and perhaps the light, but without the light of eyes. Heretofore I have been trapped in the hole of dark carelessness. I have given too little thought to how pleasant it would be to break out into the freedom and light of conscience.

2. Having cut open the veins of the heart with the scalpel of persistent inquiry into the nature of conscience, I have called upon the vital blood of the veins of a complete meditation, so that from the blood of purified contemplation, the heart may with a stylus commend or adapt what is sufficient for the writer and retain for itself what it needs to live. For something is written usefully when the author's own life is improved by the treatise and another's conscience is instructed as well. One should not think that the vein of the heart is always bled to its detriment, since it may be benignly opened. For by the outpouring of charity it flows more suitably and freely.

3. After dividing up the labor of the work which I undertake because you imposed it, I began at that point to be more ashamed of my own conscience which is corrupted in dead works. So in holy books I investigated your conscience and that of other holy people more carefully to see what conscience is or should be. Because of my dullness of mind I could not cover so difficult and large a subject in a single brief discourse, and so I have fallen into excessive wordiness. Another consideration also drew me into a long discourse; namely, that reading about or dealing with conscience should be as inclusive as conscience itself. For it is very useful that conscience take care of

itself with the massage of slow, lengthy meditations, so that it may be happy and at peace, fruitful and warm, and then, irradiated and illuminated by the sun, it may recognize itself in itself.

4. Do you think that it would recognize itself as 'beautiful among women', when it successively departed from itself 'after the tracks of the flocks' to undertake journeys through the marshes, and it 'pastured the goats' of wanton flesh? [Sg 1:7]. 'Once its sweetness and fullness had been left behind' [Jg 9:9, 11], how reluctantly do you think it would come 'among the trees of the forest' [Sg 2:3], if it knew how great a goodness is conscience which is devoted and pleasing to God? Do you think it would put up patiently with even a moment's holding back from the embrace of the spouse, if it was possessed of words? But miserable, blind and foolish because it 'embraces refuse' [Lm 4:5], it loves darkness, and what is more miserable, it even seeks misery with misery. For what in this world is more sublime has become more wretched and pitiable [1 Co 1:27–28].

5. But this difficulty does not withdraw this conscience, which meets misery on its path, from that other misery of ambition, because it is not judged misery. The deceptive comeliness and the false beauty [Pr 31:30] of the great whore [Rv 17:2] drinking from the golden chalice are judged to be delight. In fact, however, the misery which worsens the soul, the prosperity of fools, is more unhappy than the misery which strikes the body and which is a punishment of evil deeds. A good conscience does not feel the good of either kind of misery. A good conscience does not feel traveling misery, because it does not go out to that evil way which leads to hell. At the same time it avoids stationary misery, because it closes the door through which death enters our souls. Just as it refuses to go out because a lion is on the road, [Pr 26:13] so it avoids leaving its door open because there is a 'raven in the window' [Zeph 2:14]. It abhors equally the blackness of the raven and the fierceness of the lion: blackness so it will not be discolored, fierceness so it will not be devoured. It says that the stain of the raven might have swallowed up our beauty or the throat of the lion swallowed our tenderness, 'if the Lord had not helped us' [cf. Ps 124:2]. He lined the door of the ark with bitumen from the outside so that when it was exposed to the

flood it would not sink, and he took the evil beast from the road, so it wouldn't devour Joseph as he came to his brothers [Gn 37:33]. The Lord teaches in the gospel how conscience must close itself within itself when he says: 'Enter your room'. 'Your room' surely refers to the hidden place of conscience, and the door is your mouth. So, 'when you pray enter the room' [Mt 6:6] of a tranquil and quiet mind, where 'the Lord is, who dwells in Sion. His place is made of peace, and he speaks there to the heart of Jerusalem' [Is 40:2].

6. So, I say, once the door of the exterior senses is closed, the heart enters its room so that it may call to the Lord with its voice. The woman who does not disturb the atmosphere with the vocal cords in her throat, but by a secret path of the spirit importunes the Holy Spirit in spirit and in truth, is more effective in her requests. As soon as she is heard she is answered. She is heard without the pulsation of sound, so quickly does the heart's feeling move. When such affection harmonizes God and herself, she delights the symphony of heaven with her harmony. She sings and God plays an accompaniment and even exults.

7. By contrast, some pray and sing every day with other kinds of lips and tongues. When they are not answered, they tell the angels indignantly: 'We sang to you and you did not dance, we uttered a lament and you did not weep' [Lk 7:32]. That is, you were not present to congratulate us for our successes, although we chanted in the oratory every day. Nor did you commiserate with our troubles, although we were sorry to the point of tears. One can read in the prophet about this sort of tears, poured out insincerely and impurely: 'You have polluted my altar with your tears' [Ml 1:7, 12; 2:13]. A conscience which pours out feigned tears in the midst of sin's pleasure and does not wish to abandon sin, but to make up for it by this weeping and then sin again, is polluted rather than washed by its tears. Thus it was said also of Judas' 'Let his prayer be a sin' [Ps 109:7]. When a pure conscience sings it causes an angel to dance, that is, to rejoice with it; and when it laments, it causes the angel to weep, that is, to be compassionate. 'For there is joy among the angels of heaven over one sinner who is pentinent' [Lk 15:17]. Likewise, it is written elsewhere that 'the angels of peace will weep bitterly', that is, be compassionate toward the penitent [Is 33:7].

8. Behold the greatness of a good conscience. It is the sister of the angels. For the present it clings to the small breasts of the church, because it does not yet have the breasts of angelic perfection [Sg 8:8]. When it has them, it will advance all the way to a shared life with God. A good conscience is the sign of religion, the temple of Solomon, 'the field of blessing' [Dt 28:3], the garden of delights, the ark of the covenant, 'the cup of Joseph with which he was wont to take auguries and indeed to become inebriated' [Gn 44:5], the royal treasury, the palace of God, the book sealed and closed. A good conscience is whatever can be uttered or thought that is especially delightful, beautiful, honorable, useful, pleasant, good, healthful.

9. Among devout minds a good conscience is the single and singular bond of the pledge of future happiness. It is not carried around by the wandering instability of changeableness. It thinks that the dark deeds and blandishments offered to sense are beneath it. Conscience is also radiant and never droops [Ws 6:12]. It is not overshadowed by dark clouds, or scorched by the blazing sun, or infected by disease; nor does it sink back at the errant return of the stars. The world may weep, mock, turn around unstably, burn, perish, or pass, but conscience will never wither. The body may be subjected to punishment, wasted away from fasting, mangled by blows, stretched on the rack, butchered with the sword, tormented with the punishment of the cross, but what is that to conscience? These things are engraved on the mortal skin for the meriting of a crown rather than inflicted there for a guilty deed. And so what annoyance do they involve for conscience?

10. Conscience says: 'Wicked torturer, the more sharply you jab, the more becomingly you paint the skin of my flesh which is "one of the skins of Solomon's tents" [Sg 1:5]. Your piercing makes me a painting. I surrender my skin, so you may paint it when you pierce it. When you pierce it you both pierce and paint. "A man will give skin for skin, and all that he has for his conscience" [Jb 2:4]. You stretch the skin in torture, but then the painted form shows all the more. I glory in the variegated garment. When I behold the wavy lines of the wounds, the dazzling lilies, the rose on the thorn, the endeavors of each virtue, they depict the various dwelling places of the heavenly rooms. With what glory and beauty will conscience then bubble

over for joy. Would that that hour would, so to speak, spread out a pavement for conscience.'

11. Then, O God, what refreshments will the starved soul grasp with its mouth, and with what utterances will the fattened and enlarged conscience respond? Whether it wanted to or not, it could not restrain itself from the glitter of the wonders which God does for it, just as Joseph, full of new wine, could not restrain his devotion and compassion. Does conscience begrudge its grace to others? 'It does not travel with sickly envy' [Ws 6:7]. Is it difficult, and such that pious concern cannot advance to it? No. It is easily seen 'by those who seek it' [Ps 22:26]. Does it delay opening so that you feel tired and start back? No. It anticipates those who seek it in order to show itself to them first [Ws 6:14]. Is someone slow to go to it? 'It will come to you' [Ps 102:12]. 'The one who watches for it at dawn will not labor. He will find it waiting on his doorstep' [Ws 6:15]. What more can I say about conscience? One thing I say, that to think of it is the height of good sense, and the one who watches for it will always be safe [Ws 6:16]. Without any disrespect to wisdom, it is more useful to run to conscience than to wisdom, unless it wisely builds up conscience.

12. In fact, wisdom and conscience come to the mind in step, so that wisdom never comes without conscience and conscience never comes without wisdom. Both wisdom and conscience with equal gait pull the soul toward its goal as though it were their own vehicle. Let us see what this goal is according to the book of Wisdom, from which we have already taken many things. So we join the two together, so that what we say of one we may transfer to the other. The book of Wisdom speaks of the beginning and end of wisdom in the following way: 'Its beginning is a genuine desire for discipline. Concern for discipline is love, and love is keeping discipline's laws. Keeping the laws is the perfection of incorruptibility. Incorruptibility makes one close to God. So the desire for wisdom will lead to the eternal kingdom' [Ws 6:18–21].

13. Behold the fiery chariot and the fiery horses and God the driver! Where do they carry, not a jug, but the soul? To the eternal kingdom. You desire a kingdom, especially a lasting one. Pay attention and go up, not by a headlong, disorderly journey, like that of

Satan who fell like lightning from heaven into gehenna, but like the rising dawn of the sun growing toward full daylight. Take hold of discipline where the cedar tress are cut and shaped. The apostle says: 'If you are without discipline, you are not sons but offspring of adultery' [Heb 12:8]. Squared off by the cutting of discipline and fitted to the structure of the city which is arranged in a square, drawn to the width, length, depth and height of charity, grasp and hold on to that charity. 'For the one who loves fulfills the law' [Rm 13:10].

14. Love, therefore, is keeping the laws. What pay does one who keeps the commandments deserve? The Lord says: 'If anyone loves me, he will keep my commandments, and my Father will love him, and we will come to him and make our dwelling with him' [Jn 14:23]. But to the Lord who comes you should hold out and unfurl the mantle of incorruptibility, so that you may enfold with this shroud not the body of Jesus, but the grace of the Trinity which comes to you and remains in you. What have you to do with the immortal, invisible king of the ages; specifically, what will you receive from him? A kingdom and the crown of the kingdom upon your head. And there will be a collar around your neck. Rule, therefore, in the kingdom of conscience and of wisdom.

15. So much for these matters. I want this letter to be appended to the opening of the book about conscience, so that once this sample has been tasted, the reader may either spit it out, if what is said in it tastes bad, or may proceed more eagerly within the veil, behind which are contained many not altogether useless things about conscience, but also about purifying the heart. Certain matters are briefly noted below about the heart's letting go and holding on, its outpouring and dissolving, its loss and repair and recuperation.

16. To make an estimate of the years and of the family's sustenance is as much the mark of a good and prudent man, as to live not by chance but by a clear and just law. Good opinion thinks it base and burdensome to depend upon the hand or the table of another. After calculating what he has stored up and the expenditure of the following period, the prudent man already begins to have a taste of the consolations of the future rest. He is going to live his life not by accident, but in a happy and respected security. He collects suitable supplies for each

season. Otherwise, if some time of year is devoid of provisions, this lack would prove wrong the inactivity of the idle man; and when he needs leisure, he will suffer from hunger. He hastens to extinguish the annoyances of the enforcer who pillages the substance of his innards with daily growling, while an overflowing abundance of everything completely excludes scantiness of table and harvest, so that month follows month in unbroken frugality and sabbath follows sabbath with uninterrupted joy and rest. When one has investigated the deep interior places and explored the recesses of the mind, what is paid out in the storerooms of conscience for the sustenance of our soul from generation to generation is assessed. We must apply ourselves in a similar pattern and with no less concern, so that we may know what is sufficient and not fall short of the full and perfect measure of sufficiency.

17. I call your attention to these matters regarding the management of the household of your soul, Alcher, my good friend and a holy monk, a person concerned about studies. Although you do not cease daily gathering food, especially spiritual rations, from the fertile fields of holy doctors, you also extend your hand to the bare storeroom of our poverty. You ask a poor man not for a poor handout, but about conscience. And how will I give what I do not have? Certainly the only conscience I have is ragged and soggy. If you touch it, your hand will be defiled; if you look at it, your eye will blush. It will be safer to keep it detained in its lair. Otherwise, belching up dark and putrid vapors from the tomb it may arouse the winds of plague, so that it will not only not arouse to life those stupified in the death of a bad conscience; but it will extinguish those still wavering a bit, though tinged with the life of a good conscience. However, I will arise and go to my friend, whose door is now shut and whose children are in bed asleep with him. I will say to him, 'Friend, lend me three loaves of bread, so that I may know what is a good conscience and what is a bad conscience, for my friend, brother Alcher, comes to me from the road of inquiry, asking what is a good conscience, and I have nothing to set before him' [Lk 11:5–7].

18. Therefore, I now put down some things received from a friend and begin to treat of conscience. The teaching regarding all the matters to be treated may be grasped more clearly and retained more

easily, if all the material which is to be treated is laid out before one's eyes at the same time in a comprehensive, connected whole or its parts are presented in relief with clear distinctions and sure definitions. This manner of procedure has been passed on by learned men to guide the composition of treaties. Some by virtue of their fine minds utilize it in an especially outstanding way. Others, interpreting more obscurely because of the slowness of their wits which are little trained in writing, consign the received material to the understanding of their successors. Belonging to neither group, I am astonished at my presumption, in fact, my temerity. I come to produce literature when I am unlettered. I take up the office of expositor, when I am not even capable of serving as reader. However, there is one thing by which I may make excuse to myself and answer the criticism of others. I have marked myself out for this work not at my own prompting, but because admonished to do it by fraternal charity. I do not know if I do it usefully, but I do know that it was humbly that I took up the task enjoined upon me by a good and holy and very dear man.

19. So I have been asked to treat of conscience, and to say not what sort of conscience I have, but what sort I ought to have. For every conscience is not of the same kind, as though all who have a conscience may believe that they have the same innocence. The task assigned is to say what conscience is and why it is so named. Then, insofar as it is given me to call to mind hidden matters or to understand from the Scriptures, I will add certain aspects or species of consciences. Thus, as grace allows, will I finish these tasks.

20. First, however, our reader should be warned to seek in the words that follow, not science but conscience. For learning in the sciences he may consult an abundance of reading, whether of the divine sort produced among us, or of the philosophical kind pursued by the familiar inquirers into nature. He may use this little parchment for the investigation and informing of consciences. Let us see what conscience is, not by definition but by a kind of description. Conscience is knowledge of itself, either expecting good or wary of evil. The statement that conscience is 'of itself' will be made clearer by an inquiry into the etymology of the name.

21. Such is the etymology of this name that 'conscience' [*conscientia*] is 'knowledge of the heart' [*cordis scientia*]. It might seem that

according to this etymology conscience is nothing else than knowledge [*scientia*]. For knowledge of the heart is either that knowledge in the heart aimed at receiving the learning of an extrinsic philosophy or that knowledge which from the understanding of the heart remains in the heart better and is preserved more usefully. 'Knowledge of the heart' refers to both kinds, but 'conscience' only to the latter. For knowledge of the heart is understood in two ways, namely that by which one knows oneself in oneself and by oneself, or that by which one knows other things besides oneself and outside of oneself. For the heart by its own knowledge knows both itself and many other things. When it knows itself it is called 'conscience'. When it knows things other than itself, it is named 'knowledge'.

22. Finally, it is said about that wisdom which is in the heart: 'God endowed the heart of Bezalel with wisdom to make all works of gold or silver', and so forth [Ex 31:3–4]. Similarly, of a certain person it is said that 'the wise of heart is strong with power' [Jb 11:4]. Again regarding the kind which concerns oneself and not other things it is written: 'Would that God would give me to say these things with judgment' [Ws 7:15]. Similarly, 'the mouth of the just will meditate on wisdom and his tongue will speak judgment' [Ps 37:28]. Many seek science, few seek conscience. And if it came to pass that conscience were sought with as great an effort and care as doubtlessly is expanded on vain and secular knowledge, it would be grasped more quickly and retained more fruitfully. For if one sought himself within himself close by himself, and searched by grace with himself as his teacher, what wonder if he be found? It would be surprising indeed if he could find anything in himself besides himself, unless by chance he grasped the image of God descended to his own soul through the working of grace. If this should happen, what would it be? What is the creative image in the created image, if not wisdom in the soul, glory in the conscience, sanctification in the ark? For, then the soul understands itself, then conscience is illuminated, then the knowledge of the heart is complete, then does the created image receive God in itself and itself in God by mutual exchange.

23. For this mingling of our soul and God's word, grace performs the duties of God's minister, so God wishes to be poured into us. Purity undertakes to prepare the soul, so the majesty of the word will

not refuse the heart's womb. Grace leads God to our guest rooms; piety sees to faithful obedience. Grace pours a glass for the guest once he is received; purity receives him as he comes. These are the things which give joy to the soul of the just, these are the things which produce a conscience pleasing to God, a conscience to be honored by angels and men, a conscience at peace and rest with itself.

24. These are the two olive trees and the two candelabra shining before the Lord. There are two olive trees: one by which that sublime eye of majesty is turned back with compassion for our miseries toward the deplorable sickness of our dunghill; the other by which the rotting scars of our innards are washed and the confused eye of our countenance receives treatment. Likewise, there are two candelabra: one by which the will of the divine good pleasure is suggested to our minds; the other by which the majesty of renumeration is already offered to the powers of our hope. Conscience which is thus clarified by the two olive trees and the two candelabra is good and solid and clear before God and men. It is good by simplicity, solid by charity, clear by chastity.

25. In order that I may provide you with an example of this condition of conscience, not subject to the error of idolatry but in the guise of very plain teaching, fix in your mind something which will both goad the mind to the piety of devotion and be a visible example to enkindle the soul to invisible contemplation. Imagine a table filled with a variety and abundance of different dishes. Put there a king crowned with his diadem and marked with every triumphal grandeur. Have him sit at the head in the first place, and let the group assisting and ministering be most solicitous with food and drink. Let there be gold and silver vessels for every purpose. Let there be drinks seasoned with honey. Let everything set there be responsive to the wish of his palate and stomach. Let cithara, lyre and psaltery refresh the ears of his companions with melodies. There are to be found there regal clothes; the dignified carriage of young men and youths; good manners; and in the entire household a consummate sense of what is correct arranges everything, even the smallest detail and the smallest movement. So, too, on every side there are tapestries or coverings fashioned with brocade and damasked weaving. A flowered couch, cedar paneling. What else? Let everything be arranged in perfect order, so that nothing is wanting in

elegance, nothing is superfluous or boring.

26. For the time being, however, let the most spacious and beautiful place, specially prepared for the queen and mistress of the house, remain empty. Perhaps occupied with something to do with lodgings, the queen delays the solemnities of the king by putting off her arrival. Meanwhile, everything — countenances and murmurings, both faces and sighs — expresses a strong desire that her seat be occupied. Finally there comes the woman at whose beauty the sun and moon are in awe, and as she sits down the doors are closed and the wedding feast has a full complement of guests. The mystical cases of scrolls thoroughly examined and now opened declare her name to the royal court: this lady is called 'Conscience'. While conscience seeks the place prepared from all ages [Ps 93:2] and sits in it, the voice of the Spouse is heard assuring the whole court about the bride: 'She is my one dove, the one daughter of her mother, the favorite of the one who bore her' [Sg 6:9]. Without doubt conscience is one because of oneness of faith and unchangeableness of purpose; she is a dove because of her gentle simplicity; she is the only daughter of her mother, because of the perfection of her charity; she is the favorite of her who bore her, because of the grace and beauty of her chastity.

27. Learning the tone of her beauty from her apparel interpreted typologically, I summarize her character in the following description, and in the variety of colors I distinguish all the parts of her virtues. She is of great stature because of her long-standing perseverance. She has emerald eyes because of the perpetual freshness of her chastity; she has a nose like the tower of Lebanon, which faces toward Damascus, because of her wise discernment of temptation's assaults; she has rosy cheeks because of compassion for her oppressed brothers; she has lips overflowing with honey and honeycomb because of the pleasantness of her mystical utterance; she has well-shaped hands, because of the perfect functioning of obedience; her breast is firm, because of unflagging vigilance against the harmful depredations of demons; the shoes of her feet are bronze and iron to batter the heads of dragons; a golden circle about her loins symbolizes restraint of desire's inclinations. She wears clothes which breathe the scent and fragrance of the myrrh of mortification, a drop of humility, and a dab of good reputation.

28. To turn our head back to the little wings of divine fear and final judgment, let us see how confident such a conscience is of her appearance and beauty when she comes to the judgment, not fearing any lack, because of the abundant sufficiency of her virtues; nor opinion, because of her marital union; nor shame and confusion, because of the embellishment of her clothes and her perfumes. The winter of cruel necessity is already quickly overtaking the outdoors. Then there can be no plowing through merit, no reaping a reward long since acquired. This winter will last for a long, rather an eternal period, during which there will be no begging for the support of any intercession. The closed door of mercy, which now lies open and opens wider until the end of time, will then be closed. Then all opportunity of escape, all possibility of defending oneself will be closed off. Only conscience will allay the misery of the poor, provided it has a way to fill its hand; only conscience will be able to furnish a refuge; only conscience will provide a barrier against terrified fear and the face of majesty.

29. When the fire of God's vengeance burns up heaven and earth, man will be rapt into the clouds and carried off instantly from his previous state into another condition and form. Then, if he has kept a pure and intact conscience, he will not fear the crashing of thunder, nor be dazed by flashes of lightning, be driven to flight by the angels' trumpets, be driven back by the lightning bolt of the ever-present, life-giving cross or by the majesty of the envisioned lamb having horns and eyes. The lion will roar and who will not be afraid [Am 3:8]. Leviathan or Satan will be loosed [Rm 9:14], who will be able to escape? Without doubt, the person who has adequately armed the keep of conscience. 'Woe, woe', will be heard on all sides, and who will boast of security? Precisely the person who has thought of war during peacetime, and the person who has wept when others were laughing. Just as everyone who had drained the Babylonian or golden cup of worldly indulgence down to the dregs of death will be drunk and vomiting, who will choose to drink the wine of sobriety with a clear head? Clearly, it will be those who censure the impulses of impurity and look to the purity of their conscience. 'Depart from me all you who do wickedness' [Lk 13:27], will be shouted out in a loud voice, and who will ascend to God so that his face may be illumined? Of course it will be the one who has not dirtied

his clothes [Rv 3:4] or who has at least washed them in the blood of the lamb [Rv 7:14] by true confession and complete contrition of heart. There will be no bread and water, and who will live without bread and water? Without doubt the person who leads a clean life and has a pure conscience. A good conscience has full storehouses, as it is written: "Nothing is lacking to those who fear God" [Ps 34:9]. A conscience which fears God has all the instruments of blessedness at its disposal.

30. It has the walkway of truth, the meadow or garden of delight [Gn 2:8], the well of the heart's depths. It has a place where it may sleep and rest in peace. It has the table of the altar, the temple of chastity, it has the hearth or oven of charity, the bath of confession, garments of satisfaction, the stole of immortality, the shoes of the imitation of God, the ring of eternity. What more can I say? It has a gorget, a neckpiece, barrettes to part its hair, anklets, headdresses, necklaces and many similar things, the interpretation of which provides excellent patterns for good character. Their perfection is fullness, so that as a rolling wheel on a chariot is turned around quickly by four horses with the impetus determined by the charioteer, so the Lord, by a superintending and ruling justice, directs the wheel of the soul to his will with the four horses of the principal virtues, that is, prudence, justice, fortitude and temperance. Certainly conscience, whose reins prudence pulls from the front, justice on the right, fortitude on the left, temperance in the back, with harmonized rather than discordant movement, is taken up to heaven, shouting and saying: 'Our way of life is in heaven' [Ph 3:20]. It is not enough for a good conscience to be in heaven, if it does not itself become heaven.

31. It is made into heaven through the indwelling of the Spirit of him who made heaven and earth, and who dwells in heaven. 'By the word of the Lord were the heavens made and by the word of his mouth all their strength' [Ps 33:6]. Truly these three, the Word, the Lord and the Spirit of his mouth create, strengthen and adorn the heaven of conscience. The Lord creates, the Word strengthens, the Spirit adorns. Yet, the Trinity together does these things, which by us and in us according to our various merits are distinguished singly. Whatever the Father does, the Son and Holy Spirit do simultaneously.

But, wait, having put a seal on the mystery of the Trinity, let us turn our attention to the trinity or arrangement of conscience.

32. The Lord creates conscience by fear of himself. The Word of the Lord strengthens conscience by wise instruction. The Spirit of his mouth adorns it with a variety of gifts. And note that there are here, as it were, three persons with different tasks: a servant who fears, a teacher who instructs, a friend who loves and shares everything with his friend. The Lord uses the servant, the teacher uses the word, the friend employs honor and gifts. The servant precedes the Lord, wisdom sends out its word, the friend sends a present ahead. Without a servant there is no master; without words there is no teacher; without a present there is no friend. The authority of the servant corresponds to the majesty of his lord, the teaching of the word corresponds to the wisdom of the teacher, the worth of the gift corresponds to the love of the friend. If the lord is great, his servant is faithful; if the teacher is wise, the words of his mouth are good; if the friend is loving, his gifts are beautiful, good and useful. The servant should acquire all his wealth for his lord. Any word of doctrine should confer honor on the teacher and utility on the disciple. Every gift should create reciprocity with a friend.

33. Conscience originates from fear, advances and proceeds by submission, and is perfected and completed in love. Unless conscience is afraid, it attempts or commits any sort of crime; unless it submits to the words of truth, it dissipates in the wind of pride and lying; unless it loves what should be loved, it is always being urged on with spurs and supported in its resolve. Fear lays the foundation; humble submission constructs the walls; lofty love puts on the roof. Or, just as certainly, fear arranges the framework of the building; submission puts on a coat of plaster; love adds the paint. The arrangement extends to shaping the material of one's thoughts, smoothing it down, and reducing it to the manner and form of justice. From the forest of our inclinations and fantasies, we are to select timbers which are suitable and adaptable to serve as good material for the construction of Solomon's temple. These are to be worked with the tool of discipline from the knowledge of rebukes.

34. Fear approaches all this like a good workman, so that it may arrange the material of thoughts received from the heart as from a

forest, now trimming away excess, now straightening out what is crooked, now fitting unequal pieces into parts having the same measurements, planing and joining beams, columns, panels and the rest of the structure. With the nails or dowels of the fear of God the prophet hoped to fasten the fabric of his structure together when he said: 'Fasten my body with your fear, that I may be afraid of your judgments' [Ps 119:120]. Enough about the arrangement which fear makes, which is, as it were, the creation of conscience, as was said above.

35. Next to be described is the plaster or compound of God's commandments, of which it says in the psalm: 'I have understood by your commands' [Ps 119:104]. When we hasten from fear to the commandments, it is as though we put a layer of plaster on the underlying framework. Also, the fulfillment of the commandments eases the harshness of fear aggravating the soul, using hope as a grout it brings low spots of imperfection to the eveness of unity and unanimity, and it inserts itself as a better bonding, as it joins rocks together without a hammer blow. Hence, also, it is written that in the temple of Solomon 'neither hammer nor axe were heard' [1 K 6:7]. Finally, it strengthens the things which were about to collapse, indeed as the Apocalypse says, those which were about to die. For without love and observance of the commandments whatever fear proposes is unstable. So Scripture says: 'Fear God and observe his commandments' [Qo 12:13]. Look, someone may be struck by fear because of his evil deeds and return to his heart. He weighs up the guilt and punishment of his crimes, he counts the stones of torments, and on these foundations he begins to construct the walls of penance and conversion. Thus, he at least put an iron skillet or a golden or brick wall between himself and the infernal city.

36. Someone who returns to himself and who changes his old errors to a new and better life, builds a wall of fired bricks (that is, of reformed morals) or of stones (that is, of former evils). Someone who opposes sure, stable and sturdy penitence to the destroying coals of eternal tortures, puts an iron skillet between himself and the city. But who is up to doing these things? Whose strength is like stone, whose flesh like bronze? In work and affliction, in many vigils, in hunger and thirst, in cold and nakedness, in the prison of the cloister,

in the struggle of flesh and spirit—who will not collapse, who will not give out, if the Spirit does not help our weakness, if power does not put out its hand?

37. Therefore the Lord says: 'Make peace with your adversary while you are still on the road, so he won't hand you over to the judge, and the judge hand you over to the torturer' [Lk 12:58]. On the road of effort and pilgrimage the word or fear of the Lord struggles against our lusts. We make peace with it when we fulfill the law of the commandments. You need not fear the judge if you fear the law. For according to the law the judge punishes those who break the law, not those who keep it. Observance of the law mollifies the judge. Someone who keeps the commandments reduces or plasters over fears and increases the strength of love and continence. So much for the plaster of the word, the compound of subjection. What follows deals with the painting of love.

38. The vibrant and true colors of charity do not express imaginary, or rather, fanatical images of birds, animals or snakes with the seal of God's image; instead, through the nerves and veins of the principal virtues, they sketch in the soul the likeness of the adoption of sons and grace by a restorative kind of painting. For love draws on the hard shell of an obstinate heart not with an iron stylus of fear, but rather with the little feather flying toward the love of Christ which exceeds our comprehension [cf. Eph 3:19]. What beautiful and elegant forms love knows how to paint! Charity paints a well-rounded and golden head on its statue, because it produces a pure and perfect intention; it adds a dove-like gaze for innocence; nicely shaped hands for almsgiving; a broad and upturned nose for the moderation of discretion; broad ears for obedience; full breasts for the abundance of grace; straight feet for the advance of mercy; the whole body full of eyes for purposeful circumspection.

39. Charity paints the triune God on the head, the suffering Jesus on the eyes, the book of the gospels on the ears, the scourging on the back, the lance in the side, the whole body stretched so that the bones can be counted, vinegar to drink, gall to taste, a crown of thorns on the head; it paints the body bound and stripped; it paints a blindfold over the face, the slaps, the dead body; then it paints him appearing in the garden to Mary Magdalene and conversing with

her; it paints him eating with the apostles, ascending into heaven, seated and reigning at the right hand of the Father; it depicts him coming openly for the judgment with great power and majesty, awesome for those on his left, amiable for those on the right. Notice charity's sculpture and picture. But from whence and of what sort are the colors by which the immaterial image of the soul is depicted so sublimely? Take note from where and how great the colors are, and you will be more deeply moved by the images delineated.

40. His blood is scarlet and red, his passion and death black, his resurrection green, his ascension hyacinth, his mortal life earthen, the distress of his continual struggle with men and evil spirits purple. Mark the colors. But where are the little containers, or rather, the horns in which his colors are kept? What horns contain the colors of justice, if not the horns of the just one, and what are the horns of the just one, if not just hearts? The one horn in which these are best stored is that small horn of humility of which Daniel says that 'it became great against the south and the east and force' [Dn 8:9]. Indeed, a humble conscience protrudes like a horn from the flesh, but it excels the flesh in strength, hardness and length. It becomes great against the south when it conquers the heat of harmful desire; it becomes great against the east when it conquers vapid vainglory; it becomes great against strength when it conquers any diabolic temptation of the devil. The great power of conscience showed on Moses' face, so that he was said to have horns, and the overflowing holiness of the lawgiver jolted back the eyes of the onlookers. It is to be understood that the pressure of fervent grace like that of new wine is not contained in the hearts of the saints by the weight of the flesh.

41. If the law ascends the mountain of the mind with grace, it will fill all the tables with a description of the commandments. As the letter or picture is consigned to the tablets for the information of minds or the pleasure of eyes, so the memory of heavenly goods is kept in the heart either for the merit of glory or the fortification of conscience itself. The merit of glory pertains to the conscience of the innocent, the fortification of conscience to the conscience of penitents. A good conscience is not found outside these two, whether through a failure either to stand fast in the good or to abstain from evil. Steadfast is the person who never flowed down into rivers and torrents of

criminal deeds, abstinent is he who shut out descents of wickedness. Steadfast is she who resembles a flower in the wind: if she sways, she does not fade away; if she is confused, still she does not fall. Abstinent is she who through penitence puts back on her wrist the loincloth of continence which had rotted among the Babylonians, who like Samson, after the shameful cutting away of her hair, that is, her virtues, in affliction and bitterness of spirit pulls down on her body the temple of the devil's mockery and illusions along with the vice-ridden people. There is steadfastness where there are the integrity of modesty, imitation of angelic purity, the illumination of divine splendor, the love of religion, and where all of life is a standing in the presence of God. There is abstinence where there are tears like bread day and night [Ps 42:3], where there are confession, full satisfaction for transgression of the law, conversion of the whole heart, the whole soul, the whole strength.

42. But notice that charity specifically paints steadfastness, and the law began to paint abstinence. For Moses was not able to restrain completely the evil impulses of the wicked people, but wishing at least to restrain them from uncontrolled anger he imposed the bridle of moderate revenge, that is, abstinence. He said: 'Pay an eye for an eye, a tooth for a tooth, a bruise for a bruise, punishment for punishment' [Ex 21:25]. These things do not pertain to the gentlest One, but they did pertain to the judge who, because of the hardness of the subject people, although he was able to command what attains the full and perfect good, allowed what made up for the injury done without altogether exceeding the limits of fairness. Hence it is written: 'You shall not make for yourself a statue or any likeness of something in heaven above or on earth below nor of the things in the water under the earth' [Dt 5:8].

43. The words of the law are to be pondered very carefully, because the painter's fingers must paint within the round circle of its approval. And first one should notice that the law does not teach what or how you should paint, it only prohibits what you should not paint. Perhaps this is because the law speaks to bring in the servant or disciple, while charity speaks to perfect or to send in the son. The law shows the vices of art, charity restores the knowledge and perfection of virtue. Therefore the law says: 'You shall not make a statue

for yourself, [Dt 5:8]. The historical sense of this commandment is to be observed to prevent our being preoccupied with those vanities or that tablet of the inward imagination, at the moment it should enter into contemplation, being found decorated with imaginary images from a likeness of shamelessness or any worldliness perceived in a sculpture of stone or wood or iron. For we do not prevail against this entanglement of the senses by any effort made at the time of prayer to free the wings of thought from the exceedingly tenacious deeply rooted birdlime of fantasies. For a statue served to restrict vision, vision shackled the senses, sensation allured one's thoughts and thereby stole consent, consent engraved the pleasing forms on the tablets of the imagination, practice and familiarity with such things so strengthened them with lasting persistence that they neither obey reason by leaving nor give in to zeal by yielding. Therefore, O good conscience, 'Do not make a statue for yourself, nor any likeness of something in the heavens above' [Dt 5:87].

44. Guarding the truth of faith, one should note the moral significance: the pretense of hypocrites who seek not the truth but only appearance. For they show themselves off as having the likeness of the sun in the clarity of their understanding and the likeness of the moon in the uprightness of their good name, and the likeness of the stars in the variety of their pious duties and titles. Hence, 'You are not to make for yourself any likeness of something in the heavens above', so you will be on your guard against hypocrisy, and all boasting and pride. 'Nor of anything on the earth below'; hence, the worm of avarice is crushed. For 'below' are all the things which oppress the soul with the weight of avarice and plunge it in the dissolution of wickedness. Hence the psalmist asks: 'Incline my heart to your testimonies and not in avarice' [Ps 119:36]. The text continues: 'nor of the things which are in the waters under the earth'. The desire of the flesh, which is referred to as waters, is here eliminated by the law. Notice also that the law prohibited not just the reality of these things, but even their likeness. So we are to abstain not only from every evil, but also from every appearance of evil [1 Th 5:22]. We have heard the teaching of the law regarding what is not to be carved, and in this we have learned to abstain, that is, to turn from evil. Now let us again pay attention to what is to be painted by steadfastness in our souls, when charity guides the stylus.

Let love paint first, so that as it paints, we may have before our eyes the outlines and traces and points of the righteousness which is to be formed in us. This will keep us from wandering off aimlessly. In short, it paints such forms that by the sight of them, by the warmth conceived by faith, our souls receive various offspring by the fruit-fullness of their graces.

45. Thus Jacob peeled off pieces of the bark of some poplar and almond branches and placed them at watering time in view of animals in heat. In a wonderful way the soul inebriated by drink from the chalice of our redemption is aroused toward the embraces of her husband and made pregnant with the offspring of imitation of Christ's passion. Therefore, O priest, raise your eyes and look at the picture of Christ's charity, which is placed in front of you specially, and the reforming image of Him dying on the cross, that without the corruption of flesh and spirit you may strive to conceive offspring who will make up for the labor of the person carrying them and reveal the poverty of the offerer. Take the speckled and spotted upon yourself [cf. Gen 30:39] in the accusation of confession; return the white and black to your benefactor for the sake both of the sacrament of his wholly untainted conception and of the labor of his most cruel passion. What is white is to be paid him who did not see corruption, what is black is to be paid him who through the passion passed from this world to the Father. These monochrome things are to be rendered to him who is always the same by those whose life, like the moon, varies with uncertainty and never stays the same because of mutability's modification.

46. Yet we are to retain some kinds of variety with a clear conscience — such as those the apostle mentions: to one is given wise speaking, to another speaking with knowledge, to another faith in the same spirit, to another different kinds of tongues, to another the interpretation of discourses [cf. 1 Co 12:8]. The presence of these charismata should not be hidden from our foolish minds, for by our life under their wings we contemplate their going and coming in the mirror of conscience. We should accompany their departure in ashes and sackcloth and leave the bedroom of carnal delights, promising satisfaction for errors if they will return. On their return we should call our friends and neighbors together and declare a solemn day.

Then we may sacrifice a fatted calf (that is, the unruly movement of body and heart) and tune musicians in exultation of heart. Always going over the state of the interior man in the mirror of conscience, I tell you, we may make whiter than snow what seems brown and murky, by repeated use of lye and fullers' earth ourselves. We may say with the psalmist: 'You will sprinkle me, O Lord, with hyssop and I shall be clean; you will wash me and I will be whiter than snow' [Ps 51:7]. The soul which is without a mirror does not know itself.

47. Conscience is the clean, clear and unsoiled mirror of the whole religious way of life. A woman who wishes to please her husband or boyfriend arranges the prettiness and beauty of her face by looking at her image in a mirror. So, too, the soul retraces and understands in the tablets of conscience how she was adorned by the image of truth and how she receives the traces of her Creator's image. Clearly, I have not compared conscience to a mirror or to tablets ill-advisedly: it is like a mirror, because in it the form of the face expressed is interpreted to itself by just a glance of the eyes; it is like tablets, because all the impulses of the soul are depicted on them without the sound of a voice, and because what slippery memory might lose in a flood of forgetfulness is made permanent even for all the ages of the world with the aid of tablets. Similarly, the soul uses its conscience as a mirror for present things; as for past things, like a tablet it faithfully preserves the past things which flowed away in the course of time, but did not slip through the nets of conscience. Therefore, if the soul in its present state has recourse to conscience, it will be able to apprehend clear-sightedly in a mirror both what is honorable and what is dishonorable in itself.

48. If, in fact, the soul has inquired about what it was like, although now it may have altered its mental outlook, the tablets of memory should be gone over and whatever it wrote badly or well earlier in its life should be reread in an orderly way, and from the meaning of the reading it should gather the shape of its way of life. Therefore, read about your childhood in the book of your memories. But if the deeds of your childhood happen to have disappeared by being destroyed in the flood of slippery time, accept a model of this stage of life from others. Thus you may recognize yourself in another, and you may gather from the acts of other infants whom you see what and

of what sort were the deeds of your infancy. For we do not easily remember that age which, so to speak, in the course of our lives preceded the light of discernment.

49. Certainly the eye of reason here illuminates the mirror of conscience in which we may catch a glimpse of the image of God by means of a created image. According to the measure of its ability, it takes both outlines into equal account, that of the created image and that of the uncreated image, if one may speak this way. We realize that the lineaments of that eternal majesty, ineffably beyond all understanding, extend from one end to the other [Ws 8:1]. Their beginning has no beginning, their end has no end. From this let us understand nothing else than the eternity of God, which precedes all ages of the world and remains after all ages. We attribute intelligible, measurable lineaments to the soul in regard to both place and time, for the soul is not simultaneously everywhere nor does it exist forever. It can, however, make good the narrowness of its imperfection. To do so it needs to be able to expand to the measure of the full stature of Christ [Eph 4:13], the length, breadth, depth and height of the cross, in the fullness of charity, long-suffering, humility and the anticipation of heavenly desire. By these measurements the members of our soul are somehow made equal to the conforming divine image, so that the soul may make up for its imperfection with God's real perfection and complete its deficiency with God's fullness. Once the soul's ruins have been restored by the divine aid and the expensive costs paid out in Christ's human life, we must arrange, prepare, and decorate the bed of conscience within it for King Solomon whose face the whole world desires [cf. 1 K 10:24].

50. We propose to deal with conscience and to indicate at least feebly in what a good conscience consists. I intend to present in writing this, not all the things which are suitable for the disposition or preparation of a good conscience, but, with God's help, only those things which are necessary and without which it is false and deceitful to call a conscience good.

51. A good conscience lays down as its foundation the triune God, three in persons, one in essence. Shunning reckless discussion and expanding the veneration of faith, the faithful soul worships, adores and venerates this triune God, preaches him even at the cost of shedding

her blood, follows and loves him. The faithful soul worships his good deeds, adores his majesty, venerates what is hidden, preaches what is revealed, follows in heart, word and deed the examples of his mercy, and loves with all her heart, soul and strength the depths of the riches of God. That there are existence, life, knowledge, breath and hope, she attributes entirely to him.

52. Humbly and reverently, with fear and trembling, she inquires of him what God is and what a human being is, not in order not to be puffed up with knowledge, but to be built up in her conscience. Whenever a door is opened to her as she knocks, she thanks God; whenever she slow-wittedly denies subtle or sublime truths, she humbly blames her ignorance and weakness; she is eager to seek God, not to argue about him. She asks to see God's face, not to define his incomprehensibility. She rejoices if she finds what satisfies faith. She limits the pace of her inquiry, if she retreats into the darkness of her den or rests in God's wisdom.

53. Finally, when she has beheld him running along his paths and ours in the works of our creation and restoration, she follows in the footsteps of his servant. If, in fact, her Head returns into the clouds, she goes after him by sight, rather than on foot, by desire rather than by bodily walking. Until that Man returns for his work of judgment, she keeps watch, alert and devout, at his doorway. The entry and exit or return of God is especially attributed to the person of the Son, who through the incarnation of the Word went out from the Father and came into the world and ascended again to the Father through the glorification of the ascension and thus left the world, by bodily presence rather than in the power and essence of the Word.

54. The conscience which wishes to construct the tower or framework of her life on this foundation lays down and fearlessly builds up diamond, crystal, gold quartz, and every other kind of precious stone [cf. Rv 21:19], insofar as one virtue joined to and resting upon another provides a purple ascent to the golden place of rest, where the lover is joined to her beloved and made one flesh, one soul, one spirit with him, never afterwards to be parted from him. When conscience has been lifted up and is intent upon these contemplations, what does it do, or say, or wish? Without doubt it is concerned lest through its own fault it be deprived of so delightful a spectacle; it

prays to be transfered from its dark prison to such well-lighted dwellings; it wishes to dwell in the house of the Lord all the days of its life, so that it may see the joy of the Lord [cf. Ps 27:4] and remain in God's courts. Three things work together to constitute a pure, holy, devout and sound conscience: good action, prolonged prayer, and a burning desire for God. It is clear and obvious what constitute good action, prolonged prayer and burning desire. Nevertheless, since the present work is intended not only for trained minds, but also for those who are less quick to understand, let us glance at some of the things connected with good action.

55. Fraternal obedience and daily manual labor, which are performed in the cloister or in the fields as different times and needs dictate, grow out from the root of good action. Even more are almsgiving, visiting the sick, consoling the disconsolate, supporting widows, receiving paupers and pilgrims, defending the oppressed, and similar activities branches of this tree of life, not of death; it is called good action. Ultimately, good action fosters in its breast and womb everything which pertains to the manifestations of the spirit, everything which expresses a declaration of charity by evident signs. So that a work may be genuine and pure, one should be on guard against every spattering of the old yeast, the heart should be corrected of every itch and foulness of evil desire, the body should be restrained from all leprous uncleanness. For evil burns down the forest of goodness, sexual desire corrupts the harvest of chastity, indulgence or uncleanness banishes the verdant vigor of uprightness and good reputation.

56. Notice by what resistances the firmness of good action is shaken until it is overthrown. Moreover, since ancient times the devil, the inventor and instigator of evil, has drawn from the quiver of his wickedness many other subversive contrivances to assault the good works of man, and with new plans he never stops filing his arrowheads on the anvil of his treachery. He brandishes the weapons he has already made when he shoots the darts of temptation; he thinks up new ones when he has been rebuffed, bellowing that he has been tricked by the prudence, fortitude, justice and temperance of the saints. Then he blocks the stream of his wickedness in his nostrils and renews his efforts with a more venemous and vehement puff, making

the coals burn hot and the depths of the sea seethe. Then he regards a sword like chaff and bronze like rotten wood. Then the bowmen will not rout him, and the sling stones could be straw as far as he is concerned [cf. Jb 41:12, 22, 18–19]. Then how dangerous and difficult it is to wander through the streets of his palace without the shield and breastplate of divine protection. It is better to meet a mother bear whose cubs have been taken away than to meet Satan when he is so exasperated like this and indignant with anger.

57. What will you do, then, O good conscience? Will you safely rejoice over your triumph, or will you tremble uncertainly in the face of the adversary's savage madness? You should combine both, so that, on the one hand you will not be groundlessly elated over a victory, for the battle may still be renewed from the rear, and so on the other hand, you will not be thrown into confusion by cowardly fear of a snarling enemy who is already practically conquered, for he who granted you the earlier victory still has his hand stretched out to help. You should be secure, but in the help of the Creator; you should be suspicious, but because of your weak body. You conquer through God; you are conquered on your own. Thus the angel in the book of Revelation [cf. Rv 10:2] has his right foot on the land and his left foot on the sea, so that he may trust confidently in God but tremble uncertainly about himself. This conscience says: 'With my mind I serve the law of God, but with my flesh I obey the law of sin' [Rm 7:25]. This state of conscience is moderate. It keeps in front of it the saying: 'I did not know sin, if the law had not told me: you shall not covet' [Rm 7:7]. It keeps behind it the other saying: 'Death has been swallowed up in victory', and so on [1 Co 15:54]. Concerning these states of conscience something should be said, and there should be some benefit from what is going to be said.

58. One state of conscience is good, another bad, another moderate or intermediate. Since the things that are said seem to pertain to the intermediate state, let us see what it is. There is a certain intermediate state of conscience which occurs when the soul hurries immediately from the confession of errors and the deep abyss of vices toward the light of the truth which is to be acknowledged and, having put off the old man, gives evidence of the change effected in it by the newness of its way of life as well as by its clothes. As long as

reason slumbered the barque of conscience in the world was shaken by the troughs of the sea, so that the prow of leading counsel was buffeted by the blows of carnal impulses, and the stern of reasoned judgment was dashed in a collision with dangerous rocks, that is, temptations which rise up frequently. The whole perimeter of the soul was spun around in a single gyration into a deep failure. My point is that sometimes a life sunk under a load of evil habits does not reflect either on God's judgments or on his benefits in order to stop its evil actions. Instead, as a boat is filled drop by drop from the hold up to its deck with flooding waters, and immediately afterwards sinks with all its cargo, since there is no one who restrains the treacherous waves of concupiscence, so too the soul which has no law, which is not under a rule, is carried into the pit of damnation after she has committed sin.

59. For the apostle says of this state: 'Once I lived without a law' [Rm 7:9]. What, then, O holy apostle? When you lived without a law did you live without sin? You did not know concupiscence, except that the law said: 'You shall not covet'. Therefore, how did you sin, if you did not covet, and how did you covet, if you did not know concupiscence? This is really amazing, if it ever happens: to covet and not know concupiscence. Clearly such is the case. The apostle, when he lived without the law, both coveted and did not know concupiscence. He says it himself: 'I did not know concupiscence, except the law said: You shall not covet' [Rm 7:7]. Yet, who can doubt that he was not without sin, although he was without law, especially since it is a very similar thing to be under sin and to be without law? The apostle adds that sin had also existed before the law, but was dead; that is, hidden, as blessed Augustine explains [Sermon 153.7. 9; PL 38:830]. So there was sin, but it was hidden. It was hidden, but it was a goad. It was hidden from outward knowledge; it was not hidden from inward movement. It moved one's members to covet, but it did not show what it was or where it came from. The law made clear where it came from, what it was, and how much harm it caused, but the law could not remove it. So a worldy man accustomed to the worldly customs and movements under the old law does not know the limits of justice. He thinks it enough not to kill, not to commit adultery, not to steal. When the greater and weightier commandments of the new law are

violated, they bring death, but even if they are observed they do not by themselves bestow life. The law is not sufficient both to take away sin and confer life. It is already a great deal for the law not to occasion death. If the law is observed, it does not take away death, but its surpreme benefit is not to occasion it. Grace comes in addition to the law and takes away death and confers life. If the conscience of worldly people has not sinned mortally and criminally, then, even if it has not done noteworthy deeds for God, it thinks that by the works of the law it has seized the citadel of happiness. Such a conscience is undoubtedly inadequate. It is good because it draws back from evil, but it is sick and wanting because it does not do the good fully, and it is lacking in discernment because it does not understand the goal toward which it should be striving. For the construction of a good conscience it is necessary that the centrepost of the mind be discerning, prudent, just, strong and modest. When a good conscience is firmed up by this squared off stability, it is not spun around or shaken or overturned by any raging storm of impulses. But, let us hear what the apostle says about a good conscience.

60. 'This is our glory', he says: 'the testimony of our conscience' [2 Co 1:12]. How strictly must every religious weigh in a judicial appraisal his every thought, act and word, since he knows the scales of divine examination wait behind every word, act, and thought. By a habitual preliminary he must get used to the calculations of the final reckoning, and, as it were, endure the head of the household's insistence about rendering an account of the administration entrusted to him, so that by practice and habit he may prepare himself to be more ready and fit, a good and prudent servant, in settling those accounts which put an end to the necessities of service and pay out the reward for obedience. He needs to establish a fair quantity or weight for each of his actions, words and acts, if he wishes to guard himself from an error in his calculations and from the penalty of the steward whose master received an unfavorable report because he had squandered his goods. So let the authority of the superior freely arrange controls, lest he incline right judgment toward the left through hatred or turn it toward the right through favoritism. Let him prudently notice what is the weight of the blameworthy things in his subjects which keep the left hand of judgment on the left, and

similarly what is the weight of those things which fill the purse of the right hand with worthy reward. Let him accept the measured amounts, lest he force the things which are being reckoned up to deceive and give a false reckoning which undermines judgment. Beyond a doubt, the things which make a good conscience pertain to the right, and the things which make a bad conscience pertain to the left.

61. But let us find out where a good conscience comes from and what affords the opportunity for the apostle's words: 'This is our glory, the testimony of our conscience'. Fear of future judgment, the pressure of the present world, the instability and brief span of momentary prosperity, shame at eternal embarrassment, the anticipation of endless joy, the presence of the glory of the face of God in the holy mind—these serve to prepare a good conscience. Fear produces anxious care, pressure produces grief, brief prosperity produces disdain, shame makes one circumspect, expectation produces desire, the presence of God produces forgetfulness of present things. Anxious care shakes up sluggishness, grief tempers immoderation, disdain humble pride; circumspection fortifies lack of caution, desire ignites the lukewarm, forgetfulness of present things buries concupiscence. Finally, when a sluggish mind is aroused in this way it runs like a deer to fountains of water; a sorrowing mind consoles itself by reading the Scriptures; a humbled mind grasps inscrutable and secret mysteries; a fortified mind ridicules the ferocity of the demons; a mind afire sends up [as incense] the dense cloud of its affections to the holy of holies; a mind which is burying concupiscence displays on its limbs the armor of justice in order to receive God into itself and to transport itself into God.

62. Glory and riches are in this house of conscience [Ps 112:3], but what glory and what riches? The glory which comes only from God, the glory which the angel makes resound on high, the glory by which the saints are justified in the world and blessed in heaven, the glory which brings not pride but excellence, the glory with which the Son of Man is crowned, the glory by which the face of Moses is radiant, the glory which does not consume the burning bush, the glory which filled the house of the Lord when the temple of Solomon was completed, the glory of which it is said: 'Blessed is the glory of

God in his dwelling place' [Ezk 3:12], the glory which is the only true glory, glorifying and glorified. Then after glory come the riches of salvation which moths do not touch, riches which avarice does not heap up, riches which are not the mammon of iniquity but a desirable treasure, riches which fill not the purse but the affections, riches which increase as they are distributed, which wither when they are not shared. By use virtues are not consumed but rather consummated. When they are paid out, they do not become sparse. They are useful when they approach many or all people; they are useless if they stay within their own walls seeking only what is their own.

63. Therefore, a good conscience does not just seek what is its own, nor does it hide the fire of grace under the waters of avarice, as one reads about the altar fire in the book of Maccabees [2 M 1:19]. A good conscience sends out good examples through its neighbors' streets. It bestows its glory and riches not with ostentatious pride, like that Hezekiah displayed when he showed the royal treasures to the Babylonian messengers, but with a feeling of piety, as in the gospel the businessman at table counts out with interest to money changers of morals and virtues. In your conscience the conscience of another is built up when, drawn and touched by the good odor of your good reputation, he knocks at your door seeking bread for his journey, to restrain sinful desires, to prick the stubborn poisons of obstinacy, to improve the bad inclinations of former habits. For the cities to which the Lord gives no rain run to the one to which he gives an early and a late rain, that is, a conscience looked after by God in timely fashion and perfectly healed. The conversion of conscience put off till old age receives a late, rather than an early, rain. A conscience which God brings about at a young age or during youth receives an early rain. If the latter conscience, having made a good beginning does not continue on this course all the way to the end, it received an early rain from the Lord but not a late one. If only we may receive an early rain by beginning better things well and in good time, and may add a late rain by finishing with a good end the things we began well.

64. We need to look at humility which is the foundation of conscience. A good conscience does not neglect to dig out and clear away

every layer of presumption down to the bedrock of perfect humility. From every source it collects and sews together the rags of the poverty of a nature which is exceedingly shattered and weakened. It does this not to conceal the shame of its disorder from the sight of divine mercy, which condemns hidden things and absolves those which are exposed, but so that when the mass of penalty and guilt has been lumped together it may anxiously bemoan its misery, be more alert against faults, and more humbly invoke the help of grace. After its memory has been laid out flat on the bedrock of humility, conscience empties the hollow of memory to the marrow and from each vein of the inward man it draws up into the area of the mouth the rank humors of all evils, so that through the vomiting of confession any discharges and phlegm of corruption heavy on the chest may be expelled by suitable purgation. If the sorts of things that should be purged are eliminated, it comforts the tried and they, that is, the penitents, get well.

65. Meanwhile, it is necessary to rest from the burden and shock of such a treatment, for fear conscience should want to get up right away before an induced sleep or, once it returns again to its senses, presume that it is justified without any penance. The tender soul is to be restored in its new life by a gentle regimen, if I may put it that way. It is not to be forced immediately to proceed further in the Order's observance. Some of the highest and greatest structures of the Rule should not be imprudently imposed on the beginner. One should take account of the fragility which accompanies newness, the difficulty of renewing the mind, the labor involved in appropriating customary behavior and changing oneself.

66. The Lord led his people out of Egypt into the promised land with discretion. Surely it is with the same kind of guidance that the soul is to be led from the old darkness of errors to the new light and life of holiness. The Lord spoke in Exodus about the nations (typifying the vices), who impeded him from giving the land to his people, the holy nation. He says: 'I will not expel them from your sight in a single year, so that the land will not be reduced to a waste and the wild animals increase against you. I will send them out of your sight gradually, until such time as you increase and possess the land' [Ex 23:29]. These things that are said to have happened by the Lord's

dispensation are to be related to the law for novices. For if the Lord did not avoid using dispensations, although he had no need for them — for dispensation always implies some difficulty of time, activity or person — then why should human beings, why should superiors refuse the necessary dispensations, since a dispensation is never useless when it leads to a better and more fruitful recompense?

67. We must water, trench, prune and fortify the tender religious life in our novices, until it is firmly rooted underneath and bears fruit above, until it recovers the years eaten by the locust, that is, by former wickedness. In our nature, deprived of the better space and happier place of its creation, it is ineffective to eliminate old habits and establish eternal laws in one fell swoop of renewal. Therefore, the Lord, the ruler of spiritual beings, adapts some things to others. He takes into account not the rules of eternity, but the limits of human possibility with its variations over the course of time. He certainly bends the rigors of events and future occurrences toward nature's frailty, so human fragility is not hacked apart in a clash between the oppressive demands of the times and the needs of people. Things which in their time are squared off within suitable limits happen safely. In the books of Maccabees it says expressly that when Judas Maccabeus was fighting, time was on his side [1 M 12:1]. When someone begins to do a thing and time is against him, he will be kept from finishing it or will finish it only with difficulty.

68. Thinking about time and the timeliness of things to be done, the Lord said: 'I will not expel them', that is, the enemies, 'from your sight in a single year', and so on. Renewed battles could have arisen from victory, if, once the human inhabitants were destroyed, ferocious beasts had invaded the desolate forests unhindered, since deadly forests encroached on a land devoid of inhabitants. Whenever a land is desolate, the deserted area is quickly occupied by trees and woods. A more brutal hardship would threaten, if there were conflict with wild animals. It is better to wage war with a rational, than with an irrational foe, with a man rather than with a beast. Similarly, it is more useful to fight with men than with demons, with persons rather than with perversity. In short, our blockade is more treacherously assailed by the kinds of vices which yield to no reason or authority, than by those whom we rout by reason and contradict by authority.

69. We should argue and wage war with some evil spirits; from others we should flee and with them never join battle. Hence, the apostle says: 'Flee fornication' [1 Co 6:18]. And elsewhere: 'Resist the devil and he will flee from you' [Jm 4:7]. Certainly the outcome of the skirmish is doubtful, if you choose to dispute about chastity with a licentious woman, a deceiving mind. You will have to answer both the law of the members which fights against the law of the mind [Rm 7:23], and the allurements to the eye with which the sight of prostitutes bedazzles the breast of fools, and the verbal torches which occupy the whole forest of thoughts and desires. A licentious woman is a deep and hidden pit. You fall in even in retreat, and even while avoiding it, you go astray if not in deed at least in thought. These sorts of things are to be checked by a deputation sent to stall them, or they are to be avoided with the aid of flight. The vice of impatience, however, is not conquered in this same way, that is, by taking away matters requiring patience, but by diligently calling upon the practice and power of the mind. So, too, pride is conquered by experience and a comparison of human weakness; envy, by repeated reminders of one's heavenly task and service; gluttony, by fasting and abstinence from food. So, in short, each kind of vice, once overthrown by its contrary, is struck down and strangled.

70. The prudent master of novices must instruct newcomers inexperienced in mystical speech about their weapons and train them for war, so that each one may embrace religious fervor according to his age, makeup, and strength, lest he think that in one breath he can hurry through the course which Jesus, proceeding with patience and long-suffering, ran and completed in thirty-three years. Those who do not head patiently toward predestined goals, but grasp at the traps of presumption, are affected by tedium rather than by desire. They are more compliant to the movements of stealthy duplicity than to the warnings of superior and elders. Just like a dog which abandons the tracks of a hare and runs here and there ruining the trail and working apart from the rule dictated by the objective expends a great deal of energy to no advantage, so the novice, disdaining the teaching of his master and following the willful laws of his own heart, does not catch the little hare which is his objective, who is Christ, humble in his bodily state and fearful of dogs and the horns of

unicorns [Ps 22:20–21]. Christ came to do not his own will, which was certainly good, but the will of him who sent him, which earned for him the merit of obedience. The little hare advanced by not veering to the right in prosperity, or turning to the left in adversity. O good novice, if you go to the east by working, keeping vigil and praying over and above your law, more than your master wishes, you will not find him; for you are too far away and he is on this side, for he did not exceed the bound of obedience but died in obedience. Again, if you veer to the west by not rising to the levels set out by the fathers, but by acting half-heartedly, by living negligently, you will not grasp him. You are falling short, and he is beyond you, since he ran the way of God's commandments all the way to death, even death on a cross [Ph 2:8].

71. Do not, therefore, step off the road, do not extend your course to the other side, do not bring your mind to a stop on this side. In the first case, you are wrong; in the second, presumptuous; in the third, lazy. Error leads into a measureless expanse; presumption, to the pit; laziness, to banishment. Error is in darkness; presumption in a deadly flash of light; laziness squeaks under a heavy load. A person in error runs in circles; a presumptuous person is snatched by the wind; a negligent person is stoned with ox dung [cf. Si 22:2]. A person in error is like a drunk; a person who is presumptuous is like a madman; a person in the throes of laziness is like an idler swinging exhaustedly on a hinge. Someone who has been turned back like the Jordan and is annoyed with his conversion errs; someone who stretches his wings upward too soon in his conversion by acting beyond his strength is convicted of presumption; someone who is enervated by lethargic sleep and does not keep watch on time in the light of the common observance is condemned for laziness. Therefore, do not rush to the other side through vain glory, nor stay on this side through idleness, nor jump down outside through stupidity.

72. The prophet says you will become known in the midst of two animals [Hab 3:2, Old Latin]. Always keep to the middle, because he is the middle, Jesus Christ, the mediator of God and men [1 Tm 2:5]. This, dear soul, pertains to the discernment of a good conscience by which she parts the hair of her actions and movements and smooths out everything she has with a level surface. Therefore, once conscience

has arranged her head, either she never renounces her locks, according to the law for Nazarites, through the loss resulting from cooled fervor or, if she finds her hair too heavy, she cuts it three times a year, but not without weighing it, following the example of Absalom, who cut his hair and weighed it [2 S 14:26]. She cuts the golden locks of her head three times a year if she multiplies consciousness of the law in her heart by extracting scriptural meditations from the historical, allegorical and moral senses.

73. At this point she reaches the state of conscience where she is embellished not so much by bodily adornment as by spiritual and invisible ornament. The clothes of conscience should not be fancy, because that feast day has not yet arrived on which all her dirty clothes will be taken away, when this mortal being will have passed into immortality and a tiara will be placed on her head. Let her clothes not be overly shabby through the dark life of faith, because she has sprinkled their pure woolen cloth with the blood of the passion and whitened them with the clay of the altered body with the glory of the resurrection. The apostle says: 'If we knew Christ according to the flesh, we know him so no longer' [2 Co 5:16]. Let this clothing be ivory, set with sapphires, so that it may be a body of chastity, that it may be a beautiful, chaste generation with charity. Let the house be ivory through purity and decorated with sapphire through heavenly grace. For, as the apostle says: 'Some have glory, but not before God' [Rm 4:2]. Someone who glories in having a chaste heart, but from himself and not from God, has glory in his own eyes but not in God's. For what is it to attribute the grace of chastity to oneself except to keep a jewel in a rotten manure pile? In its sordid beauty a conscience without God is filthier than a manure pile. Therefore, whenever you expel God from yourself by presuming on your own self, if you have pretended to any purity, from the glory of the flesh you have generated in the flesh abominable rottenness. The appearance of virtue combined with the reality of presumption soils the mind worse than naked treacherous temptation. Do you wish to see conscience in regal clothes, so that even the king desires her elegance and beauty? The psalmist says: 'The queen stood at your right hand in a golden garment, surrounded with variety' [Ps 45:9].

74. We divide the kinds of consciences as follows. Claustrals have one kind of conscience, worldlings another. Similarly, one conscience belongs to those who deserve ill and is called infernal. Another conscience belongs to those who deserve well and is termed heavenly. There are some others around: about them we will say something after examining these. Meanwhile, let us first turn our attention to the conscience of claustrals.

75. As a furnace tests gold, so the cloister tests the conscience of claustrals. For from the devil's envy arises an ever more violent temptation of the flesh, from restful quiet a more forceful stirring of passion, and from the prohibition of forbidden desire, fiercer insult. The spiteful king of Babylon especially increases the forces of temptation on the sabbath of the saints with any kindling he finds available, that he may strip the flesh from the men of desires and reduce it to ashes. In the kingdom of confusion the proud person blushes if anyone floats who does not adore and worship the statue of his vanity and malice. He rages still more bitterly because a few disregard the idolatrous public decrees of prostration, or rather prostitution, and spurn the common law, obeying truth rather than custom, attentive to the religion of the few rather than to the error of the many. He is surprised that the Israelite captives act more bravely in a foreign kingdom than do his people in their own homeland. For even in captivity freedom of spirit contradicts the rule of impiety. In the land of confusion every native is bent over in subjection to sin, every free man bows before justice.

76. So, once the devil has collected twigs of evil and wickedness from all around, he lights the furnace of temptation, where he brings together some things to stir up ignited desire, other things to foment evil already begun, still other things to strengthen an evil resolve and drag it out still longer. He brings together hemp and twigs and green branches for the burning of the innocent: hemp ignites quickly, but it also burns down quickly; twigs and pitch spread the edge of the fire upward; green branches nourish it in their breast for a long time and take care of the smoke and heat of the lighted hearth. Nebuchadnezzar used these three kinds of fire to burn up the royal boys with handsome faces, who were unfamiliar with the royal food [Dn 1:15]. There were our young men whose way of life was

suspect to him because of religious differences, but admirable nonetheless; because it was pure and above reproach, it never stopped insinuating itself and warning against worshipping his statue, when he presented the glory of the world, when he urged the pleasure of the flesh, when he instilled greed for gold and silver.

77. By the common law of human weakness, he generally tempts our hermits and claustrals in these matters, but he adds something special because of the singular struggle and more excellent crown of their holy vow and intention. Without doubt he rages heart and soul. The venom of malice serves as arms for the destruction of those who rebel against him. He multiplies new and meticulous plans; he opposes the shields and breastplates of new assaults and struggle, in order to avoid the spears of prayer and the arrows of confession. Finally, he hinders the purity of the penitent's confession and his intention to confess, either by the infection of pretence or by cutting away something so it is no longer complete. What swords does he use for this? The swords of shame, fear, presumption and envy. Shame amputates the intestines and genitals of confession, thereby subtracting from the sacrifice for the Lord. Fear amputates tongue and arms, presumption, the head, envy, the feet.

78. For anyone who, because of shame, does not mention the rottenness of his sin also, as it were, keeps a store of wickedness in himself, as long as in his confession he hides from his superior the occasion of sin and the opportunity of sinning, unless by chance it had been taken away from him. This is the way a person acts who offers money without a purse, when without such a container the money cannot be taken away. O greedy confession! You pay your money when you express your sin, but why do you then act fraudulently about the purse? For handing over the purse also pertains to settling and paying off the debt. If you are stealing the purse, why pay the debt? Get full credit for yourself, so that you pay everything and keep nothing back. Show the Lord the dead Lazarus, show him the tomb of the already decaying body. Do not be ashamed to open up your shame. To whom? To the ridicule of someone who defames you in the streets? No, but to a doctor, a guardian, a consoler, a person who will keep it quiet and lament with you. So much for shame.

79. But if shame acquiesces to our advice and stretches out the hand of confession, then, another member of the wicked assembly,

worldly fear, will contradict this good decision, to stop us from confessing all our sins to the Lord and to our superior. This fear says: 'I do not want to confess my evils to my superior. For he is cruel and strict. He tortures those who confess to him by assigning excessive penance, by inflicting severe abstinence, and by imposing heavy and unbearable burdens' [Mt 23:4]. This fear is resisted by the evangelical wedge which drives out fear of temporal punishment with a consideration of eternal evil. One key forces out the other, the large one forces out the small one, the strong one forces out the weak one. O penitent, if you are afraid of fasting, you should be afraid of an eternal fast more than one a day long, a sterile more than a fertile fast, a dead more than a vital fast. This fast is temporary; it is not eternal, fruitless or lethal. Its end is advantageous, profitable, salutary. By contrast, the eternal fast has no end, no fruit, no utility.

80. Similarly in other punishments, all the evils of the world are, as it were, the positive degree, which does not admit of comparison with future things, because in that allocation of eternal misery are established in the superlative of sorrow and duration the penalties which are paid back to each in proportion to his merits. It is pleasanter to receive unpleasant things in confession for our sins, evils assigned here by positive decree for the remission of sins, as Lazarus was exposed to the tongues of dogs, rather than to wait with the rich man for the superlatives of a merciless future judgment. The mercy of God, with the patience with which it now awaits the repentance of sinners, here lays down its positive decree which is wholly concerned with mercy, remission and absolution. But, the judgment which will be merciless for a person who did not act mercifully will be dealt entirely in the superlative of an irrevocable sentence, with power, majesty and irrevocable condemnation. After this superlative there are no comparatives. Once passed, the sentence is not later rescinded. This real fear should really be feared. Otherwise, in the present, that is, in confession, someone may be afraid to confess where there is nothing to fear. For in confession you ought to fear the wrath of God, not that of a superior; the punishment of the soul, not that of the body; eternal condemnation not temporal affliction. Note this also about fear; it made the tongue of the sinner stick to the roof of his mouth, so that he acted mute and did not accuse

himself. He tied up the arms of his sins, indeed he cut them off, so that like Dagon dead in his sins before the ark of the Lord's covenant [1 S 5:3–4] that is, before the priest, he constituted himself a sinner. As a result he did not hold to the example of Christ's cross, he did not attain pardon for himself and ask for it with extended hands, that is, by displaying all his evils.

81. Once this fear has been removed, there remain the battles with presumption. The origin of this presumption is marked by a noble splendor, but it is disfigured in its shoots and branches. It is born from the indestructible treasury of divine goodness, but the sweetness of the root turns bitter in the branches. For it is good to hope — not to presume — in the Lord; to hope in the mercy extended to those to be forgiven through penance, not to presume for evils hidden and held back through stubbornness; to hope humbly not to presume obstinately; to hope if one has confessed, not to presume if one has continued in sin. For it is just as bad to despair of repentance after confession as it is wicked to presume forgiveness without confession. Presume on God, but without presumptuousness and with fear. Presume on God, only if you are submissive to his commands, and do not presume empty handedly. Presume, only if your conscience decrees you should; otherwise, if you presume you will experience a ruinous fall. Someone who presumes on God's goodness without humility and without correcting his sins exposes his bleary eyes without any protective shade to the scorching and glaring light of the sun.

82. Further, this may be said about the presumption which blocked access to the way of confession, thinking it superfluous to reveal one's leprosy to a priest's eyes, when the hand of divine goodness can justify the sinner without a priest. This is certainly true, provided power is so joined to goodness so that justice suffers no loss. The psalmist says: 'Two things I have heard: that power belongs to God, and to you, Lord, belongs mercy, because you will repay each according to his deeds' [Ps 62:11–12]. Therefore, O presumption, do not think that God is lenient because of his mercy, and do not consider him harsh and cruel because of his justice. He is merciful, so hope; he is just, so fear. Fear so that you may recover from the coma of evil; hope so that you may hope for kindness from him who is good. When you

sin, fear the just one; when you confess, turn your gaze toward the kindly one. He brandishes his sword when you do evil, he puts it in its scabbard when you stop sinning. He holds and keeps it ready for a long time so that you may stop, he puts it back quickly so that you may hope.

83. When presumption has finally been eliminated, all that remains in the way of confession is despair. As we said earlier, this cuts off the feet of confession so it doesn't come to the sinner's mind. The ultimate evil is to despair. Just as presumption makes God out as unjust, so despair depicts him as loveless. Despair deprives us of our share of God. For human fragility would have nothing in God, if his kindness were taken away. Better that the lovelessness of despair were taken from us rather than the kindness of mercy from God. But the enormity of their faults drives some people to despair. But what about Peter's denial, David's adultery and murder, Mary Magdalene's promiscuous prostitution? I shall not mention the evils of lesser persons whose offenses are not so celebrated and whose correction not so renowned. If you have tripped up while belonging to the clerical order, perhaps as pope, religious, abbot, holy monk, hermit of outstanding merit, are you better, loftier or worthier than the apostle Peter? If in a worldly army or in worldly dress, perhaps as emperor, king, duke, knight, farmer, can you be greater than David in uprightness, office, dignity, power, holiness, or justice? Who of the weaker sex will be more beautiful, more noble or more lovable than Mary Magdalene? But Peter is restored, David is renewed, Mary is received back, washed, justified, and made beloved by the Lord before all others. Therefore, do not despair if you are prostitute, apostate, adulterer, murderer. Or perhaps it is not enormity but long-standing duration which persuades you to despair. What about the thief on the cross who in an instant at the last moment of his life repented, died and departed into paradise? So let no station, no sex, no transgression against your state of life, no sinful abomination, no disorder, nor the imminent prospect of death lead you to despair.

84. Look! If these four factors are excluded, the prince of this world will be cast out by genuine confession. When he has been cast out, will the claustral enter his conscience in order to celebrate the

renowned solemnities of the Lord and not to do servile work? On the delightful sabbath the true Israelite must perform no heavy or agricultural work, but only refined and enjoyable things. The sabbath of souls recalls to mind the ultimate sabbath of the angels: where they are, how they exist, what they do, what they say, what they see, what they hear, what they desire, what they hope. These things must be constantly pondered by our minds, and we must devote our whole sabbath to them. Even if you are not able to resolve your musings about what those joys of the world to come are, still, thinking which carries the mind toward the unknown is never useless.

85. We must believe that the other state to come after this one is either better, equal or worse. That it should be equal is contrary to reason and to the authority of the Scriptures. The remaining alternatives are that it be better or worse. It will be charged into something similar, but intensified. For in payment for works done in the present the good man will be rewarded with a better state, the evil man with a worse one, insofar as the one who abides in virtues will rise to the highest state of happiness, and the one who stood in vices will be drawn down into the ultimate punishment. Therefore, our mind is divided regarding ascent or descent to the abodes which will receive the soul after its release from the body. It ponders within itself the weight and moment of present and future delights, and bitterness and distress of temporal afflictions and eternal straits. It compares one with another, one with many, many with one.

86. It considers that those who administer the punishment, who heartily inflict the torments enjoined on the wretched recipients, choose never to be satisfied with the punishments, not even with their own, because of their wicked hate. It reflects that the ministers of glory always wish to add to our merit and especially to our reward. The devil does a bad job of counting up the good deeds of the sinner; he strongly belittles their weight and merit. But, he counts up evils strictly and with interest. He would also use fraudulent scales if he were not afraid of the One who judges fairly. By contrast, the angel of counsel, the angel of peace, weeps bitterly if anything is wanting in the number or merit to which salvation is due. He pleads weakness of body and bad times. He declares it a

wonder that the dove escaped from the fowler's snare, because of the savagery of the adversary's hate and plots.

87. Meanwhile, like a tree leaf tossed by a great wind and like the watery surf rumbling as a violent surge breaks over it, the wretched soul is torn within and wasted with shaking as he awaits the sentence of the judge. This is the sabbath reflexion which the claustral way of life fosters in accordance with a permanent law. Hence it is written: 'Remember to keep holy the sabbath day' [Ex 20:8]. One remembers to keep holy the sabbath day, if he has known how to reflect thoroughly and continually on the things which occur during the quiet rest of souls. Someone who passes from reflecting on future good to a deep sense of abiding love [*affectus*] also keeps holy the sabbath. For holy reflexion truly sanctifies when it does not blow away ineffectively, like smoke from the smoke house, but usefully puts down the affective roots of a firm resolve. So let reflexion pass into affection [*affectio*], so that the vein of the heart will not merely be touched by a passing movement, but that the good spirit will make an abiding halt and fill everything in the soul with grace and surround it completely with its blessing. Then you will proceed amid plenty, O religious mind, O tomb of the heart! Then you will enter the bedroom, then you will exult in glory, then you will rejoice on your beds.

88. To what will I compare a heart so gloriously glorified? Certainly to a glass dish containing unmixed balsam or undiluted wine. Obviously, a pure heart is like a glass which is clear and transparent to the eye. The holier and purer a human heart is, the more hateful it is to evil spirits. A pure conscience, like a dish, holds up before God all our interior and exterior goods, as though they were old and new wine. Balsam or wine in the dish is faith with love in the conscience. Our Lord hurries to drink it, as a deer wants springs of water, that he may be inebriated by the purity of conscience, that he may be cheered by the fervor of the heart longing for eternity, and finally that, in return, he may fill our saucer to a full and perpetual overflowing of virtues with the wine of devotion. Thus the dish becomes a fountain of life, conscience becomes the dwelling place of grace.

89. O you claustrals, drink waters from the spring of the Saviour. It is the water not of contradiction, but of sanctification. It is the well of the person who lives and sees, who lives by good action and sees by holy

contemplation, who lives by mortification of the body, who sees by purification of his thoughts, who lives by patience, who sees by wisdom. It is the well of the living God in his majesty, who sees our frailty in human flesh. Streams run out from this font or well to your eyes that they may flow with tears, and to your ears that they may hear the voice of God's praise, and to your hands that they may be clean of the blood of cruelty and lust, to your feet that the dust of earthly desires may be shaken off, to the whole body that it may be full of eyes [cf. Ez 1:18]. The fountain and well of living waters in the pool of Siloam (which means 'sent') not only illuminates the eyes' darkness. It also heals blindness.

90. Finally, flowing down from the heights to what is lower, this stream goes around the workshops of our cloister. It decorates the chapel with pools—both for washing the animals offered up for sin and for cleansing the very sanctuary of our soul—in such a way that it has a channel next to the altar at the priest's foot. At the entrance to the sanctuary the person who is going to make the immolation washes his hands and feet, making satisfaction for thoughts as well as through confession and compunction. He scrubs himself clean from every impurity, just as one day God will wipe every tear [Ro 7:17] from the eyes of the saints. Here, however, tears are needed because of the many impurities. Tears will cease there, where there is no misery arising from guilt or punishment. But here the more copious the tears, the rarer the impurities. Note how the claustral conscience directs its thoughts according to the measurer's rope, adjusts his affections according to the measure of the sanctuary [Ex 38:24], weighs out compunction for guilt, so that he may take his drink in measured tears. So much for the claustral conscience.

91. The life and conscience of seculars is as far from purity as it is from claustral quiet. The quality of one's conscience is born of the quality of one's life. Holiness of conscience points to goodness of life. For it says in the gospel about the Father of lights and the Son of God that 'no one knows the Father except the Son' [Mt 11:27], and again that no one comes to the Father except through the Son' [Jn 14:6]. We can say something similar about life and conscience for each person's life is known only by his conscience, and one comes to a good conscience only through a good life. From the window of quiet and contemplation,

let us survey how the wheel of secular life rolls around and then we shall be able to grasp the great inconstancy with which secular conscience spins around.

92. As wandering, worldly care knows no stable foundation, so secular conscience furnishes no sure and stable signs of itself. It changes its expressions not just from day to day and year to year, but hour by hour and practically every moment. Look at the forum, the pub, the theatre, the brothel; look at all the workshops of errors of all sorts. Secular man is here, there, everywhere. These mutations, indeed mutilations, are very, very bad. Anyone who mutates in vices like this will certainly be mutilated in eternal punishments. What is the conscience of a cheater, a deceiver, an adulterer, an incestuous person, a perjurer, an evil doer, a murderer, a false witness, and others like them? Surely their consciences are darkened by infernal smoke, smeared with sin's abomination, grim at the threat of eternal punishment, apprehensive at the anticipation of the future judgement.

93. An evil conscience already judges itself, because all wickedness is apprehensive. It catches the outline of future dungeons of chastisement in the depravity of present evils, as it holds the ropes of torments untied from the corpses of sins. Someone who has accepted the shadow of sin at the urging of convenience is designated by a just sentence to undergo no uncertain punishment, but the already known and familiar slavery of malice. And if subsequently the soul tries to escpae this tent and get away, the familiar punishment of vices will meet him, demanding a down payment as he tries to hide, and turning him back to his tent by the law of the commandments. For it is a commandment that you will be attached in the future life to the one to whom you were subject in this life. Scripture says; 'Where the tree falls, either to the north or the south, there it will remain' [Qo 11:3]. But since there are two grinding at the mill, of whom one will be taken and one left, we need say no more about the one who will be left.

94. Let us take a look at the conscience who will be taken. Secular men, who, while keeping the name of faith and Christianity, are overly concerned about earthly business and cares, build with wood, hay and stubble upon the foundation which is Christ. No one can be free of sin, at least the venial kind, who travels the paths of the sea, buying, selling,

letting contracts, accepting contracts, marrying a wife, begetting children, defending and claiming property, and doing other secular business of this kind. But time after time he returns to the tent of the covenant to offer what the priestly law requires for crime and sin. He exposes his leprosy and what is not leprosy and every sort of uncleanness under the eyes of the priests. By the prescibed obedience he is prepared to expiate what he failed in through intemperance. Thus the good conscience which sinned by excess or defect as a result of slippery mind's fall is gathered back by penitence into the lap of the church which mourns the sins of her son. One's conscience shows signs of new growth when one's life is reformed. We need say no more about the conscience of secular people.

95. What shall I say about the infernal conscience, at the very mention of which my eye, my soul, and my stomach turn queasy? Clearly this conscience and interpretation of it belongs to those who hate the Lord, as Daniel told Nebuchadnezzar regarding his dream and its interpretation. The stench of death arises from an infernal conscience. Let my eye not see it, my hand not handle it, my soul not know it, because death is doing all it can in that pot.[177] What has been cherished in it blossoms into a rule.

96. "Woe, woe," resounds the infernal conscience. The melody of psalms and hymns does not soothe it, the consolation of the gospel does not call it back, the passion of the Lamb and the outpouring of chrism does not moisten the dryness of its horns. A pile of mercies does not lessen its madness. It is turned into adamantine rock by obstinacy, into an eternal fire by the endless burning of evil lusts, into a pit by the disorder of ignorance. Awake, it displays the infernal workshops in a welter of illicit ambitions and schemes of depraved desires. Asleep, it increses the residue of evils, as if with dead ashes; with real grief it stirs the soul which dreams of future miseries. The snares of the penalties with which it is constantly tortured are as interminable as the payment of its mistakes. This is enough about the infernal conscience.

97. The heavenly conscience is the outstanding inheritance of the servants, or rather, the children of God. Of this conscience it is said: 'You are the one who will restore my inheritance to me. For me the measuring lines have fallen on excellent places, so that my inheritance

appears outstanding to me' [Ps 16:5–6]. A heavenly conscience is certainly an outstanding inheritance, which envy does not dim, which unregulated heat does not blacken, which rust does not devastate, which insect, locust and caterpillar do not enter, under which spiteful thieves do not burrow, which foxes do not demolish, which not even a single wild boar eats, which a hailstorm does not knock down, which hoar-frost does not scorch, which the wind does not buffet, which an enemy does not plunder. Its foliage is green, its flower never lacks scent or color, its fruit never fails to have a pleasing taste and to satisfy. Its springtime climate excludes whatever is harmful, whatever is contrary to happiness. God is in its midst, filling the soul with splendors of simplicity and purity which outshine the sun and the moon. Thousands upon thousands of inward impulses attend his throne, with the order and reverence of the angelic ministers, with the countenance of their heart downcast and their step and pace measured. They put their fingers to their lips, because they are afraid to say something which does not edify. They strive to be present on time for the divine command; they take pains not to be away too late. They clearly direct their countenance toward the propitiatory, so that their whole ministry will be at the service of propitiation.

98. What if Satan should be present among the children of God? What happens is described by the apostle: 'If any brother named among you is a fornicator or adulterer or murderer, or anything like that, do not eat with him' [See 1 Co 5:11]. A heavenly conscience certainly is afraid to take the food of the Lord's body and blood when it discovers that lustful impulses have profaned God's sanctuary. Finally, what is more, the perfect conscience does not dare touch simple food, unless it first has vomited out through confession whatever contamination appeared in the temple of glory through the devil's entry. What else? Whatever is contained in the heavenly conscience is dedicated to holy services. The necessities of this life are distasteful to this conscience, and superfluities an abomination. Apart from God it regards all else not as dung, but as death [cf. Ph 3:8]. It is fattened on fasts, is enlivened by moritifications, glories in affronts, is consoled in solitude, rejoices in adversities, is expanded by poverty, is strengthened by weakness, and turns all the adversities of this life into the grace of glory. I have been able to say only a little

about the heavenly conscience, because I have never tasted it. Someone who has tasted it will come up with more and better things than these. And these remarks may suffice here regarding the heavenly conscience.

ABBREVIATIONS

General

CCL	*Corpus christianorum latinorum.* Turnhout, Belgium. 1953-
CCCM	*Corpus christianorum. Continuatio mediaevalis.*
PL	J.-P. Migne, *Patrologia cursus completus, series latina,* 221 volumes. Paris, 1844–1864.

Works of Peter of Celle

References to the editions of Peter's works not translated here will be given as follows:

E   *Epistolae.* For letters in PL 202, references will include the number of the letter in arabic numerals followed by the column and paragraph indication; e.g., E 39: 452C. For the letters edited by Jean Leclercq, 'Nouvelles lettres de Pierre de Celle', *Analecta Monastica 5,* Studia Anselmiana 43 (Rome: Herder, 1958) 167–179, the number of the letter will be given in Roman numerals, followed by the page; e.g., E II:168.

Pa   *Liber de panibus.* PL 202:929–1046. By chapter number, followed by reference to PL: e.g., Pa 7:959B.

Pu   *De puritate animae,* ed. Jean Leclercq, *La spiritualité de Pierre de Celle,* Etudes de théologie et d'histoire de la spiritualité, 7 (Paris: J. Vrin, 1946) 174–192. By page and lines; e.g., Pu 186:17–29.

R   *Commentaria in Ruth,* ed. Gérard de Martel, CCCM 54 (1983) 1–170. The number of the commentary, the pages, the lines; e.g., R 2:101:640–645.

S   *Sermones.* The number of the sermon, followed by the column and paragraph in PL 202:657–926; e.g., S 32:735A.

T   *De tabernaculo,* ed. Gérard de Martel, CCCM 54 (1983) 171–243. By number of the commentary, page, and lines; e.g., T 1:181:72–79.

References to the works translated in this volume will be to the
paragraph numbers introduced into the translation (for SC chapter
numbers will be given as well); e.g., C 46; SC 17:2.

AR *On Affliction and Reading.* Translation of *De afflictione
et lectione,* ed. Jean Leclercq, *La spiritualité,* pp.
231–239.

C *On Conscience.* Translation of *De conscientia,* ed. Leclercq,
La spiritualité, pp. 193–230.

SC *The School of the Cloister.* Translation of *L'école du cloître,*
ed. and trans. Gérard de Martel, Sources chrétien-
nes, 240 (Paris: Cerf, 1977).

Se *Sermons 29, 33, 39, 44.* Translated from PL. References
by sermon number and paragraph; e.g. Se 33:4.

NOTES

[1]Most of the following summary of Peter's life is drawn from two works of Gérard de Martel, OSB: 'Pierre de Celle à Reims', *Mémoires de la Société d'Agriculture, Commerce, Sciences et Arts du départment de la Marne* 89 (1974) 71–103; 'Pierre de Celle', *Dictionnaire de la spiritualité* 12 (1985) 1525–1526. Also helpful is the introduction to the same author's edition and translation of Peter's *L'école du cloître*, Sources chrétiennes, 240 (Paris: Cerf, 1977), pp. 11–18.

[2]Jean Godefroy, 'La maison d'Aunoy-les-Minimes souche de Pierre de Celle', *Revue Mabillon* 41 (1951) 33–35; Gérard de Martel, 'Une notice inédite sur Pierre de Celle', *Mémoires de la Société d'Agriculture, Commerce, Sciences et Arts du départment de la Marne* 97 (1982) 81.

[3]John of Salisbury, *Ep.* 138 to Thomas Becket, PL 199:117B.

[4]E 9:412AC; E 10:413BD. Peter mentioned the controversy in a letter to John of Salisbury, E 74:521B.

[6]E 159:603C.

[7]E 161:605B.

[8]E 22:425B.

[9]E 25:430D–431A.

[10]Hugh: E 26–29:431D–438C; Mont-Dieu: E 40–48:455B–474A. For Bernard of Clairvaux, see de Martel, 'Notice', p. 79; for the Cistercians generally, Gilbert Wellstein, 'Die freundschaftlichen Beziehungen des Benediktiners Petrus Cellensis zu den Cisterciensern (1150–1183)', *Cirstercienser-Chronik* 38 (1926) 213–218, 249–252.

[11]E 20:423AC.

[12]E 19:421AC.

[13]See E 21:423C–424C, a thank you letter to Henry, bishop of Beauvais from Peter, abbot of Celle.

[14]E 111:562AB.

[15]It is not clear when Peter gave his nine synodal sermons: S 83–91: 889C–917C. He might have given them at Chartres after he was made bishop or even before he became abbot of St. Remi. Some of the theological content of these sermons is discussed later in this introduction.

[16]E 77:525A; see E 78:526B, and de Martel, 'Notice', p. 84.

[17]E 79:527BC.

[18]E 104:554D–556A.

[19]E 108:559B–560B.

[20]E 80:528A–529A.

[21]E 82:529C–530C. As abbot of Reims Peter wrote at least eight letters to Alexander III: E 77–78, 80–85; 525A–526C, 527C–532D. As abbot of Celle Peter wrote to Alexander before and after the latter's accession to the papacy: E 1–5, 7:405A–409A, 410BC.

[22]Alexander III, PL 200, passim. Most of Alexander's correspondence to Peter is included in letters numbers 808–982, dated between 1170–1172.

[23]E 24:426AC (= Ep. 333 in the letters of Thomas Becket, PL 190: 675D–676B); E VI:178–179; Ep 334:PL190:67BD (*Petrus Cellensis qualiscunque minister* to Thomas, archbishop of Canterbury). See Roger Ray, 'Rhetorical Scepticism and Verisimilar Narrative in John of Salisbury's *Historia pontificalis*', *Classical Rhetoric and Medieval Historiography,* ed. Ernst Breisach, Studies in Medieval Culture 19 (Kalamazoo, MI: Western Michigan University, 1985) 88–90.

[24]See E 73:519C–520B; E 75:522BC.

[25]E 127:576B.

[26]E 121:570B–571C.

[27]The correspondence of John to Peter was published in PL 199, epistles 75, 76, 81, 82, 85, 96, 97, 115, 280. Peter's letters to John and Richard are the following: to John, E 67–75:613B–622D; E 118–120w.f.:568A–570B; E 124–125:573B–575A; to Richard, E 162–166:605D–610A; to Richard and John, E 121–123:570B–573B. See Ronald E. Pepin, '*Amicitia jocosa:* Peter of Celle and John of Salisbury', *Florilegium* 5 (1983) 140–156.

[28]E 154:598AB; see E 158:602D–603A; E 166:610A; de Martel, 'Notice', p. 86; Anne Prache, 'Saint-Remi de Reims', *Congrès archéologique de France* (135ᵉ session, 1977, Champagne) (Paris: Société française d'archéologie, 1980) 109–121, especially 117–119. Anne Prache, *Saint-Remi de Reims, l'oeuvre de Pierre de*

Celle et sa place dans l'architecture gothique (Geneva-Paris: Société française d'archéologie, 1978) gives details.

[29]PL 200:1371B. P. Glorieux, 'Candidats à la pourpre en 1178', *Mélanges de science religieuse* 11 (1954) 20–21.

[30]E 95:546A; E 83:530D–531B.

[31]E 94:543AC. For Peter's other correspondence with Bernerède see E 93, 95, 97–99, 101–102, 148:540D–541A, 543D–546B, 547B–550A, 551B–554A.

[32]E 174:632B–633B.

[33]Only the beginning (life) and the end (works) of this preface were published in the edition. For the story of this preface and an edition of the previously unpublished sections see Gérard de Martel, 'Mabillion et la préface aux oeuvres de Pierre de Celle', *Revue Mabillon* 58 (1970–1975) 245–269. Mabillon cited only Peter's letters. References to the preface will be by the chapters and pages of Dom de Martel's edition.

[34]Mabillon 'Préface', 8:257–258; E 143:586D–587A; see E 46:467A–470B, and the discussion of Peter's christology below.

[35]Mabillon, 'Preface', 22:268; see his sermons for liturgical feasts and E 37:448AC.

[36]E 49:474AB.

[37]Mabillon, 'Préface', 10–13, 18:259–261, 265; Jean Leclercq, *La spiritualité de Pierre de Celle,* Études de théologie et d'histoire de la spiritualité 7 (Paris: J. Vrin, 1946) pp. 15–23; Peter's praise of charity, 'the virtue of virtues', in his letter to Clairvaux, E 57:484BD; the letter to a friend on the subject of friendship, E V:177–178.

[38]E 114:564BC; Mabillon, 'Préface', 14:261–262.

[39]Mabillon, 'Préface', 16, 19–20:264–266.

[40]Mabillon, 'Préface', 20–21:266–268. In *La spiritualité* Leclercq emphasized the contemplative character of medieval (French) monasticism and of Peter himself: see, for example, pp. 47–51, 82–90, 99–107, 139–144.

[41]The vocabulary of prayer is discussed in Leclercq, *La spiritualité,* pp. 82–90, 105–107. Examples of Peter's use of 'contemplation' are found in SC 7:3, 12:2, 17:3, 18:3, E 25:427B; E 136:580B; E 161:605BC; E 167:610C.

[42]Jean François, *Bibliothèque générale des escrivains de l'ordre de saint Benoît* (1777; repr. Louvain-Héverlé: Bibiothèque S. J., 1961) 398.

[43]de Martel, *L'école,* pp. 19–24; de Martel, 'Pierre de Celle', 1526–29; de Martel, 'Pierre de Celle à Reims,' p. 102; Leclercq, *La spiritualité,* pp. 15–23.

[44]Heinrich Hohenleutner, 'Die Briefsammlung des sogenannten Walter von Dervy (Montier-en-Der) in der Oxforder Handschrift St. John's College, MS 126', *Historisches Jahrbuch* 74 (1955) 673–680.

[45]Jean Leclercq, 'Nouvelles lettres de Pierre de Celle', *Analecta monastica 5,* Studia Anselmiana 43 (Rome: Herder, 1958) 160–179. Dom de Martel's study of the manuscripts of the letters is to appear in *Scriptorium;* he is preparing an edition of them.

[46]Leclercq, *La spiritualité,* pp. 24–30; Jean Longère, *La prèdication médiévale* (Paris: Etudes Augustiniennes, 1983) 54–55; Gérard de Martel, 'A propos d'un semon attribué a Pierre de Celle', *Studia Monastica* 19 (1977) 46–55; Gérard de Martel, 'Recherches sur les manuscripts des sermons de Pierre de Celle', *Scriptorium* 33 (1979) 3–16. PL 202:637A–926D, which reprints the edition of Dom Janvier, includes 95 sermons. Of these S 92:917C–918B is a doublet of S 88:907D–908C. S 35 seems to be two sermons: 742C–745D, 745D–748A. Dom de Martel has identified and edited an additional sermon of Peter's in 'Recherches', pp. 7–9. Emma del Basso, 'I *Sermones* di Pietro di Celle', *Atti dell'Accademia Pontaniana* (Naples), 17 (1968), 97–154, was not available to me when I wrote this section. She gives a more extensive summary of the contents of the sermons.

[47]S 176:610AD.

[48]E 19:421D; E 34:446A. That in both cases Peter replied that he had been too busy to comply with the requests suggests that he wanted to devote some time to the writing of the texts.

[49]The sermon edited by Dom de Martel, 'Recherches', pp. 7–9 is entitled *De nativitate sanctae Mariae,* but it may be a sermon for the Annunciation.

[50]*Petri Cellensis Commentaria in Ruth. Tractatus De tabernaculo.* CCCM 54 (1983). Dom Leclercq published an edition of the second

treatise *De tabernaculo* and of the end of the second commentary on Ruth in *La spiritualité*, pp. 147–173. The first treatise *De tabernaculo* was published by Dom Janvier and is included in the PL 202:1047A–1084B.

[51]PL 202:929A–1046D. John of Salisbury asked Peter to write a sequel on the wines of scripture, but there is no evidence Peter attempted such a work: Ep 85 (PL 199:72AD).

[52]*La spiritualité*, pp. 174–192.

[53]E 164:608AB.

[54]E 165:608BD.

[55]See de Martel, 'Notice', p. 78n; John Benton, 'The Court of Champagne as a Literary Center', *Speculum* 36 (1961) 551–591.

[56]Dom de Martel detected an even clearer outline in the first ten chapters: Origin of claustral discipline (1–2)

General desciption of claustral discipline (3–4)

Goal of claustral discipline (5–6)

Relation to other disciplines (8–9)

Symbols of claustral discipline:

angel of resurrection (10)

stadium (11), etc.

[57]Edited by Dom Leclercq, *La spiritualité*, pp. 231–239. On moderation in asceticism see E 93:546B.

[58]Leclercq, *La spiritualité*, p. 87; E 46:467B; AR 1, 8, 20–22.

[59]AR 21.

[60]The first part of the treatise was printed in PL 202:1084D–1098A. Dom Leclercq edited the entire work in *La spiritualité*, pp. 193–230. Three studies are Phillippe Delhaye, 'Dans la sillage de saint Bernard: Trois petites traités *De conscientia*', *Cîteaux* 5 (1954) 92–103; Emma del Basso, 'Il *De conscientia* di Pietro di Celle', *Sapienza*, 23 (1970) 26–40; Ermenegildo Bertola, *Il problema della cosceinza nella teologia monastica del xii secolo*, Il pensiero medioevale, ser. 2, vol. 1 (Padua: CEDAM-Casa Editrice Dott. Antonio Milani, 1970) 78–102.

[61]For Bernard's ideas on conscience see, in addition to the works mentioned in the previous note, Phillipe Delhaye, 'La conscience morale dans la doctrine de S. Bernard', *Analecta Sacri Ordinis Cisterciensis* 9 (1953) 209–222; Albino Babolin, 'Il problema della

coscienza in Bernardo di Chiaravalle', *Actas de V Congreso inter-
nacional de filosofía medieval* (Madrid: Editorial nacional, 1979)
1:531–534.

[62]*On Purity* and, perhaps, *On Affliction and Reading* are unfinished,
and the two treatises on the tabernacle and the second treatise on
Ruth end abruptly.

Peter may have written a few other works. One which survives is a life of St Mary Magdalene. See Pierre Courcelle, 'Treize
textes nouveaux sur la 'region de dissemblance' (Platon, *Politi-
que,* 237d)', *Revue des études augustiniennes,* 16 (1970) 278; V. Sax-
er, 'La 'Vie de sainte-Marie Madeleine' attribué au Pseudo-
Raban Maur, oeuvre claravalienne du xiie siècle', *Mélanges Saint
Bernard,* 24e Congrés de l'Association bourguignonne de sociétés
savantes, Dijon, 1953 (Dijon: Association des Amis de Saint
Bernard, 1954) 408–421.

[63]Self-knowledge, C 5–6; prayer, C 7; SC 4:4; tears, Pa 12: 984D,
C 7; confession, SC 4:4; SC 21; actions, E 17:419C.

[64]Peter condemns hypocrisy in C 44; SC 4:2, and emphasizes the importance of good example and good reputation in C 63; SC 4:1,
7:2, 8; E I:168; T 1:178:140–142.

[65]The fullest treatments are de Martel, *L'école,* pp. 65–74; Leclercq,
La spiritualité, pp. 47–69; see Delhaye, 'Dans la sillage', p. 100;
Bertola, pp. 79–81.

[66]C 18; SC letter to Count Henry and Prologue 4.

[67]Some of Peter's images are quite charming, others silly or repellant.
He had a disconcerting penchant for images of putrefaction,
manure, and menstruation; e.g. C 17; C 24; C 73; C 79; SC 4:3; SC
24:6; SC 27:6; S 40:768B; Pa 11:978A. He also liked metaphors of
food and banquets: AR 12; Se 39:2; Pa, passim; C 25–28.

[68]*La spiritualité,* pp. 27–28, 47–69, 99.

[69]Nicholas of Clairvaux was able to prod Peter to some technically
theological observations on the Trinity in E 64:496D–498A. In
this uncharacteristic letter Peter cites as authorities Augustine,
Isidore and Jerome, as well as the Bible. See Pa 7:958D–959D.

[70]C 31.

[71]C 51.

[72]Pa 12:983C.

[73]Pa 7:959A. Inos Biffi, 'Aspetti dell' imitazione di Cristo nella letteratura monastica del secolo XII', *La scuola cattolica* 96 (1968) 451-490; Leclercq, *La spiritualité,* 127-138.

[74]Pu 174:14-21.

[75]On the theme of the fashioning of humanity in the image and likeness of God, see Leclercq, *La spiritualité,* pp. 108-111. The 'region of unlikeness' is mentioned in SC 20:2; E 143:587B; S 61; 826A. On this much studied topos see Pierre Courcelle, 'Treize textes' 277-278.

[76]Pa 7:959B.

[77]Pa 7:959D.

[78]S 66:845BC; S 35:746B (cf. Se 39:9); S 1:637D.

[79]Se 29:5: S 51:789C.

[80]SC 16:3.

[81]SC 7.

[82]SC 19:3; Se 44.2.

[83]S 47:782D; Se 29.1-2; SC 19:3: 'a bow, stretched between the divine and human natures against the devil'.

[84]S 50:787D.

[85]S 50:787C.

[86]Se 39:3.

[87]S 30:728D; S 47:782D.

[88]Se 33:10.

[89]Se 29:8-10.

[90]SC 16:4; cf. SC 23:2; Se 44:3.

[91]S 35:745D; S 37:753CD, 756A; E 40:454D.

[92]S 51:789C; see Se 29:6.

[93]Pa 4:949AB; C 38-39; Pu 174:14-21.

[94]Se 29:1, 7; Se 33:5; Se 39:11; S 43:775D-776A; S 30:728CD.

[95]SC 33:8; T 1:178:137-139; Se 33:1, 8; Pa 1:929C, 932AB; Pa 2:934C; Pa 9:971CD; Pa 22:1024B.

[96]S 94:921C; SC 5:2.

[97]SC 6; see SC 16:1; T 1:201:61-202:94.

[98]Pa 7:965BC; cf. Pa 2:937D-938A.

[99]Pa 18:1006C-1008B.

[100]S 12:672CD.

[101]S 13:677B; cf. S 30:729C.

[102]Bernhard Poschmann, *Penance and the Anointing of the Sick,* rev. and tr. Francis Courtney (New York: Herder and Herder, 1964) 156–167; A. G. Martimort, ed., *L'église en prière,* 3rd ed. (Paris: Descleée, 1965) 595; Jean Leclercq, 'S. Bernard et la confession des péches', *Collectanea Cisterciensia* 46 (1984) 122–130.

[103]C 43; C41; AR 4–5; SC 21.

[104]SC 20:1. Claustrals suffer some especially virulent temptations because of their way of life: C 75–77.

[105]See Leclercq, *La spiritualité,* pp. 121–122.

[106]Pu 184–186.

[107]Se 39:12–13; E 155:598C.

[108]C 29: C 60; C 82.

[109]SC 20:3.

[110]C 77. On concealing nothing in confession see SC 12:1.

[111]C 90; Pa:939C; Pa 12:982D–986D; AR 5; SC 27:8.

[112]C 5–6; C 48; AR 21.

[113]C 68–69.

[114]C 32–33.

[115]SC 27:1.

[116]See Leclercq, *La spiritualité,* pp. 32, 94; S 40:766B–769B.

[117]S 41:770D: At the Last Supper Christ 'transubstantiated' bread and wine into his body and blood.

[118]Foretaste: S 38:761B. Joining the angels in the vision of God: E 41:457BC; S 27:720D–721A.

[119]SC 27:14–15; S 94:923C; E 154:597CD; R 1:28:80–91.

[120]S 91:917C. For the synodal sermons see above, note 15.

[121]SC 1:1; 17:2.

[122]SC 2:5. These Peter treats in SC 18–26. In SC 18.1 he refers to the first four of them as the things he considers more desirable and necessary.

[123]SC 3:1–2.

[124]In E II:168, Peter lists the things regarding which he constantly admonished the brothers at Celle: moral integrity, observance of the *ordo* (i.e. their particular way of life), reception of guests, chaste love, divine praise, mutual obedience, fulfillment of the gospel and the rule of Benedict. In E 100:551A Peter expresses the hope that after a period of turmoil the monks of his former

monastery at Celle will experience a reflowering of holy obedience, the virtue of silence, claustral reading, rigor in chapter,
psalmody, unity, and the devout reception of guests.

[125]E 19:421AB. Contemplation in this context is an aspect of sermon
preparation. Pu 178:32–34, could be taken in the sense of this
passage or to indicate the possibility of an identity of action and
contemplation.

[126]E 176:635AB.

[127]E 95:545A.

[128]Pa 7:962BD.

[129]Pa 7:961C. Elsewhere Peter gives a description of good action:
fraternal obedience, daily manual labor, almsgiving, visiting the
sick, consoling the disconsolate, support for widows, reception
of poor people and pilgrims, defense of the oppressed—'anything which is a declaration of charity by evident signs' (C 55).

[130]Leclercq, *La spiritualité*, pp. 78–80; Pu 183:8–11; T 2:240:203–204;
Pa 7:961CD, 963D–964A, 966A.

[131]E 17:419C: 'Ardent desire in restful leisure and fervent work in
action are equally compensated'.

[132]E 41:458B.

[133]C 94.

[134]E 73:519A–520B = H. Denifle and E. Chatelain, eds., *Chartularium
universitatis parisiensis* (1899; repr. Bruxelles: Culture et Civilisa-
tion, 1964) 1:24.

[135]T 1:207:4–5.

[136]T 1:186:28–29.

[137]E 144:588B.

[138]S 86:898C; T 1:186:18–30; E 173:629C.

[139]S 66:847D.

[140]SC 5:4–5. In a letter to Cardinal Peter of St Chrysogonus Peter
recommended a cleric who attended the schools of Paris: E 91:
539A = Denifle-Chatelain, *Chartularium* 1:25.

[141]Seneca: E 25:430B; E 31:439B; E 37:449B; E 64:495C. Horace:
E 89:537B. Plato: T 1:171:25–28. Aristotle: E 175:633B. See E
64:496D–498A.

[142]Logic: C 85; SC 27:14. Scientific theology: S 40:768B–769B;
E 43:464A–465D; E 64:496A–498A.

[143]Se 39:17.

[144]The two commentaries on Ruth expound the allegorical and moral senses respectively. The commentaries on the tabernacle deal with the same two senses. For the four senses of Scripture: T 1:218:21–23; S 69:858A; S 70:860D; S 86:899D. For Scriptural expositions in the treatises see SC 17 (Ez 27); SC 21 (Heb 4:12); SC 19–20, 23–25 (Rv 6).

[145]For these four Fathers see the indices of the critical editions of Peter's works. Most of T 2 is a summary of Bede. Among the contemporary authors mentioned in E 167:610B—Masters Hugh, Gilbert and Peter, St Bernard—the latter held a special place in Peter's esteem. John of Salisbury wrote Peter to ask for Bernard's epistles (Epp. 96, 97; PL 199:87C, 89A) and Peter cites Bernard as an authority in his polemic with Nicholas of St Albans (E 171:613A). Peter's two sermons for the feast of St Bernard are vague, but they mention Bernard was an 'expositor of the Scriptures' (S 76:875B).

[146]AR 8.

[147]C 22. On the wordplay *scientia/conscientia,* see Leclercq, *La spiritualité,* p. 91.

[148]AR 21.

[149]SC 8:1. By 'philosophers' in this passage, Peter seems to aim at both the pre-christian thinkers and Christians who were engaged in philosophical pursuits in his own time.

[150]E 75:520A: S 89:879C; S 91:916A; SC 1:2.

[151]AR 14. Note the reference to the trivium.

[152]T 1:207:2–6.

[153]Death: SC 24–26; judgment: C 29, C 61; heaven: C 97; hell: C 80, C 86; C 96.

[154]SC 26:1–3.

[155]Bernard's opposition is spelled out in his *Ep.* 174 to the canons of Lyons, *Sancti Bernardi Opera,* ed. J. Leclercq, H. Rochais, 7:388–392. Peter's letters to Nicholas are Ep. 169, 171, 173 (Pl 202:611–613, 613–622, 628–632). A letter of Nicholas to Peter is printed in PL 202:622–628. A tract attributed to Nicholas was edited by C. H. Talbot, 'Nicholas of St. Albans and Saint Bernard', *Revue Bénédictine* 64 (1954) 92–117. His article (pp. 83–91) and

A. W. Burridge, 'L'immaculée conception dans la théologie de
l'angleterre médiévale', *Revue d'histoire ecclésiasticque* 32 (1936)
570–597 discusses the controversy about the feast. Further
bibliography is given in de Martel, ed., *Commentaria in Ruth,* pp.
xxxi–xxxvii. Peter remarks on Nicholas's Englishness in E
171:614A, 621D–622B, E 173:629C, and terms him 'magister'
in 617B, 629D. For Peter's opinion on the doctrine of the immaculate conception see Se 29:9; SC 7:3. Luka Modrić, 'Gli
scritti di Nicola di S. Albano sulla concezione della B. V. Maria',
Antonianum 53 (1978) 56–82, argues that the Nicholas with
whom Peter corresponded did not write the treatise edited by
Talbot.

[156] E 171:614D; E 173 629C; 632A; Pa 11:477D; E 122:572BC.

[157] E 171:616D–617A; E 173:632A.

[158] E 171:613D, 617D–618B.

[159] E 171:619B, 620BC, 621B; see E 173:629AB.

[160] E 173:630AD.

[161] AR 13.

[162] For negative attitudes toward theological argument see SC 20:5;
27:17.

[163] SC 27:16.

[164] Se 39:7.

[165] Pa 927–928.

[166] de Martel, 'Recherches', pp. 3–16.

[167] de Martel, ed., *Commentaria,* pp. xiii–xviii.

[168] The liturgical texts which influenced the making of this sermon
were the entrance antiphon (Ps 43:1–3) and the gospel (Jn
8:46–59).

[169] This quotation has not been identified.

[170] Peter here quotes the hymn *ut queant laxis* used on the feast of John
the Baptist (June 24).

[171] Starting here, Peter devotes several pages to a detailed commentary on Ezk 27.4–11, 13. He follows rather closely the treatment
in the eighth book of St. Jerome's *Commentary on Ezekiel,* ed.
Franciscus Glorie, CC 75 (1964) pp. 357–367, lines 709–1013
(PL 25:246C–253C). At the end of his commentary Peter observes
that the reader might prefer a more straightforward account,

and so he gives a summary of 'the nerves and joints of claustral discipline'. To make sense of the commentary itself, it is almost essential to have at hand the biblical text which Peter is explaining, which is here translated from the Vulgate with the help of Jerome's commentary and the *Jerusalem Bible*.

(1) The word of the Lord came to me, saying: (2) 'Son of Man, take up a dirge over Tyre. (3) You will say to Tyre, which stands at the edge of the sea and does business with people of many islands, this is what the Lord says: O Tyre, you have said, "I am [a ship] of perfect beauty". (4) Situated in the heart of the sea [were] your frontiers. Those who built you perfected your beauty. (5) They built you with firs from Senir for your planking. They brought a cedar from Lebanon to make a mast for you. (6) They fashioned oaks of Bashan into your oars. Your thwarts they made of Indian ivory and your decks from [products of] the islands of Italy. (Jerome explains that these 'decks' were compartments in which the most precious merchandise was stowed.) (7) Varied linen of Egypt is woven to make your sail for the mast. Hyacinth and purple from Elishah formed your deck-tent. (8) The inhabitants of Sidon and Arvad were your oarsmen. Your wise men, O Tyre, were [aboard as] your helmsmen. (9) The elders and wise men of Byblos had sailors to take care of your fittings. All the ships of the sea and their sailors were involved in your commerce. (10) Persians and Lydians and Libyans were fighting men in your army. They hung up their shields and helmets on you as decoration. (11) The sons of Arvad were with your army around your walls. But the Pigmies who were in your towers hung their quivers on your walls all around and perfected your beauty. . . . (13) Greece, Tubal and Meshech are your retailers. . . .'

[172]Peter here echoes Gregory the Great, *Pastoral Rule* 2.4 (PL 77:31A–32A). cf. Pa 1:933CD.

[173]The verse which Peter comments on during the rest of this chapter is Rv 6.2. He first gives an allegorical application to Christ, then a moral application to reading. His Latin version reads: 'And

behold a white horse! The rider on it was holding a bow. A crown was given him, and he went away, so that conquering he might conquer.' The theme of the seven seals was already broached in SC 18.2–3. SC 19–25 will continue the allegorical reflections on Rv 6. Each of the four horses of Revelation is associated with one of the four evangelists and his traditional symbol: SC 19:3–Matthew; SC 20:3–Mark; SC 23–Luke; SC 25:1–John.

[174]The Scripture text which Peter comments on in this paragraph is Rv 6.3–4: 'I heard the second living creature say: "Come and see". And another horse, a red one, went out. It was given to its rider to take peace from the earth. . . . He was given a great sword'.

[175]Peter is following Gregory, *Homilia in Evangelia* 2.25.8–9 (PL 76:1194C–1196A).

[176]Peter here quotes, with some alterations, Gregory the Great, *Hom. in Ezech.* 1.8.6–7, ed. Marcus Adriaen, CC 142 (1971), p. 105, lines 157–172 (PL 76:857BD).

CISTERCIAN PUBLICATIONS INC.

Kalamazoo, Michigan

TITLES LISTING
THE CISTERCIAN FATHERS SERIES

Texts and Studies
in the
Monastic Tradition

THE CISTERCIAN STUDIES SERIES

Temporarily out of print

†Forthcoming